Rural Livelihoods in India

The Editors

Biswajit Chatterjee is Professor, Department of Economics, Jadavpur University, Kolkata has earned the reputation as an acclaimed economist, an excellent author and editor, learned scholar and researcher of good repute, a very effective and inspiring teacher and research guide and outstanding administrator and organizer. He has also served as Dean, Faculty Council of Arts at Jadavpur University, Kolkata for eight years and Head, Department of Economics, Jadavpur University. He is at present the President of the Indian Society of Labour Economics and was President of the Indian Econometric Society during 2011-12 and 2012-13, besides being President of BEA during 2005-2014. He has contributed many research papers in reputed journals, authored several books and edited volumes on themes of development economics, international trade and labour economics which are being used in many Indian and International Universities. Recently two edited books entitled *Analytical Issues in Trade, Finance and Development* (2014) and *Agriculture, Sustainable Development and Microfinance* have been published in His Honour.

Asim K. Karmakar is Assistant Professor, Department of Economics, Jadavpur University, Kolkata and Life Member, Indian Society of Labour Economics. He is presently the Executive Council Member of both the Indian Economic Association (IEA) and The Indian Econometric Society (TIES); formerly the Managing Editor (2011-2014) of the Quarterly Referred Journal *Artha Beekshan* of Bengal Economic Association. He has contributed many research papers in reputed journals at home and abroad, and written books and edited volumes.

RURAL LIVELIHOODS IN INDIA

Issues, Measurement and Policies

Edited by
Biswajit Chatterjee
Asim K. Karmakar

CONCEPT PUBLISHING COMPANY PVT. LTD.
NEW DELHI-110059

ISBN-13: 978-93-5125-151-4

First Published 2015

Published and Printed by

Concept
Since 1974

Concept Publishing Company Pvt. Ltd.
A/15-16, Commercial Block, Mohan Garden
New Delhi-110059 (India)
T: 25351460, 25351794, *F*: 091-11-25357109
E: publishing@conceptpub.com, W: www.conceptpub.com
Editorial Office: H-13, Bali Nagar, New Delhi-110 015, India.

Cataloging in Publication Data--Courtesy: D.K. Agencies (P) Ltd. <docinfo@dkagencies.com>

Rural livelihoods in India : issues, measurement and policies / edited by Biswajit Chatterjee, Asim K. Karmakar.
pages cm
Includes bibliographical references and index.
ISBN 9789351251514

1. Rural development--India. 2. Rural development--India--West Bengal. 3. Rural poor--India--Case studies. 4. Rural poor--India--West Bengal--Case studies. 5. Poverty--Government policy--India. I. Chatterjee, Biswajit, editor. II. Karmakar, Asim K., 1956- editor.

HN690.Z9C6 2015 DDC 307.14120954 23

Preface

This book is a venture to cater to different views on the aspects of Rural Livelihoods in India written by reputed economists of the country as well as by young scholars. Admitting that trickle-down theories do not address the legitimate aspirations of the poor and cannot eliminate poverty and with the fact that while the Indian economy has grown to 10th largest in the world, it also accounts for one-third of the world's poor people (around 230 million), a sharp increase from one-fifth in 1981 in the background, the present book with the little *Rural Livelihoods in India: Issues, Measurement and Policies* is an attempt to capture the various issues of rural livelihoods in India, and the state of West Bengal I particular. It also brings together a wide range of evidence with the objective of identifying key trends in the agricultural sector, highlighting vulnerable populations that need to be addressed to provide such support. Also it assimilates current debates and development around the poor and their plight, the potential livelihood opportunities, and policies that advance the possibilities for strengthening the livelihoods of the poor.

This book contains a set of 19 chapters on "Rural Livelihoods in India" and several districts of West Bengal in particular. We hope that this book will not only provide a very good reading material on rural livelihoods in India but also help the students, teachers and researchers of economic discipline for better understanding of the issue, and will help the government and policymakers to take appropriate decisions to tackle the livelihood problems of our country.

We are thankful to the contributors without whose cooperation this book could not be published in time. Last, but not the least, we thank book could not be published in time. Last, but not the least, we thank Shri Ashok Kumar Mittal of Concept Publishing Co. Pvt. Ltd., New Delhi for his cooperation and help to publish this book in an elegant manner.

Kolkata

Biswajit Chatterjee
Asim Karmakar
Editors

Contents

List of Contributors

Dr. Ananta Kumar Bhukta, Associate Professor in Commerce, Santipur College, Nadia, West Bengal.

Anasuya Kar, Associate Professor in Economics, Netaji Nagar College, 170/436, N.S.C. Bose Road, Regent Estate, Kolkata, West Bengal-700 092. Email: kar.anasuya@gmail.com

Dr. Asim K. Karmakar, Assistant Professor, Department of Economics, Jadavpur University, Kolkata, West Bengal-700 032. Email: iasimkkarmakar@gmail.com

Bhajan Chandra Barman, Assistant Professor, Department of Economics, Netaji Nagar College, Kolkata, West Bengal-700 092. Email: bhajanbarman@gmail.com

Bipul De, Assistant Professor, Department of Economics, Sonamukhi College, Bankura, West Bengal.

Prof. Biswajit Chatterjee, Professor of Economics, Jadavpur University, Kolkata, West Bengal-700032. Email: chatterjeeb@vsnl.net

Dr. Biswambhar Mandal, Assistant Professor, Department of Commerce, University of Kalyani. Email: biswambhar.mandal@gmail.com

Chandrasekhar Hajra, Assistant Professor, Department of Economics, Nistarini College, Purulia, West Bengal-723 101. Email: hajrachandrasekhar@gmail.com

Dr. Debasis Mukhopadhyay, Assistant Professor, Department of Economics, Bejoy Narayan Mahavidyalaya, University of Burdwan, West Bengal. Email: Mukhopadhyay.debasis@yahoo.co.in

Debjani Ray, Assistant Professor in Economics, Dum Dum Motijheel College, Kolkata, West Bengal. Email: debjaniray1969@gmail.com

Dr. Jayanta Hajra, Assistant Professor in Economics, Deptartment of Economics, J.K. College, Purulia, West Bengal-712 401. Email: jayantaeco@yahoo.com

Dr. Mahasweta Bhattacharya, Assistant Professor in Commerce, Santipur College, Nadia, West Bengal.

Mamataj Uddin Ahmed, Research Scholar, Department of Economics, Vidyasagar University, Midnapur, West Bengal.

Mriduchhanda Chattopadhyay, Department of Economics, Jadavpur University, Kolkata, West Bengal-700 032.
Email: Mriduchhanda29@gmail.com

Piyali Chatterjee, Lecturer, GNK Institute of Management Studies, Sector-I, Salt Lake, Kolkata, West Bengal-700 064.
Email: piyalich3@gmail.com

Poulomi Bhattacharya, Department of Economics, Jadavpur University, Kolkata, West Bengal-700032.
Email: poulomi.ju.eco@gmail.com

Pritha Ghosh, Department of Economics, Jadavpur University, Kolkata, West Bengal-700032.
Email: Ghoshpritha9@gmail.com

Dr. Ranjanendra Narayan Nag, Associate Professor, Department of Economics, St. Xavier's College (Autonomous), Kolkata, West Bengal-700 016. Email: rnnag12@rediffmail.com

Sadhan Chandra Kar, Associate Professor in Economics, Dinhata College, Cooch Behar, West Bengal-736135.
Email: sadhanckar@gmail.com

Dr. Sangeeta Kundu Project Assistant, Planning and Development Unit, Jadavpur University, Kolkata, West Bengal-700 032.
Email: sangeetakundu9@gmail.com

Dr. Sebak K. Jana, Associate Professor in Economics, Vidyasagar College, Midnapur, West Bengal.
Email: sebakjana@yahoo.co.in

Shilpi Majumdar, Department of Economics, Jadavpur University, Kolkata, West Bengal-700 032.
Email: Shilpi.majumdar90@gmail.com

Shubhashrita Basu, Department of Economics, Jadavpur University, Kolkata, West Bengal-700 032.
Email: Shubhashrita2106@gmail.com

Soumik Banerjee, Department of Economics, University of Calcutta, Kolkata, West Bengal-700 032.

Suhas Roy, Assistant Professor in Economics, Department of Commerce, Bethuadahari College, Bethuadahari, Nadia, West Bengal-741 126.
Email: roysuhas@rediffmail.com

Surya Narayan Ray, Assistant Professor of Commerce, Dinhata College, Cooch Behar, West Bengal-736135
Email: surya_tqm@rediffmail.com

Dr. Swapan Kumar Roy, Assistant Professor in Commerce, Department of Commerce, Bethuadahari College, Bethuadahari, Nadia, West Bengal-741 126. Email: Swapan651@gmail.com

Uttam Haldar, Assistant Professor in Economics, Surendranath College, Kolkata, West Bengal-700056. Email: haldaru@gmail.com

Introduction

The term 'livelihood' represents 'means of living' or that which comprises the capabilities, assets and activities required for the means of living. In modern parlance, a livelihood comprises the assets (natural, physical, human, financial and social capital), the activities, and access to these (mediated by institutions and social relations) that together determine the living gained by the individual or the household. However, the term 'Rural Livelihood' invariably points towards the day-to-day means of living of people in the rural areas and the varieties of means available to the rural society today.

It is in the above context, the papers presented in this edited volume especially deal broadly with three areas of rural livelihoods in India: Conceptual Issues, Determinants of Livelihoods and Case Studies. Within each of these areas, the individual papers have dealt with a wide variety of topics.

Development of the rural economy and diversification of livelihood patterns of the rural people in India beyond the production of primary goods, are important pathways from the morass of poverty, deprivation and backwardness to which the inhabitants of the rural areas are subject to for ages. For a vast country like India with lots of heterogeneity across its population over multiple dimensions, it is extremely difficult to pin down the exact causes and determinants of rural livelihood diversification and their impacts on the incidence of vulnerability of the poor rural households. Diversification of livelihoods enhances the incomes of the rural people as well as reduces the incidence of risk or vulnerability in the face of shocks or unknown events. As a coping strategy, diversification of livelihoods may be useful, but its success depends on a number of factors—both economic and social. While the literature has talked about push and or pull factors affecting diversification, there are scopes for the interplay of both these sets of factors, if one concentrates only one aspect of livelihood. Diversification, namely employment and income diversification, then all the contesting issues concerning rural livelihood and diversification thereof boils down to finding the nature of causality between rural non-farm employment and selected macroeconomic and development indicators in Indian states that contribute to our understanding of the phenomenon of livelihood diversification in rural areas. In the above backdrop, the chapter entitled *Rural Livelihood Diversification in India: Concepts, Measurement and Determinants* by Biswajit Chatterjee and Sangeeta Kundu delves deep into various questions associated with rural livelihoods in India, analyses the dimensions of livelihood security and their measurement, discuses the pattern of rural livelihood in India as evidenced from the literature, and brings out the policy challenges faced by the government in furthering diversification of rural livelihood patterns in India. Their study pinpoints to the fact that among the various factors and determinants, the state-specific effects are not robust for all types of relationships postulated as classified into push as well as pull factors. They find that while unemployment rate is significant for the female workers and the subsidiary workforce, it is not an important determinant of growth in the male non-farm employment in the rural areas. Higher education has a positive and significant effect on rural non-farm employment in India, but not for male and female principal workforce. For the manufacturing workforce they find that unemployment rate, population density and degree of urbanisation have positive and statistically significant impact on the UPSS and MPS workforce, but the female principal manufacturing workers are being influenced by only population density significantly. The diversification in income and employment patterns of rural population of India therefore connotes to the importance of economic and demographic factors which in turn depend on the variety of social and non-economic factors and their interactions. But the primary focus of policy of rural development in a country like India is to maintain stability of the relationship between such push and pull factors so as to ensure a sustainable pattern of livelihoods, and to insulate the people from the vulnerabilities generated in the development process through various shocks.

Biswambhar Mandal in his chapter *Rural Livelihoods in India: Some Areas of Concern* argues that out of the total of 1210.2 million populations in India, the size of rural population is 833.1 million. Majority of the rural inhabitants still find it difficult to ensure their basic amenities of life. Tackling rural poverty still remains a pressing challenge for rural India. Rural poverty causes concern for the overall growth of our nation. Majority of population in rural India sustains on agriculture and linked occupations. Agriculture and allied activities that support the livelihoods of nearly 70 per cent of India's rural population, has lost its importance. In recent years, land-based livelihoods of small and marginal farmers are increasingly becoming unsustainable. As their land has failed to support their family's requirements, they are forced to look at alternative means for supplementing their livelihoods. The rapid changes at the macro level that India witnessed since the early nineties has contributed to the instability of the livelihood systems of the poorer section of rural households. Searching jobs for the millions remain a challenge for rural India. Every year millions of poor families migrate in search of work. They are forced to migrate due to a livelihoods collapse in the villages. India ranked 94th out of 118 countries in the Global Hunger Index. Understanding the livelihood systems of the poor is crucial to effective poverty reduction. Livelihoods of the poor can never be understood in any one-track logic—be it economic, social, technical, cultural or political. The Indian government has passed legislation to benefit rural citizens. The benefits are inequitably distributed between the rural and urban areas. The rural-urban divide in accessing infrastructure services coupled with inability of civil society organizations to utilize the existing provisions has contributed to the slow growth of livelihood opportunities in rural areas. Slowdown in agricultural growth and productivity, changing cropping patterns, increase in distress migration, changing consumption patterns, government policies favouring industrial houses, among others have seriously undermined the food and livelihood security of the poorer households. An integrated, multidimensional and holistic approach to poverty eradication efforts is crucial to preserve and enhance the livelihoods of the poor.

Soumik Banerjee, Shubhashrita Basu and Ranjanendra Narayan Nag in their chapter *Globalization and Rural Livelihood: A Three-Sector Model* make an attempt to look into the various issues and perspectives of rural livelihood and analyze the effects of the development and displacement on the various sections of rural society. In their paper they construct a General Equilibrium Model to examine effects of globalization on factor prices, income distribution and sectorial composition of output which have profound bearing on rural livelihood. The model consists of 3-sectors that can apply to a large class of emerging market economies.

The sectors under consideration are an import-competing industrial sector, a non-traded traditional agricultural sector and an export-oriented agricultural sector. The different comparative statics pertain to agricultural trade liberalization, tariff liberalization, a fall in foreign interest rate and technological progress in the agricultural sector. The results in this chapter depend on existence of non-traded good, factor intensity rankings and multiple cross-effects embedded in a general equilibrium framework.

Pritha Ghosh in her chapter *Rural Livelihoods in India* makes an assessment of rural development efforts that have been initiated in past recent years in India. It also looks into the matter of social and economic changes and their impact on rural communities and tries to provide some suggestions regarding implication of agricultural extension and development plans. Economic changes include increased agricultural and industrial production, liberalization of economic and export policies, increase in number of rural bank branches and increase coverage of rural masses under different credit programmes. Implications of these changes for rural development agricultural extension include designing programmes for farmer families with limited land, public policy, education to farmers regarding land subdivision, fragmentation and consolidation and developing linkages with other disciplines to understand better the problems and suggest solution strategies. India's strong economic growth has consistently sought to include the rural poor, who are concentrated in areas where rainfed agriculture is the main economic activity. However, poverty persists because of limited and equitable access to productive resources such as land, water, improved inputs and technologies and microfinance as well as vulnerability to drought and other natural disasters, but low level of literacy and skills conspire to keep people in the poverty trap, preventing them from claiming their basic rights or new activities to earn income or build assets.

Large numbers of India's poorest people live in the country's semi-arid tropical region. In this area shortages of water and recurrent droughts impede the transformation of agriculture that the Green Revolution has achieved elsewhere. There is also a high incidence of poverty in flood-prone areas such as those extending from eastern Uttar Pradesh to the Assam plains, and especially in northern Bihar. Poverty affects tribal people in forest areas, where loss of entitlement to resources has made them even poorer. In coastal fishing communities people's living conditions are deteriorating because of environmental degradation, stock depletion and vulnerability to natural disasters.

A major cause of poverty among India's rural people, both individuals and communities, is lack of access to productive assets and financial resources. High levels of illiteracy, inadequate health care and extremely limited access to social services are common among poor rural people. Microenterprise development, which could generate income and enable poor people to improve their living conditions, has only recently become a focus of the government.

Rural poverty alleviation programmes were revamped and re-focused during the Ninth Plan to increase their effectiveness. Rural poverty alleviation programmes were revamped and re-focused during the Ninth Plan to increase their effectiveness. Programmes that provide self-employment and wage Employment to the poor were implemented with greater vigor during the eleventh Plan. SGSY would provide opportunities for self-employment to the rural poor. The programme would shift to a process-oriented approach in four stages.

- Social mobilization for formation of self-help groups;
- Savings among the group and internal lending among its members;
- Provision of a revolving fund; and
- Micro-finance and Micro-enterprise development.

Network of institutions that promote the self-help movement was created during the 11th Plan period. Partnership was forged between NGOs and other community-based organizations, government agencies and other financial institutions. There was system of identifying and training local facilitators. Key activities were planned to respond to the needs of the area. Training programmes for beneficial linkages with training institutions would be forged. Greater attention would be paid to marketing. Rural hats/markets at the taluka/district were set up for display of products.

Linkages were developed with private channels, industrial enterprises and export houses for higher value realization for SGSY groups. Special attention was paid to provide technical support for upgrading technology and standardization of products. Use of information and communication technology was promoted during the plan period in this regard. The SGRY was the single wage employment programme. The programme had three streams which would seek to address the need of rural infrastructure at the village level, ensured guaranteed employment of at least 100 days in areas facing chronic unemployment/migration and provide relief in natural calamities such as floods, droughts, earthquakes and other contingencies.

The projects under SGRYwas chosen with a view to taking up schemes that enlarge the scope for increased economic activity. Access to land was an important element in the poverty reforms, record of rights of land owners and tenants, computerization of land records, prevention of alienation of tribal lands, and issue of land rights for women were the major tenets of the land reform agenda. The promotion of a movement which enhances social capital and forges linkages with other formal and informal stakeholders engaged in developmental activities was a major thrust during the Plan. PRIs have created a space for the involvement of the community in governance. There is a need to provide greater attention to effective empowerment of PRIs. The Government recognises the necessity of building capabilities at the local levels for planning, implementation and monitoring of development programmes. These would be undertaken on a large scale during the next Plan period.

Asim K. Karmakar in his chapter titled *In Search of Rural Livelihoods in India* attempts to compile some important informations relating to the overall context in which livelihoods, particularly rural livelihoods in India, need to be understood. The analysis of the major trends over the past two decades indicate that the livelihood base of rural population in the country has been transformed significantly due to the workings of a multitude of forces. An important aspect of this transformation is that the structure of the economy of almost all the states has shifted away from agriculture towards other sectors. The challenges to livelihood diversification are particularly serious for the poorest states—Jharkhand, Chhattisgarh, Madhya Pradesh, Bihar, and Odisha—as they lag behind others in terms of human development achievements also. Initiatives to promote livelihoods in these states hence need to be anchored effectively on the goals of expansion of economic opportunities, alleviation of human poverty, improvement of capabilities, and reduction of inequalities.

Sadhan Chandra Ray and Surya Narayan Kar in their joint chapter entitled *The Challenge of SHGs in Generation of Rural Sustainable Livelihoods: Bridging the Gap between "Shining India" and the Country* make an attempt to state that SHGs can bridge the gap between 'Shining India' powered by GDP driven growth model that has led to unbalanced development and the "Rural India" where nearly 75 per cent of the population of the second largest democracy resides. Out of the 553.92 million rural population who are either employed or are interested in working, 10.1 per cent representing nearly 55.95 million rural population are still unemployed. The primary rural employment generating sector is agriculture which is over-saturated. The organized sector is not employment-intensive and organized self-employment through the formation of sustainable SHGs is the only opportunity to provide for multiple livelihood opportunities in the rural sector especially among the socially and economically disadvantaged groups. Their study based on field survey data of Dinhata subdivision of Cooch Behar district in West Bengal clearly demonstrates the positive effect of the formation of SHGs on the incidence of employment in rural Dinhata by making a comparison between SHGs and non-SHGs households; as well as establishing the creation of more employment opportunities among the employable rural female workforce.

Debasis Mukhopadhyay in his chapter *Poverty Eradication through SHGs: The Changed Face of Rural Livelihoods in West Bengal, India* voices forth that poverty eradication efforts in India which initially concentrated on supply of agricultural technologies, inputs and services that were often 'production' oriented were not targeted towards the poor. Now the approach changed towards 'capacity-building' in sector organizations to equip people and organizations with the skills and resources to do a better job. The concept of livelihoods and livelihoods analysis emerged in the mid-nineties—closely associated with poverty reducing strategies.

In 2010, GoI approved the restructuring of SGSY programme into the National Rural Livelihoods Mission (NRLM) to reach down to the household level to support formation of institutions which aggregate to form an institutional platform—the Self-Help Groups (SHGs).

SHGs have become the common vehicle of development process, converging all development programmes. SHG-Bank Linkage Programme launched by NABARD way back in 1992 envisaging synthesis of formal financial system and informal sector has become a movement throughout the country. It is considered as the largest micro-finance programme in terms of outreach in the world and many other countries are keen to replicate this model. At present, a large number of Self-Help Group Promoting Institutions (SHPIs), all the banking agencies and MFIs are pursuing this programme for the uplift of the poor. This is also recognized as a part of priority sector lending and normal banking business by Reserve Bank of India. Nearly about 10 crore poor households are covered under the programme.

Slowdown in agricultural growth and productivity, changing cropping patterns, increase in distress migration, changing consumption patterns, government policies favouring industrial houses, among others have seriously undermined the food and livelihood security of the poorer households. An integrated, multidimensional and holistic approach to poverty eradication efforts is crucial to preserve and enhance the livelihoods of the poor, mainly in the rural areas. This paper thus enquires into the changing faces of rural livelihoods in India and the role of the SHGs those come to the rescue of the poor.

Debjani Ray in her chapter entitled *Impact of MGNREGA on the Rural Livelihoods of West Bengal* articulates that the MGNREGA comes at a crucial juncture of the Indian Economy when it is passing through a period of jobless growth. Between 1993-94 and 1999-2000, the employment growth fell to 1.07 per cent per annum from 2 per cent during 1983 while GDP went up from 5.2 per cent during 1983-93 to 6.7 per cent during 1993-2000. Both male and female unemployment rates in rural India have gone up in 2004-05 as compared to 1993-94. The National Rural Employment Guarantee Scheme (NREGS) based on the NREG Act, 2005 is the outcome of the policy agenda outlined in the National Common Minimum Programme of the UPA Government. Its context has been prepared by the Goal 1, i.e., eradication of poverty and hunger of the Millennium Development Goals (MDGs), the decline of per capita availability of foodgrains in the 1990s and the failure of the series of wage employment programmes in India since 1960s. Hailed as the world's biggest welfare project that has helped to create community assets and increase the income of the rural people, it has the potential to create history.

Unemployment rate is quite high in West Bengal, therefore NREGA has a special significance for the improvement of rural livelihood in the state. A district level study on different facets of the implementation of NREGA is done for the impact assessment of the scheme on West Bengal.

Uttam Haldar in his chapter *Food and Livelihood Security in Rural West Bengal –An Experience* focuses that despite economic growth, green revolution, government employment generation programme, the rural livelihood in India is still enamoured with poverty and hunger. Chhatna Block in Bankura district of West Bengal is known to be a backward area in terms of socio-economic development. Mono-cropping agriculture led by limited Irrigation facility is the major economic activity. To earn their livelihood, tribal people (Santhals) migrate three to four times in a year and suffer a lot. Economic backwardness among Scheduled Tribe population is manifested through high illiteracy rate, poor health status, ignorance, superstition and poor consciousness about sanitation, family planning etc. In this background objective of the study is to analyse the prospect of rainwater harvesting in drought prone areas of Bankura District with community participation in making food and livelihood security of marginalized people and to highlight the development activity initiated by a tribal lady in raising the standard of living of tribal population in Chatmagara village of Chhatna block. The study finds out that the development of rural infrastructure like water harvesting structure through community participation with strong leadership using government development programme will lead to sustainable cultivation and hence food and livelihood security in drought prone areas of Bankura district where opportunity of alternative livelihood is limited. Distress migration has been stopped. Empowerment of women breaks the vicious circle of food and livelihood insecurity.

Jayanta Hajra and Chandrasekhar Hajra in their joint chapter entitled *Food Deprivation as a Choice among Poor People in Backward Rural India during Liberalization* forcefully argues that the dichotomy of high growth rates and persisting hunger among the Indian population has become an important area of concern to the policy-makers. The shift of focus of public support measures from capability enhancing programmes to social security programmes has widened regional inequality. The need of the hour is the capability enhancement of these rural folk by government attempts not just the social security programmes as advocated by present day policy-makers; otherwise sustainability of this high Indian GDP growth rate will face serious challenges in near future.

Poulomi Bhattacharya in her chapter *Focusing on the Factors influencing the Rural Livelihoods in India* delves deep into the fact that not just Growth but Growth with Development-Inclusive Growth, is what should be focused on. India's economic growth includes the rural poor. Despite an impressive economic growth, the rural livelihoods persist in poverty and hunger. The rural people depend on rainfed agriculture for their survival which is uncertain and statistics indicate that on average a farmer commits suicide in every 30 minutes. Lack of education and skill prevents them from having an alternative means of survival. Many other behavioural, geographical, technical and financial factors can be attributed for the worsening conditions of the rural people. Despite having an intense and intrinsic endowments of natural resources, the rural-urban prosperities differ. While an unprecedented economic growth brings prosperity to urban livelihoods, the crisis faced by the rural people are kept unnoticed or not been given the proper concern.

Rural development policies are sound, but it requires a change in its implementation to achieve long-lasting poverty reduction. The Department for International Development of United Kingdom has made a substantial contribution in improving rural livelihoods in India by reducing poverty. In this chapter she presents a comparative overview of past and present scenarios of rural livelihoods which will highlight the significance of certain factors required to be focused on. The paper also shows how a change in one factor can affect the lives of rural people and tries to estimate what the scenario will look like in the near future based on the comparative study.

Mriduchhanda Chattopadhyay in her paper *Rural Livelihoods in India Viewed from the Perspective of Women* has observed that in India with men moving to the expanding urban industrial sector in search of better job opportunities and higher wages, women are playing a major role in agricultural sector and rural economy. Though women play a pivotal role in agriculture, women are still dominated both socially and economically even at the household level. In rural India, many families that are female headed, lies below the poverty line. Women try their level best to alleviate poverty of their households by taking part actively in rural credit market. Micro-financial institutions prefer rural women over men as they are more likely to return the credited amount within time-frame in case of self-help groups due to their high self-esteem.

Shilpi Majumder in her chapter *Dalits and Rural Livelihoods* explores the concept of caste system, its historical background and its implications on the society which is followed by the origin of *Dalits* and their status in the Indian society, the various atrocities against the *Dalit* women and children and the policies prescribed for them. The first section gives a brief idea about the origin of caste system. It voices that the first traces of caste system were found in the *Rigveda* and also in the *Bhagavad Gita*. It is a term which is used to specify a group of people having a specific social rank. Each *jati* has been arranged in a hierarchical order to fit into one of the four basic varnas—the Brahmans, the Kshatriyas, the Vaishyas and the Shudras. However there's one more *jati* which doesn't fit into any of these *varnas*, and they are the Untouchables or the *Dalits*. These people are supposed to do all sorts of menial jobs and aren't allowed to attend any kind of social gathering. The second section tells about the Millennium Development Goals. Even after successful implementation of the Millennium Development Goals (MDG's), it has been found that still a section of the society is excluded. The mortality rates of *Dalit* children are high as the mothers lack sufficient nutrition and care. The Drop-out rates of *Dalit* children are high. It also shows the various socio-economic indicators like size of the landholding, population below poverty line, monthly per-capita consumption expenditure, health status indicator, death rates, and literacy rates which are important to understand the position and status of *Dalits* in the society. The third section focuses on the various crimes against *Dalits—Dalit* women and *Dalit* children. *Dalit* women are subjected to various atrocities for mostly two reasons. First because they are *Dalits* and second because they are women. They are subjected to crimes such as verbal abuse, sexual assault, naked parading and murder. The *Dalit* children also aren't excluded. They serve mostly as child labour and *Dalit* girls are sexually abused as they reach their puberty. The children are forced to leave schools and are forced to work for their families. The fourth section focuses on the various policies prescribed to uplift their socio-economic status.

In her chapter *Rural Livelihoods in India: Issues, Measurement and Policies,* Piyali Chatterjee articulates that the picture of rural India is a queer blend of the traditional farm and the widely spread non-farm sector while the latter is gaining overwhelming importance through the passing years. Her chapter explores the existing avenues for generating employment and income in rural areas, and also to evaluate the rural livelihoods scenario in India. The rural sector of India has undergone a sea-change in the post-Independence era. The years after Independence saw severe poverty all-around the economy. The then Government of India through the Second Five Year Plan regime undertook heavy investment in different sectors of the economy for the macroeconomic development of the economy. The First Five Year Plan mainly focused on improving the agricultural sector and the living standards of the people. The allocation in agriculture and community development was around 17.4 per cent of the total planned budget. The government took several steps to rehabilitate the landless workers, whose main occupation was agriculture. These workers were also granted fund for experimenting and undergoing training in agricultural know-how. However, the plan was able to attain its objectives in the agricultural sector. The liberalisation period starting from 1991 saw a couple of changes as well, in the rural livelihoods scenario. The opening up of the economy intensely affected the rural economy through its various policies related to the farm and non-farm sector.

The study of rural livelihood in the context of the Indian economy is of immense significance even in today's 'modern' industrialised scenario. Given the fact, that the country's industrial capacity is increasing day-by-day coupled with the consequences of more jobs and higher per capita income, one cannot deny the importance of the 'traditional' sector which is comprised mainly of the agriculture and allied activities. As per 2012 statistics, agriculture is the dominant sector of the Indian economy having an average growth rate of 2.8 per cent. For over 58.4 per cent of India's population draws its livelihood from agriculture. It is also worth mentioning here, that agriculture contributes approximately one-fifth of total GDP (Gross Domestic Product). According to a Corporate Catalyst India (CCI) Survey, "India is the second-largest producer of food in the world and holds the potential of being the biggest on global food and agriculture canvas." Hence, this paper also intends to highlight the importance of its study in the context of globalisation. Along with this, the rural non-farm sector (RNFS) has its own importance. The RNFS is comprised of economic activities as follows, household and non-household manufacturing, handicrafts, construction, mining and quarrying, transport, trade, livestock rearing, self-help groups, etc. It is undeniably a support sector beside the agricultural sector, creating huge employment opportunities and of course, income for further sustainable development. It is as such of equal importance to analyse and study RNFS along with RFS. The study of the present topic is based mainly on secondary data analysis and also on other studies by different authors. The data has been compiled in tables for facilitating analysis and evaluation of it.

Anasuya Kar in her chapter *Disaster—A Menace to Rural Livelihoods* via *Environmental Hazards* stresses that India is regarded as one of the most disaster-prone areas in the world on account of her critical geographical position, climate and huge population. And history of disasters has proved it time and again. To stop or avoid natural disasters is not under human control—rather it is the 'so called' development drives by the man that stands responsible to some extent for increasing the attacks by the natural disasters.

In India about 60 per cent of the land mass is prone to earthquake of various intensities, 68 per cent of area is susceptible to drought and over 40 million hectares is prone to floods. Disaster not only results in loss of thousands and thousands of lives but also in terms of losing private, community and public assets along with wiping out the means of livelihood for millions, especially in rural areas. It is well recognized that the poor and the vulnerable sections of the society are affected disproportionately by disasters. Often quite they lose their homes, assets and livelihoods—whatever little they have.

Natural as well as man-made disasters, having direct impact on economy, agriculture, food security, water, sanitation, environment and health, have forcibly made it one of the single largest concern for most of the developing nations including India. Apart from the economic aspects, such disasters have social and psychological dimensions, manifested later on lives and livelihood of the affected persons, directly or indirectly.

Her chapter unfolds the monstrous sides of the disaster as a whole with special reference to rural livelihoods and throws some policy framework as it is the poor and underprivileged who are worst affected by the calamities and disasters.

Suhas Roy and Swapan Kumar Roy in their joint paper titled *Livelihoods of Rural Van-Rickshaw Pullers are at Stake: A Case Study in a Selected Village of Nadia District of West Bengal* focuses that Van-Rickshaws are very common means of rural transport, especially in remote villages. During devastating flood of the year 2000, they proved as the most effective means of transport in the villages where roads were almost absent. They were equally effective in the muddy, water-logged and uneven rough surfaced pavements. As because van-rickshaws can accommodate four or more passengers in a van, they enjoy cost leadership in relation to ordinary cycle-rickshaws. Until recently they were profitable for both to the pullers and commuters. With the introduction of motor-run van-rickshaws (locally known as lachhiman, city-service van and bhatbhati van), number of passengers of van-rickshaws is declining sharply. Rural unemployed youths, en masse took pulling these van-rickshaws as their livelihood because it was one of the easiest ways of earning their bread. The monopoly of carrying passengers and goods by van-rickshaws is being challenged due to improvement of village roads under PMGSY, NABARD's RIDF Schemes. In many places, kuccha roads have been laid under MGNREGS. Moreover, with economic development, villagers also using own motorcycles and scooters. Besides, a number of models of a few reputed car manufacturing companies have launched small passengers as well as goods carrying vans to ply on all-weather roads of the villages. All these factors are working simultaneously to cut down the demands of the van-rickshaw pullers.

Their chapter focuses on the factors responsible for the challenges facing the rural van-rickshaw pullers in earning their livelihoods and possible remedies thereof from the feedback received from a study conducted in Bethuadahari -I and Bethuadahari-II Gram Panchayat under Nakashipara Development Block in the district of Nadia covering data of fifty van-rickshaw pullers.

Bhajan Chandra Barman in his chapter *Impact of Microfinance through SHG on the Livelihoods of the Rural Poor: A Case Study of a Village in Nadia District of West Bengal* argues that providing easy finance and micro credit has always been the primary objective of microfinance linkages. Micro finance (MF) in the form of SHG-Bank linkage model has been able to inspire hope in the lives of thousands of rural poor, especially women and enable them to contribute to their families' well being through savings and borrowings. Microfinance, a new anti-poverty programme, influences the quality of life and is considered to be a powerful tool for positive socio-economic changes in modern society. The main objective of this paper is to analyze the socio-economic impact of microfinance through SHGs on the livelihood of the rural poor in Nadia District based on primary data collected from a village. Specially prepared SHG scheduled and household schedule are used to collect information about the functions of the SHGs. He has taken 10 SHGs and 130 women from the study area and results are interpreted by tabular analysis.

Mahasweta Bhattacharya and Ananta Kumar Bhukta in their joint paper *Handloom-Oriented Livelihoods of the Weavers of Nadia – A Case Study of Santipur* endeavour to assess how far the traditional handloom oriented activities in the district of Nadia, West Bengal has become effective in reducing poverty and income inequality among the people who are readily associated in this particular trade.

The district of Nadia is essentially an agricultural district and the bulk of her working population is found engaged in various agricultural pursuits. However, an interesting feature represented in the last population Census is that in the Nadia district of West Bengal, a considerable number of people are engaged in household industries than in any other part of the State and handloom-weaving particularly is the main household industry there. In the art of handloom industry, Nadia district occupies a very important place in the State of West Bengal and handloom plays a pivotal role in placing them in a standard socio-economic status. Surprisingly enough in the last Weavers' Census 69,713 people are engaged in this traditional industry particularly in the rural area of Santipur to earn their livelihoods.

The above paper has been divided into six sections. Section I, appears with a brief discussion of the state of poverty and inequality persisting in the LPG era across the globe and it is followed by the "Objective of the Study" in Section II. In Section III and IV they have tried to depict the geographical features of Nadia district in short and a brief introduction of the industry in Nadia subsequently. In Section V titled "Economic analysis and findings", they have basically tried to find out the financial aspects of the weaving industry at present in rural areas of Santipur classifying the weavers into three main categories viz., (i) weavers producing and selling Individually, (ii) weavers producing and selling under Co-operatives, and

(iii) weavers producing and selling under Mahajans and others. Here they have used a very simple statistical device in analyzing the available data, i.e., computation of the Covariance of income of the income earners and observed that individual weaving is the best in generating surplus (R-C) consistently with their greater marginal productivity than that of weavers working under Co-operatives and Mahajans and hence suggested for their various impetus. In conclusion, they have tried to focus on some problems faced by this industry at present along with the future policy prescriptions.

Sebak K. Jana, Bipul De and Mamataj Uddin Ahmed in their chapter *Forest Dependence of Households: A Study on Joint Forest Management in the Districts of Bankura and Paschim Medinipur in West Bengal* utter that Non-Timber Forest Products (NTFPs) are an important source of livelihoods for a significant portion of the rural populations all-over the world. The present study attempts to explore the dependence of households on forests managed under JFM based on the primary data collected from 220 households from 24 FPCs in three forest ranges in Bankura district and one range in the Paschim Medinipur district of West Bengal. The Study reveals that households in forest fringe areas are still very much dependent on forest for their livelihoods. The factors behind such dependence have also been analyzed.

The present book addresses a series of exceedingly important rural livelihoods issues in India as well as other intricate issues associated with employment and social development and these together provide useful clues towards a critical understanding of the contemporary rural Indian economy.

No thanks are adequate for Shri A.K. Mittal, the Managing Director, Concept Publishing Company Pvt. Ltd. for his meticulous publication of this book despite many hazards.

Kolkata

Biswajit Chatterjee
Asim K. Karmakar
Editors

SECTION I
Conceptual Issues

1

Rural Livelihood Diversification in India

Concepts, Measurement and Determinants

Biswajit Chatterjee and *Sangeeta Kundu*

I. Introduction

For a country of India's size, heterogeneity and diversity, the issue of development is of paramount importance, and since the majority of its population is concentrated in rural areas, rural development has assumed important place in our national developmental agenda. Development of the rural economy, and diversification of livelihood patterns of the rural people beyond the production of primary goods are important pathways from the morass of poverty, deprivation and backwardness to which the inhabitants of the rural areas are subject to for ages. In this chapter, we propose to delve into various questions associated with rural livelihoods in India, analyse the different dimensions of livelihood security and their measurement, discuss the pattern of rural livelihood in India as evidenced from the literature, and bring out the policy challenges faced by the government in furthering diversification of rural livelihood patterns in India.

In a developing economy like India, there exists tremendous inequality in income distribution, endowments, opportunities and access to various services across the rural population, and these inequalities and disparities are significantly higher compared with the urban segments. The rural economies with relatively much intense and intrinsic relationship with natural endowments are generally oriented to production of primary goods and as such, the aggregate income accrual to the rural households from production of such primary goods is in general higher than of the urban households. As net suppliers of primary goods, and net buyers of secondary and tertiary goods and services, the rural sector provides important structural linkages to the rest of the economy in terms of demographics, human capital and natural endowments, which lead to varying permutations of the economic activities and income generation process of the rural people and the resultant inter- and intra-regional differentiations in livelihood and well-being. The rural-urban divide is sharper and more dynamic in developing countries than in the developed ones due to essentially three reasons. Firstly, to meet the food security of increasing population, the food sector (i.e. the primary agricultural production) would have to be operated more intensely and this process, being land based, would remain located in non-urban areas with practically no scope of relocation of agricultural activities. Secondly, the urban expansion and contraction of the share of primary sector in the GDP is adjunct to the overall development process—if demographic structures in a region are rigid or less dynamic than the pace of restructurings of subsectors resultant to economic growth, the rural urban divide in terms of per capita income accrual is poised for further widening. Thirdly, in medium and long-term, growth of agrarian segments cannot be placed at the ambitious levels of urban based and urban biased manufacturing and service sectors. It may be argued that even in the event of accelerated economic growth, as witnessed in some of the developing countries with prominent agrarian presence such as India and China, the growth ambitions from agriculture sector would need to be moderate and sustainable with concern for stress on natural resources of water and soil and due to the technological constraints. The demographic pressure and socio-economic inequalities in rural domains of developing countries further complexes the relationship between humans and endowment. For example, about 30 per cent of world population is in the developing countries of South and South-East Asia with less than 7 per cent world landmass. The FAO Statistics (FAO 2005) indicates that this region has almost 40 per cent of world's agricultural dependent population with less than 20 per cent global arable land resources. With such uneven distribution of production assets, low levels of literacy, skills, awareness and connectivity and limitations of alternative options for livelihood, the high prevalence of poverty in these regions becomes the natural corollary. There is concern on the incidence of deep rooting of poverty amongst the households depending on single income from farm activities (UN-Wye Group, 2007). But, the scope of increasing real income of farmers and bringing sustained improvement in their well-being, solely through farming operations, is seriously constrained. The rural economies in developed countries are relatively more diversified and majority of their rural households have larger share of non-farm income accrual. The expansion of non-farm activities in the rural areas is crucial in diversifying the economic activities in the rural economy, and to generate employment and narrow down the rural-urban differentiation in income distribution during the growth process of such developing nations. While emphasizing the catalytic role of accelerated agricultural growth for development and overall economic growth, the planning processes in developing countries have also viewed (World Bank, 2008, Planning Commission of India, 2007) that agricultural growth may not to be the source of increasing direct employment and earning per head. Considering the negligible employment elasticity to agricultural growth, creation of non-agricultural opportunities, diversification of rural economy and expansion of Rural Non Farm Employment are adjunct to the strategies of managing vulnerabilities associated to the farm sector and bringing meaningful structural change in the socio-economic conditions of the rural economies.

II. Rural Livelihoods—Concepts and Measurement

Livelihoods are the ways in which people satisfy their needs, or gain a living (Chambers and Conway, 1992). The livelihood literature discusses how rural people make a living and whether their livelihood is secure or vulnerable over time. Livelihoods emanate from a variety of sources and activities for each given household—more often than not even for each working member, which may change even within a year, and, of course, vary over time. Flexibility of households' livelihoods determines the type of strategies that rural households adopt to make it secure and responsive to changes. The livelihood strategies are the sum of all diverse activities that people do in the context of their livelihood, and are based on the access to and combination of five forms of capital assets, namely, human capital, natural capital, financial capital, social capital, and physical capital (Sconner, 1998; Bebbington 1999). A livelihood comprises the capabilities, assets (including both material and social resources) and activities required for a means of living, and is sustainable when it can cope with and recover from stresses and shocks, maintain or enhance its capabilities and assets both now and in the future, while not undermining the natural resource base. Sustainable rural livelihoods are critically linked to the enhancement of these five capitals. In an agrarian economy, rural livelihoods are intricately linked with the access of rural people to natural resources such as land, water and biotic resources.

It is important to note that the terms *'assets* or *capitals'* in livelihoods analysis are conventionally associated with a stock, whereas in the dynamics of livelihoods operations there are many aspects of the five assets that are akin to flows. A better understanding of these concepts can be gained by looking at them in relation to entitlements theory (Sen, 1982, 1985; also Scoones, 1998). With this perspective, the livelihoods assets can be seen as a capability or a potential that can be deployed to undertake, or be 'invested in', livelihood activities. They are not uniform in character: for example under natural capital, access to water resources is contingent upon the flow of water through the hydrological cycle, whereas social capital can take the form of the network of social relationships which households possess that have potential to influence the viability of livelihood activities. From this perspective, livelihood capitals will accumulate where the potential to which the household has an entitlement increases.

Improvement in all the five capitals, and less dependence on vulnerable (less resilient) activities or strategies, could be termed 'strong SRL', while improvement in some of the capitals should at least compensate any decline in other capitals and high dependency on vulnerable strategies, which could be termed 'weak SRL'. These five capitals are complementary to one another and natural capital, especially, has a pivotal role in the livelihoods of rural people: "predominantly the poor of the world depend directly on natural resources, through cultivation, herding, collecting or hunting for their livelihoods" (Rennie and Singh, 1996: 16). Improvements in each of these capitals are in turn dependent on various indicators.

In the context of rural livelihoods, physical capital is measured in terms of a household's possession of durable assets (excluding land) such as house, machinery, livestock, and so on. Watershed related structures reflect the physical capital created at the village level under the watershed programme. Increases in natural capital are measured in terms of changes in access to or improvements in land, water and other common pool resources (CPRs). It is essentially a flow—the availability of productive potentials as inputs into livelihood activities that come from the dynamics of ecosystems functioning. Of course, natural capital can be treated as a stock in the short run, for example, by felling trees in a forest or over-fishing a lake, but this is not sustainable and is at variance with the concept of sustainable livelihoods. Changes in land values over the period are taken as a proxy for land quality, as land prices are often directly linked with area and quality (Reddy, 2001). Changes in availability of drinking water are measured in terms of quantities consumed and time spent in fetching water at the household level. In the case of irrigation water, changes in area under irrigation, number of wells and the depth of the water tables are taken as indicators. The changes are taken over a period of five years and seasonal variations, especially during summer, are also elicited. Use of fodder from CPRs and time spent in fetching it, is taken as a measure of improvements in CPRs other than water bodies. Education, skill and health are the main elements of human capital. Changes in human capital are measured through changes in education and medical expenditure, as this can best capture variations within communities, and these can be measured directly. Social capital is represented by changes in the migration pattern at the household level, the status of women in the decision-making process at the household level, as well as women's participation in self-help groups, active participation of the community in the watershed activities land equity in terms of beneficiary coverage and benefit flows. Financial capital is measured in terms of savings – that part of income that is not used for consumption or social payments. Income can be derived from various livelihood activities such as agriculture, wage labour, livestock, non-farm activities, returns on investments, and so forth, at the household level. Stability in livelihoods is assessed in terms of the security of the income sources and diversification of income generating activities.

The major problem in measuring these indicators is that some of them are measured at the household level and some at the village, community or group level. Synthesizing these levels in a coherent manner is difficult, though the SRL framework is capable of integrating local and global aspects of change. Similarly, integrating quantitative and qualitative aspects is also difficult, as quantification is not possible in all cases. While measurement of changes in some of the variables such as income, employment, assets and saving is straightforward, measurement of change in variables like water, CPRs and migration is rather tricky. On the other hand, measurement of change in some of the variables such as collective action and gender is difficult, as these variables are qualitative in nature.

The livelihood, either in terms of income or activity participation, needs to be measured first in its micro existence where it relates to the individuals residing in different population domains. However, from the point of view of generation of statistics on socio-economic characteristics, an individual is identified through the household. *"A central feature of the household is that there is a high degree of pooling of income and expenditure. This means that assessment at the level of the household is more meaningful in representing the potential command over goods and services than would be the case if the incomes of the individual members were treated separately. (The Wye Group Handbook 'Rural Households Livelihood and Well-Being'* United Nations, 2007, p. 181)". Since household is a multi-activity unit, the rural farm households in the context of their farm and non-farm own account enterprises are the managerial units with varying degrees of participation of their members. The derivatives of livelihood diversification in terms of employment and labour force participation can be obtained from the household labour force surveys (e.g., National Sample Survey in India) which dissect the household to capture the labour force and the work participation of its members in different industries and occupation. There are, of course, some limitations and constraints in deriving household income and its distribution over individuals as well as in the industry-occupation classifications. The estimation of household income requires assessment of financial flows in the matrix of individuals and the activities within the households. These financial flows may accrue from the wage work, imputations of non-wage work and flows from the savings and stocks. When the household activities are unorganized, informal and overlapping as is the case for farm related activities mixed with off-farm and non-farm activities, accounting such flows becomes difficult during survey investigations.

III. Diversification of Rural Livelihood—Issues and Dimensions

Livelihood diversification is defined as a process by which household members construct a diverse portfolio of activities and social support capabilities in their struggle for survival and in order to improve their standards of living. Livelihood diversification can take place through both agricultural diversification i.e., production of multiple crops or high-value crops; and non-agricultural livelihood diversification i.e., undertaking small enterprises, or choosing non-agricultural sources of livelihood like casual labour or migration. A recent study by Food and Agriculture Organization (FAO) on farming systems and poverty has suggested that diversification is the most important source of poverty reduction for small farmers in South and South-East Asia.

The basic rationale for diversifying the livelihood strategies by the rural households is two-fold: first, to increase household incomes; and second, to minimize risks of livelihood failure. Diversification reduces the risk of livelihood failure by spreading it across more than one income source. Diversification assists to reduce vulnerability, to generate financial resources in the absence of credit markets, and confers a host of other advantages in the presence of widespread market failures and uncertainties. Broadly, the rationale for diversification emanates from the opportunities for more employment and generation of higher incomes through more efficient use of resources and through exploitation of comparative advantage (World Bank, 1990).

Diversification is a core strategy of contemporary rural livelihood systems in developing countries (Ellis, 2000). In reality, rural household's resource allocation decisions are fundamentally constrained by conditions of livelihood asset endowments and related socio-political and institutional factors. Households may choose to adopt various strategies to secure their livelihood. They may be classified as: the *ex ante* risk coping mechanisms adopted by the households like crop diversification, varietal diversification, income diversification, livelihood diversification, etc.; and, the *ex post* mechanisms such as reduction in consumption expenditure, selling of animals, implements and other assets, increase in use of family labour and distress sale of assets to cope with losses. Thus, it is worth mentioning that the adoption of coping mechanism leads to the improvement in the standard of living of the households. Diversification of economic activities at the household level can occur through two processes. Firstly, the household may diversify its activities by increasing the number of workers engaged in different economic activities in the household. Secondly, it may diversify by letting each member to participate in more than one economic activity. In the micro-context, diversification of economic activity by an individual worker/household can be analyzed as: first, an occupational shift from one sector to the other over a period of time; and second, participation in more than one economic activity in either sector at a point in time (Unni, 1996). In the macro-context, the process of livelihood diversification of the employment structure or growth of non-agricultural employment can be analyzed as consisting of two components: first, new entrants to the labour force entering the non-agricultural sector; and second, a shift of workers from agriculture to non-agriculture (Unni, 1996).

Although the term "Economic Diversification" relates to the production of diverse goods and services in a production boundary, it also relates to pursuance of diverse economic activities by the people of a geographic domain for producing larger range of goods and services. The diversity of production and economic activities of the people is triggered by the use of resources for production of goods and services from available alternatives, and results into income flows from diverse sources. Such diversification process also takes into account the efficiency of resource use as well as the opportunity of resource use. In general, not only the economic condition of rural household improves with the blending of non-farm economic activities with farm activities—it also has positive impact on efficiency of their farm enterprises. It integrates with the multi-pronged strategy in the framework of action against poverty, stimulating enhancement of entitlement and access. The *opportunities, empowerment and security* are the three factors that have complimentary and supplementary role in neutralization of economic deprivation. These three factors are also closely associated with the process of economic diversification. If the opportunity of doing multiple activities enhances returns and exposure and thereby empowers the economic and social well-being, the empowerment through literacy, skill, knowledge, awareness, resources and connectivity improves the capacity and scope of harnessing the opportunities. The resultant derivatives are augmented remuneration and returns from diverse sources, contributing to stability of economic condition, security, reduction in vulnerability and risk mitigation.

One of the basic forms of rural economic diversification is the *crop diversification.* The diversified cropping pattern in a region emerges due to allocation of arable land resources for cultivation of number of alternative crops. The Indian agrarian space is endowed with diversity of agro-climatic conditions and varying degree of augmentation of farming resource through irrigation infrastructure, crop specific farming technologies, diversified demand and post-harvest linkages. Such on farm diversification helps in reducing farming risk due to climatic, market and other such aberrations and often improves resource use efficiency. However, the crop diversification has been subjected to resource endowment of farmers in terms of land, water, technology, seeds and soil besides externalities such as agro-climatic conditions, sustainability and the response to market (Haque 1999, Mehta 2005). The skewed distribution of infrastructure such as road, transportation, market, post-harvest handling, irrigation and power are found to be the impediments for both horizontal and vertical diversification. Nevertheless, the crop diversification not only indicates the options and opportunities of cropping, it also harmonises the supply to demand of diverse commodities and in the process diffuses the price volatility in the market. One may note that in India, at micro level, the operational holding size is small (Average operational holding is 1.3 Hectares) and individual farmers have limited scope of diversification in their farms. A generalization of crop diversification takes the form of *farm sector diversification* through animal husbandry, poultry and fisheries and its measurement in terms of value of outputs. It is widely acknowledged that in semi-arid central and western India having lesser scope of multiple cropping, animal husbandry reduces the vulnerability of farmers. In the regions where forward integration of small cattle holders has been strengthened by institutions such as cooperatives, the economic conditions of farmers have improved. The cooperatives, self-help groups and other institutions of marketing etc. have stimulated the process of on-farm and off-farm diversification by putting the opportunity, empowerment and security as the rural development package. The extension of farming activities to certain on farm post-harvest operations not only adds to the farm gate value creation it also expands the production entrepreneurship of the farmers to services.

From the point of view of diversification of economy in the production boundary, one may also look into the existence of enterprises in the rural areas and producing non-agricultural goods and services. In India, there is a significant presence of small and tiny non-agricultural enterprises in the rural areas. There is preponderance of informal and unorganized enterprises in the rural economy, both in terms of their number as well as workforce. Out of total own account enterprises (without hired workers), 11.1 million (92%) non-agricultural manufacturing and 9 million (91%) of service sector (excluding domestic trading) enterprises are located in rural sector (NSS 62nd and 63rd Round, reference period 2005-06 and 2006-07 respectively). However, in terms of GDP, these rural enterprises have much smaller share. The rural non-agricultural entrepreneurial diversification may not be simply assessable in terms of their number and GDP share. There are aspects of economy of scale, operating efficiency and technology used in the corresponding large enterprises located in industrial hubs, which are not easily measurable but impinge on efficacy of rural non-farm diversification.

The diversification through crops and on and off-farm production offers limited perspective of rural economic diversification. For the rural economy to sustain in the long run, the scope of its diversification would necessitate expansion to the wider dimensions of *livelihood diversification*. The vulnerability of livelihood in rural agrarian segments of developing countries has been acknowledged and the livelihood security is one of the central theme needing attention in the liberalized and market reformed agricultural trade regime. The rural livelihood diversification therefore is an integral dimension of development agenda for strengthening rural livelihood and sustaining livelihood security.

There are two ways to look into livelihood diversification. First, the individuals and/or their groups perform different activities, i.e., the individuals are capable of engaging in the alternative choices in the labour market and undertake different forms of rural employment; both farm as well as non-farm. From the point of view of rural development, the *rural employment diversification* is considered to be driving force (UN-Wye Group, 2007). Secondly, the *rural income diversification* enabling individuals or households to have income sourced from the diversified sources. There is differentiation in employment diversification and income diversification as both are broadly complementary but may not necessarily be synonymous. The employment diversification is measured in terms of labour force participation in diverse industries and occupation. The wages and remunerations from different employment would add up to income. However, the income diversification is more comprehensive, since it would also account for transfer payments (rents, interests, dividends etc.) to individuals. The domain of rural livelihood may extend beyond the rural production boundary. The commutation of rural people to urban neighbourhood for their work and jobs as well as income transfers from urban to rural add to the wider dimensions of livelihood diversification.

Diversity of modes of livelihood at any given time is also closely related to the *diversification* of livelihoods over time. A broad comparative review of a process described as 'de-agrarianisation' in sub-Saharan Africa concluded that perhaps 60-80 per cent of rural household income in the late 1990s was derived from non-farming sources, by comparison with an approximate 40 per cent in the 1980s (Bryceson, 1999). There were several reasons for such changes: structural adjustment programmes, sharply worsening terms of agricultural trade, the collapse of meso-level infrastructures of support for small farmers, devalued currencies, new opportunities and necessities of cross-border smuggling and trade, etc. It is important to recognize that it is not only poor households that are forced to diversify in order to make ends meet as best they can. Richer households also diversify their economic activities—as for example in the case of businessmen who are 'weekend' farmers—and this can be a path to accumulation. It is also important to note that migration for work elsewhere is one typical mode of diversification in the livelihoods of the rural poor that has arguably been inhibited by politicians and undervalued by policy-makers (de Haan, 1999). Three main questions arise out of recent research work in the mid 1990s and the late 1990s, under the auspices of different projects, for example by the African Studies Centre at Leiden University, the Institute of Development Studies at Sussex and the Overseas Development Institute in London. The first question is how, in view of the complexity of individual household trajectories of change it is possible to derive defensible generalisations about the experience of large numbers of the rural poor over time. The second question is how to achieve a better understanding of the links and the tensions between different levels of analysis: the micro-level of the household, the meso-level of institutional intervention through local government, development agencies or regional markets, and the macro-level of national policymaking. The third question, relevant in the context both of prevalent neo-liberal policy prescriptions and of the reality of diversified rural livelihoods across a number of conventionally discrete economic sectors, is how policies are to be devised in practice that will have an effective impact upon the disparate livelihoods of the rural poor.

IV. Determinants of Rural Livelihood Diversification

Livelihood diversification in rural areas of developing countries is influenced by the interplay of economic and non-economic factors. While the economists' approach to explaining diversification stems from the decision-making of rural households as outcomes of freely-made choices, albeit subject to economic constraints, e.g., resources, assets, skills, incomes and so on. Social and familial constraints also, of course, apply, as not only what people do, but their capability to change what they do, is influenced by their social context (family, kin, caste, ethnic group, community, belief systems and so on). For example, the social institutions through which livelihoods are mediated may act to suppress opportunities for some members of a community (for example, landless, women, low caste) while enhancing those of other members. This 'social-embeddedness' of individual or household actions is indeed important in identifying factors influencing rural livelihood diversification. The literature identifies a range of different motives and pressures that contribute to explaining why diversification occurs and the patterns of diversity that are observed. Some main determinants of diversification are seasonality, differentiated labour markets, risk strategies, coping behaviour, credit market imperfections, and inter-temporal savings and investment strategies.

Seasonality on its own explains many of the patterns of diversity in rural household incomes, especially those involving on-farm diversity and off-farm agricultural wage earnings. In economic terms, seasonality means that returns to labour in both on-farm activities and off-farm labour markets vary during the year, causing seasonal changes in occupation as labour time is switched from lower to higher return activities. Seasonality means that continuous household consumption needs are mismatched with uneven income flows. Leaving aside risk and market imperfections, this would not constitute a problem provided that total income was sufficient to cover annual consumption requirements. Crop storage, output sales and savings could be used to convert unstable income into stable consumption. In practice, of course both risk and market imperfections abound in the rural economy. Income instability and consumption smoothing are real problems confronted by households, and therefore an important motive for income diversification associated with seasonality is to reduce income instability. The economic motivation for diversification cited in relation to seasonality applies more generally—when the marginal return to labour time in farming for any individual falls below the wage rate or the return to self-employment attainable off the farm, then the household is better off switching that individual into off-farm or non-farm activities. Work opportunities vary according to skills (for example, in trading, vehicle repair, brick making), education (for example, for salaried jobs), and by gender (for example, male wage work in construction or mines *vs*. female opportunities in trading or textile factories). Economic considerations of labour allocation may be overlaid and modified by social rules of access both within the family and in the community, and these rules may result in the 'social exclusion' of individuals and households from particular income streams.

Aside from considerations of static comparative advantage in the deployment of labour time, rural households are observed to take a longer term strategic view of future income sources. Investment in social networks is one manifestation of this. Investment in education, often linked to migration and remittance behaviour, is another.

Risk is often cited in the literature as the primary motive for income diversification. Risk is the subjective probability attached by individuals or by the household towards the outcomes of the various income generating activities in which they are engaged. In the face of probabilistic outcomes in relation to income streams, the social unit diversifies its portfolio of activities in order to anticipate and to mitigate the threat to its welfare of failure in individual activities. In terms of the static allocation of labour time across different activities, it is then the risk-discounted marginal returns to labour that determine the patterns of engagement and specialisation by household members. Since households are risk averse, they are often prepared to accept lower income for greater security. A basic characteristic of rural livelihoods in developing countries is that most of the income earning opportunities open to poor households, that is, own farm production and agricultural wage labour, exhibit high correlations between risks attached to alternative income streams; in other words, if there is a drought or flood in a particular locality, all income streams are adversely affected simultaneously. While on-farm diversity can take some advantage of differences in the risk-proneness of crops or crop mixes to adverse natural events, the protection this affords is only partial. Diversification into non-farm incomes, by contrast, can result in low risk correlations between livelihood components. At this stage, one must distinguish between *ex-ante* risk management and *ex-post* coping strategy with crisis. A complementary way that risk and coping have been distinguished is to interpret risk as *ex-ante* income management and coping as *ex-post* consumption management in the wake of crisis. While the former involves spread of activities as deliberate household strategy, coping is the involuntary response to disaster or unanticipated failure in major sources of survival. Following this distinction, coping strategy includes tactics for maintaining consumption such as drawing down on savings, using up food stocks, gifts from relatives, community transfers, sales of livestock, other asset sales, and so on. Coping behaviour takes place in sequential phases, which, typically seek first to protect the future income generating capability of the household, even if current consumption is compromised. It is only as a last resort that assets critical for future survival are sold or abandoned to stave off starvation. Therefore, the term coping can be used to encompass distress and crisis reasons for the emergence of new livelihood patterns, and these differ conceptually and in practice from risk management determinants of livelihood patterns.

The concept of coping is inextricably linked with the notion of vulnerability of rural families to livelihood collapse in the face of disaster such as drought, floods, cyclones and so on. Vulnerability is defined in this context as a high degree of exposure to risk, shocks and stress; and proneness to food insecurity and is linked to the resilience and sensitivity of the livelihood system, where resilience means the ability of the system to absorb change or even utilise change to advantage; while sensitivity refers to the susceptibility of the natural resource base to change following human interference. Adaptation to shocks constitutes strategies for diversification of livelihoods, and vulnerability enhances when the adaptation strategies fail to restore the balance in livelihood patterns. Diversification explicitly draws attention to a variety of dissimilar income sources (farm, non-farm, remittances etc.) as its chief characteristic. This is one potential outcome of adaptation but not the only one— new ways of trying to sustain the existing income portfolio are also forms of adaptation. Adaptation may result in the adoption of successively more vulnerable livelihood systems over time. By contrast, the prime motive and consequence of successful diversification by the poor is to reduce vulnerability. Since credit market failures in the rural economy of developing countries of Africa and Asia are cited as principal reasons for rural poverty, livelihood security can be enhanced through expansion of non-farm activities in rural areas, whereby the farm households can generate cash income to substitute for the absence or high cost of credit, thus permitting them to purchase cash inputs into production, or to make farm investments. Credit market considerations also illustrate how closely interrelated in practice are the different determinants of diversification. Cash generated to overcome a credit squeeze also contributes to mitigating the seasonality problem of managing unstable income, and this in turn may help to reduce risk-aversion in farm production decisions.

Attempts to list out separate determinants of diversification often miss the multi-dimensionality of the process shaping rural livelihoods. Each of the above-listed determinants—seasonality, labour market imperfections, risk, coping, credit, accumulation—may be conceptually distinct but are rarely separable in practice, and in fact are mediated through social institutions, including ties of community and kinship, property rights and obligations, and gender relations within the household. They are also often shaped by interactions with the physical environment, and by changes over time in the larger economy, including the impact on income-earning opportunities of structural adjustment and market liberalisation policies. Migration decision by rural labour basically as a coping strategy to spread the risk of income uncertainty in rural occupations, flow of remittances to family members and ability to fall back upon land and other assets including assets expected at inheritance, are cited as valid examples of interdependence of factors operating simultaneously affecting the status of rural livelihood diversification. The migration literature has dwelt on both 'pull' and 'push' reasons for migration to occur—income differentials are seen as the major 'pull' factor; while seasonality, risk, market failures, erosion of assets (for example, land subdivision at inheritance), landlessness, and disasters leading to livelihood collapse are seen as 'push' factors. The literature is abound with evidences supporting both the forces—for example, Bigsten (1996) finds that the pull of high wages is more important than the push of land scarcity in explaining migration decisions in Kenya; while Adams (1993) finds precisely the reverse in a study of the factors explaining international migration from rural Egypt. The notions of push and pull are similar in descriptive intent to the juxtapositions of involuntary versus voluntary and desperation versus choice as ways of broadly categorising alternative sets of circumstances that result in livelihood diversification. While it is often useful to dichotomise cause and effect in this way, the ease of so doing should not be confused with the accuracy of the description thus achieved. In practice, individuals and households are influenced by a multiplicity of factors determining the livelihood changes they undergo. While on occasions a single factor may dominate over all others for an entire community or location, more often a cumulative combination of factors will represent variable pressures and opportunities for different individuals and households within the community.

V. Diversification of Rural Livelihood in India

According to the conventional theory of economic development, the share of non-farm income and employment in the total income and employment of the rural households increases in the developing countries in the process of their development, and a combination of farm and non-farm income at the household level provides resilience against adverse situations in either of the sectors. Although economic opportunities in the non-farm sector have increased in India in recent periods, a comparative account of the non-farm sector in the rural *vis-à-vis* the urban sector shows significant disparity in terms of its size and growth. Given the lopsided pattern of growth in India's non-farm sector, its importance in the rural sector for the potential of generation of employment and diversification of livelihoods needs to be assessed. The rural non-farm sector (RNFS) in India encompasses all non-agricultural activities: mining and quarrying, household and non-household manufacturing, processing, repair, construction, trade and commerce, transport and other services in villages and rural towns undertaken by enterprises varying in size from household own-account enterprises to factories. The RNFS thus comprises diverse activities and sustained growth in the RNFS depends on a varied set of factors, depending on the kind of impetus, positive or negative, that these factors provide to the rural economy. RNFS will experience development-and-distress-related rural diversification depending on the importance and strength of such diverse factors.

Rural diversification may be defined as the economic development of non-agricultural activities. At the micro-level this refers to a livelihood which has multiple, part-time components. Rural diversification may be associated with a booming or recession economy or with accumulating or immiserating livelihood strategies. The available studies explain positive or negative outcomes of rural diversification with pull and push factors. In the pull or development-led proposition for rural diversification there are again different strands of arguments. While Mellor (1978) argued that technology-led growth in agriculture gave rise to several linkages, which led to an expansion of employment in the non-agriculture sector, Visaria *et al.* (1994) argued that development of urban centres gave impetus to non-farm employment in the adjoining rural areas because of low factor (land, labour) prices in the rural areas. In the development-led proposition for rural diversification, some researchers argued that infrastructure facilities and supportive institutions encouraged rural non-farm employment (Acharya and Mitra, 2000). In general, the urbanization and extension of infrastructure facilities in a region are highly correlated. Several human resources related parameters like education and skill development of rural workers, credit availability for non-farm activities have also encouraged the process of rural diversification (Islam, 1997).

The second set of arguments explains the phenomenon of employment diversification in rural India with distress-related indictors. Vaidyanathan (1986) found a positive association between the unemployment rate and the incidence level of rural non-agricultural employment in states, and argued that in a situation where the labour absorptive capacity of agriculture was limited and the urban industrial sector was not able to accommodate the ever-growing labour force, the RNFS tended to act as a 'sponge' for the surplus labour. The RNFS thus acts like a residual sector in which rural workers concentrate on account of their distress conditions. This is popularly known as the push phenomenon or distress hypothesis which was subsequently, supported by several scholars.

The above discussion suggests that pull as well as push-related factors promote rural non-farm employment (RNFE) growth. However, the pattern of RNFE growth in either of the situations would be different. In fact, the non-farm sector consists of several heterogeneous industries, and is influenced by a host of separate factors often independent of other industrial categories. The state-wise employment trends in non-agriculture industrial categories and several related indicators at the level of state also support this premise (Jha, 2005). Demographic pressure accompanied by increase in per capita income, for instance, influences construction activities; whereas, rural literacy and infrastructure facilities by and large promote finance-insurance-real estate and business services (FIREB). Employment in trade and transport is highly correlated and is most affected by basic infrastructure facilities like roads. From certain states there are also evidences of road facilities encouraging employment of the rural workforce in urban industries like manufacturing, business services. Infrastructure other than roads is also important for employment growth in other non-farm sectors. Manufacturing for example, requires assured power, business services require more reliable communication facilities, etc. (for details, Jha 2005).

A detailed study by Uma Rani *et al.* (2004) lists reasons for particular trend of employment and income in the manufacturing sector. Their study found that in manufacturing activities undertaken in the organized and unorganized sectors during the years 1984-1999, the growth of employment, value-addition and capital in the organized manufacturing sector has grown during 1984-95 and declined subsequently. The trend is somewhat different in the unorganized sector, where growth had peaked up during the 1984-90, flattened during the 1989-95 and surged ahead in subsequent years (1995-2000) following the adoption of promotional policies towards unorganized segments of small-scale industries. This growth has been particularly high for the organic as compared to the inorganic manufacturing units. Employment growth in construction peaked during the 90s, though it was fairly high (1.75%) even in the 80s. In the urban sector, construction activity had peaked early (in the 80s) while in rural India a high growth was experienced during the 90s. The extension of basic infrastructure like roads in rural India might have contributed to employment growth in rural construction during the 90s, apart from adoption of certain policy initiatives by the government.

Transport-storage-communication (TSC) and finance-insurance-real estate-business (FIREB) services were the industrial categories where employment increased in both the rural and urban sectors. Employment in TSC appears to be more influenced by increased investment in infrastructure such as roads, which increased the quality of real estate and consequently, the income and employment in real estate. This in turn had spread effects on the growth of business services. Trade, hotels and restaurants (THR) were the other industrial categories where employment growth was positive and significant in both the sectors, though the rate of growth was higher in the urban sector. The employment growth was negative in mining and quarrying, utilities and community services during the 1990s. These industries, largely within the domain of the public sector, experienced decline in employment because of policies of downsizing. In mining, the decline in employment could also have been accentuated because of the strict environmental regulations and an increased focus on clean technologies. Switch to more capital intensive methods of resource extraction had its negative impact on the employment despite increase of income in mining.

In sum, the employment situation in the rural non-farm sector had deteriorated in the 90s. Manufacturing, the most important non-farm sector was marked by a decelerating rate of growth of employment during the 90s. Though mining, utilities, and community services accounted for only a small proportion of rural employment; employment growth in these sectors was negative. Construction, trade, transport, and business services emerged as the most important sources of rural employment growth in the 90s. These industries had, however, a small base, which accounts for around 11 per cent of rural employment in the country. The NSS survey of enterprises presents a trend similar to the NSS quinquennial survey on employment. The situation on the quality aspect of rural employment was also not encouraging as there was persistently high underemployment and casualization of the workforce. In spite of all these discouraging trends, the real wages of rural workers had increased while the gap between rural and urban wages in non-farm activities has decreased during the 90s.

According to the study by Brajesh Jha (2006), in order to investigate the possible determinants of rural non-farm employment (RNFE), the RNFE per cent in selected states and districts can be regressed separately with agriculture income per hectare (PHAI), agricultural output per capita (PCAO), infrastructure indices (INFI) in per cent and population density (PDS) per sq. km. The estimated relationships can be either linear or non-linear. In Jha 2006, the regression is accomplished in 10 states with information from 20 districts.

Linear OLS estimates:

$$\text{RNFE} = -22.61 + 1.6\ \text{PCAO} + 0.3\ \text{INFI} + 2.8\ \text{PDS}\ \ N = 30,\ \ R^{-2} = 0.54$$

$$t\text{-stat.}\ (2.6)\ (1.1)\ (3.5)\ (3.2) \qquad \ldots\text{eq. (1)}$$

$$\text{RNFE} = -20.42 + 0.4\ \text{PHAO} + 0.3\ \text{INFI} + 2.3\ \text{PDS}\ \ N = 30,\ \ R^{-2} = 0.56$$

t-stat. (2.4) (1.4) (3.7) (2.7) ...eq. (2)

Log-linear OLS estimates:

RNFE (ln) = –5.26 + 0.2 PCAO (ln) + 0.8 INFI (ln) + 0.5 PDS (ln) N = 30, R^{-2} = 0.54

t-stat. (3.7) (1.6) (2.6) (3.5) ...eq. (3)

RNFE (ln) = –4.72 + 0.1 PHAO (ln) + 1.1 INFI (ln) + 0.4 PDS (ln) N = 30, R^{-2} = 0.50

t-stat. (2.4) (1.4) (3.3) (2.9) ...eq. (4)

In all four sets of specifications though, the adjusted R-square was not very high, signs of the coefficients were along the expected lines and also estimated coefficients for variables other than agriculture were robust (significant at the 1% level). It is interesting to note that variables related to agriculture are found to be the weakest determinants of rural non-farm employment. In a linear form of relationship, the infrastructure index is the most important determinant followed by population density, both of these variables are significant at 1 per cent. The importance of these variables in RNFE growth can be corroborated from certain studies of the late 80s and 90s. These studies emphasize the role of infrastructure development in increasing rural non-farm employment growth. Population density however reflects the role of push or distress-related phenomenon in promoting RNFE.

Several studies at the national and state-levels have attempted to understand the growth in rural non-farm sector employment by analysing the probable determinants which influence occupational diversification of the rural workforce from agriculture to the non-agricultural activities. We propose to probe into the dynamics of the growth in the share of non-agriculture in rural workforce and attempt to estimate its major macro-level determinants relating to the economic environment affecting the demand for non-farm jobs in the rural areas. The diversification of workforce towards the non-farm sector can be distress-driven or growth-driven, and it is important to know which one is the dominant force because the impact on rural poverty and income-inequality will be different in the two cases.

The factors identified in the literature in order to explain the growth of rural non-farm employment can broadly be grouped into the following categories—(i) Agricultural growth led diversification (Inter-sectoral Linkage Hypothesis), (ii) Distress led diversification (Residual Sector Hypothesis), (iii) Factors external to agriculture such as rural infrastructure, human capital and per-capita public expenditure on rural development, and (iv) Factors external to the rural economy such as degree of urbanisation and urban agglomeration. In the early 1970s, it was postulated that due to increase in agricultural productivity a virtuous cycle could emerge between agricultural and non-agricultural activities through inter-sectoral consumption and production linkages (Mellor, 1976). With increasing levels of agricultural income, the relative share of consumption expenditure of the rural population on non-food items tend to increase and this in turn stimulates the growth of rural non-farm employment. Moreover, agricultural growth leads to an increased demand by the agriculturalists for inputs such as fertilisers, tools, machinery equipments and their repairing services, as well as an increase in the demand for processing of the agricultural products. These backward and forward production linkages also lead to the growth of non-farm sector employment in the rural areas.

A different set of literature argues that due to lack of employment opportunities in agriculture a large section of rural labourers gets 'pushed' into low-productive casual activities in the non-agricultural sector. In the absence of inter-sectoral linkages or due to non-existence of a mechanism for conversion of agricultural growth impulses into non-agricultural employment opportunities, the growth in rural non-farm employment can thus bc seen as distress diversification. Vaidyanathan (1986) observed a strong positive relationship between unemployment rate (as an indicator of excess labour supply problem in agriculture) and rural non-farm employment and formulated this spill-off of excess labour force from agriculture to the non-agricultural sector as the 'Residual Sector Hypothesis'. It may be noted that the distress movement of labour force into non-agricultural activities from agriculture cannot completely be ruled out in the Indian context, and alternative distress-causes like population density, proportion of marginal land-holdings and casualisation of agricultural labour force have been suggested and they are found to have positive impacts on rural non-farm employment in many of the studies. The growth of rural non-farm employment was also found to be determined by factors external to agriculture but within the rural economy, like rural infrastructure (particularly road density, telecommunications, banking facilities and electricity consumption), human capital, government programmes etc. Taking literacy rate as a proxy for human capital, Chadha in his studies (1997, 2001a, 2004) has found that at the all-India level that the proportion of illiterate workers were higher in agriculture than non-agriculture, the participation in non-farm activities tended to increase with increase in the level of education and there is a shift from casual non-agricultural jobs to regular employment. Apart from the above-mentioned determinants, researchers have attempted to understand the role of factors external to the rural economy like degree of urbanisation, urban agglomeration, size of nearby villages/cities, non-agricultural value added per capita, macro level policy environment and the like in influencing the growth of rural non-agricultural employment. At the NSS regional level Unni (1991) has found a strong positive impact of urbanisation (defined as the share of population in urban areas to total population) on male participation and a weak negative impact on female participation in rural non-farm employment.

For our study we will focus on a mix of these 'pull' and 'push' determinants to estimate their impact on the growth of rural non-farm employment in India during the post-reform period. We will be analysing the growth of the rural non-farm sector employment in terms of the share of non-farm workforce in total rural workforce, but unlike most of the other studies which focus on the non-farm sector as a whole, we would like to take a look at the growth of the sector at a disaggregated level also. Since there are differences in the participation pattern of the male and female workers in rural employment, we have attempted to analyse the determinants of male and female rural non-farm employment separately.

The dependent variables chosen for our analysis are—

- RNFE-UPSS – % Share of non-farm workers in rural usual ps+ss workforce;
- RNFE-MPS – % Share of non-farm workers in rural male usual ps workforce;
- RNFE-FPS – % Share of non-farm workers in rural female usual ps workforce;
- MFG-UPSS– % Share of manufacturing workers in rural usual ps+ss workforce;
- MFG-MPS– % Share of manufacturing workers in rural male usual ps workforce;
- MFG-FPS– % Share of manufacturing workers in rural female usual ps workforce;
- CON-UPSS – % Share of construction workers in rural usual ps+ss workforce;
- CON-MPS – % Share of construction workers in rural male usual ps workforce;

CON-FPS– % Share of construction workers in rural female usual ps workforce;

TRD-UPSS– % Share of trading and related workers in rural usual ps+ss workforce;

TRD-MPS– % Share of trading related workers in rural male usual ps workforce;

TRD-FPS– % Share of trading related workers in rural female usual ps workforce;

TRA-UPSS– % Share of transport workers in rural usual ps+ss workforce;

TRA-MPS – % Share of transport workers in rural male usual ps workforce;

TRA-FPS– % Share of transport workers in rural female usual ps workforce;

SVS-UPSS– % Share of other-services workers in rural usual ps+ss workforce;

SVS-MPS – % Share of other-services workers in rural male usual ps workforce;

SVS-FPS – % Share of other-services workers in rural female usual ps workforce.

To find out how these shares have been changing over time and across regions we have chosen the following variables as the macro-level determinants –

UNEMP-UPSS–Rural usual ps+ss unemployment rate;

UNEMP-MPS–Rural male usual ps unemployment rate;

UNEMP-FPS–Rural female usual ps unemployment rate;

DENSITY–Rural population density (person/sq.km.);

AGRI–Per-capita agricultural value-added (Rs.'000);

LITERACY–Rural literacy rate (%);

LITERACY-M–Rural male literacy rate (%);

LITERACY-F–Rural female literacy rate (%);

SECONDARY–Secondary-passed population among rural literates (%);

SECONDARY-M–Secondary-passed population among rural male literates (%);

SECONDARY-F–Secondary-passed population among rural female literates (%);

URBAN–Degree of urbanisation (% urban population in total population).

Here UNEMP and DENSITY represent the distress-driven factors, AGRI represents the inter-sectoral linkages, LITERACY and SECONDARY are the proxies for human capital and URBAN is the extra-rural influence.

Our work comprises 16 states (entities) and 5 NSSO rounds (time points) for India, thus making the data set possessing some characteristics of both the cross-sectional studies and time-series studies. We attempt to utilise the panel regression methods which examine individual-specific effects, time effects or both, in order to deal with observed or unobserved heterogeneity, which are not captured in the regressors. These effects are either fixed or random effect. A *fixed effect model* examines if intercepts vary across group or time period, whereas a *random effect model* explores differences in error variance components across individual or time period.

If individual effect u_i (cross-sectional or time specific effect) does not exist (i.e. u_i =0), ordinary least squares (OLS) produces efficient and consistent parameter estimates.

OLS model: $y_{it} = \alpha + \beta X_{it} + \varepsilon_{it}, (u_i = 0)$

If individual effect u_i is not zero in longitudinal data, heterogeneity may influence some of the core assumptions of OLS estimation. Then panel data models provide a way to deal with these problems.

The functional forms of one-way fixed and random effect models are as follows:

Fixed effect model (FE): $y_{it} = (\alpha + u_i) + \beta X_{it} + v_{it}$

Random effect model (RE): $y_{it} = \alpha + \beta X_{it} + (u_i + v_{it}),$

where u_i is a fixed or random effect specific to individual (group) or time period that is not included in the regression, and errors are *independent identically distributed*, $v_{it} \sim$ *IID* $(0, \sigma v^2)$.

Fixed effects are tested by the F test, while random effects are examined by the Lagrange multiplier (LM) test (Breusch and Pagan, 1980). If the null hypothesis is not rejected in either test, the pooled OLS regression is favoured. The Hausman specification test (Hausman, 1978) compares a random effect model to its fixed counterpart. If the null hypothesis, that the individual effects are uncorrelated with the other regressors, is not rejected, a random effect model is favoured over its fixed counterpart.

We have taken the data corresponding to the 16 major states and the 5 NSSO Employment-Unemployment rounds. Thus we have 80 observations for India. Table 1.1 shows the summary statistics of the Indian data-set, for the dependent and explanatory variables.

We can now summarise the estimated equations 1.0 to 6.0 as given below, to see at a glance how the share of non-farm employment in rural workforce is getting affected by our chosen 'push' and 'pull' factors. We have performed the tests for the choice of the fixed effect model of regression *vis-à-vis* the random effects model, and find the following relationships with *** and ** signifying statistical significance at 1 per cent and 5 per cent levels respectively.

Determinants of RNFE Workforce

RNFE-UPSS = 0.81 + 1.14 UNEMP*** + 0.03 DENSITY***
– 0.33 AGRI + 0.13 URBAN + 0.07 LITERACY
+ 0.56 SECONDARY** ...(1.0–RE)

RNFE-MPS = – 5.43 +0.38 UNEMP–MPS + 0.05 DENSITY**
– 0.26 AGRI + 0.48 URBAN + 0.07 LITERACY-M
+ 0.34 SECONDARY-M ...(1.1 – FE)

RNFE-FPS = – 0.84 + 0.30 UNEMP-FPS** + 0.07 DENSITY***
– 1.16 AGRI + 0.35 URBAN – 0.17 LITERACY-F
+ 0.45 SECONDARY-F ...(1.2 – FE)

Determinants of MFG Workforce

MFG-UPSS = 2.13 +0.49 UNEMP*** + 0.01 DENSITY***
–0.02 AGRI + 0.11 URBAN**–0.02 LITERACY
–0.04 SECONDARY ...(2.0 – RE)

MFG-MPS = 3.06* + 0.43 UNEMP-MPS*** + 0.01
DENSITY** – 0.06 AGRI + 0.14 URBAN***
–0.02 LITERACY – M-0.01 SECONDARY-M
...(2.1 – RE)

MFG-FPS = 1.07 + 0.07 UNEMP-FPS + 0.03 DENSITY***
– 0.02 AGRI + 0.01 URBAN – 0.05 LITERACY-F
– 0.01 SECONDARY-F ...(2.2 – RE)

Table 1.1: Summary Statistics for the data set on India – state-level analysis

DEPENDENT VARIABLES		Mean	Std. Dev.	Min	Max	Obs	
RNFE_UPSS	overall	27.09	10.00	10.10	64.80	N	80
	between		8.75	13.72	52.32	n	16
	within		5.23	16.27	40.29	T	5
MFG_UPSS	overall	7.37	3.52	3.10	16.60	N	80
	between		3.42	3.58	14.90	n	16
	within		1.12	4.17	10.29	T	5
CON_UPSS	overall	5.22	4.10	0.60	20.20	N	80
	between		2.80	1.80	11.36	n	16
	within		3.06	0.30	14.06	T	5
TRD_UPSS	overall	5.48	2.36	1.60	13.20	N	80
	between		2.13	2.64	11.26	n	16
	within		1.12	3.30	7.72	T	5
TRA_UPSS	overall	2.33	1.38	0.40	7.30	N	80
	between		1.16	0.60	5.74	n	16
	within		0.79	0.39	3.93	T	5
SVS_UPSS	overall	5.87	2.51	2.60	15.50	N	80
	between		2.29	2.94	11.52	n	16
	within		1.14	3.25	11.01	T	5
RNFE_MPS	overall	33.31	11.25	13.00	68.20	N	80
	between		9.94	16.90	57.26	n	16
	within		5.72	20.01	46.65	T	5
MFG_MPS	overall	7.49	2.80	2.10	13.80	N	80
	between		2.65	2.80	12.92	n	16
	within		1.10	3.69	10.09	T	5
CON_MPS	overall	7.07	5.49	0.80	24.90	N	80
	between		4.37	2.32	17.60	n	16
	within		3.47	1.23	16.75	T	5

INDEPENDENT VARIABLES		Mean	Std. Dev.	Min	Max	Obs.	
UNEMP	overall	2.02	2.14	0.23	11.46	N	80
	between		2.06	0.58	8.96	n	16
	within		0.76	0.09	4.52	T	5
UNEMP_MPS	overall	2.64	1.96	0.57	12.50	N	80
	between		1.73	0.80	7.90	n	16
	within		1.00	0.41	7.24	T	5
UNEMP_FPS	overall	4.54	6.61	0.15	31.01	N	80
	between		6.02	0.55	22.48	n	16
	within		3.05	0.92	22.17	T	5
DENSITY	overall	297.70	177.45	80.00	732.00	N	80
	between		177.37	95.40	644.20	n	16
	within		40.29	169.30	434.30	T	5
URBAN	overall	26.38	10.26	8.37	47.89	N	80
	between		10.09	9.38	41.55	n	16
	within		2.93	18.97	38.48	T	5
AGRI	overall	5.49	2.23	2.26	11.83	N	80
	between		2.16	2.50	11.25	n	16
	within		0.72	3.45	7.39	T	5
LITERACY	overall	53.22	13.98	24.99	86.60	N	80
	between		11.23	38.72	82.25	n	16
	within		8.70	37.80	71.20	T	5
LITERACY_M	overall	62.40	11.70	38.80	87.90	N	80
	between		9.10	49.89	84.80	n	16
	within		7.65	48.12	77.79	T	5
LITERACY_F	overall	43.59	16.73	9.80	85.30	N	80
	between		13.88	24.10	79.86	n	16
	within		9.84	25.45	64.22	T	5

(Contd.)

(Contd.)

DEPENDENT VARIABLES		Mean	Std. Dev.	Min	Max	Obs	
TRD_MPS	overall	7.21	2.86	2.20	16.30	N	80
	between		2.53	3.62	14.64	n	16
	within		1.45	3.77	10.11	T	5
TRA_MPS	overall	3.55	1.97	0.60	10.20	N	80
	between		1.63	0.96	8.28	n	16
	within		1.16	0.87	5.77	T	5
SVS_MPS	overall	6.83	2.46	3.70	17.20	N	80
	between		2.18	4.06	11.40	n	16
	within		1.25	4.33	12.63	T	5
RNFE_FPS	overall	22.29	15.35	4.00	70.00	N	80
	between		14.56	8.24	53.70	n	16
	within		5.86	1.09	45.59	T	5
MFG_FPS	overall	8.90	7.92	1.20	35.80	N	80
	between		7.87	1.74	30.52	n	16
	within		1.97	3.92	14.18	T	5
CON_FPS	overall	2.43	2.97	0.00	20.30	N	80
	between		1.71	0.70	6.60	n	16
	within		2.46	0.45	16.85	T	5
TRD_FPS	overall	2.70	1.59	0.20	7.20	N	80
	between		1.40	0.76	5.52	n	16
	within		0.82	0.36	5.86	T	5
TRA_FPS	overall	0.23	0.40	0.00	2.40	N	80
	between		0.24	0.04	0.94	n	16
	within		0.32	0.42	1.99	T	5
SVS_FPS	overall	7.75	8.61	0.90	49.30	N	80
	between		8.11	1.40	31.72	n	16
	within		3.42	0.87	25.33	T	5

INDEPENDENT VARIABLES		Mean	Std. Dev.	Min	Max	Obs.	
SECONDARY	overall	18.29	6.72	7.21	37.21	N	80
	between		4.62	11.74	26.41	n	16
	within		4.98	6.35	30.86	T	5
SECONDARY_M	overall	20.95	6.88	8.17	39.23	N	80
	between		4.44	14.52	27.87	n	16
	within		5.34	9.06	33.74	T	5
SECONDARY_F	overall	14.36	7.74	4.08	37.48	N	80
	between		5.50	7.53	24.66	n	16
	within		5.58	1.50	27.95	T	5
UNEMP Rural	Unemployment Rate (UPSS)						
UNEMP_MPS	Rural Unemployment Rate (MPS)						
UNEMP_FPS	Rural Unemployment Rate (FPS)						
DENSITY	Rural Population Density						
URBAN	Degree of Urbanisation						
AGRI	Per-capita Agricultural Value-Added						
LITERACY	Rural Literacy Rate						
LITERACY_M	Rural Male Literacy Rate						
UTERACY_F	Rural Femele Literacy Rate						
SECONDARY	Share of Secondary-passed among rural Literates						
SECONDARY_M	Share of Secondary-passed among rural male Literates						
SECONDARY_F	Share of Secondary-passed among rural female Literates						

Source: Own calculation using Stata-12.

Determinants of CON Workforce

CON-UPSS = –1.55 +0.10 UNEMP + 0.002 DENSITY–0.65 AGRI-0.04 URBAN + 0.07 LITERACY + 0.39 SECONDARY*** ...(3.0 – RE)

CON-MPS = –16.35** + 0.29 UNEMP-MPS + 0.03 DENSITY** –0.78 AGRI + 0.42 URBAN* + 0.05 LITERACY-M +0.20 SECONDARY-M ...(3.1 – FE)

CON-FPS = 7.83 + 0.003 UNEMP-FPS + 0.003 DENSITY–1.82 AGRI* –0.05 URBAN + 0.06 LITERACY-F + 0.16 SECONDARY-F* ...(3.2 – FE)

Determinants of TRD Workforce

TRD-UPSS = –1.49*** + 0.21 UNEMP*** + 0.01 DENSITY*** + 0.03 AGRI + 0.02 URBAN + 0.06 LITERACY** + 0.03 SECONDARY ...(4.0 – RE)

TRD-MPS = –3.89*** + 0.23 UNEMP-MPS*** + 0.01 DENSITY*** + 0.09 AGRI–0.01 URBAN + 0.12 LITERACY-M*** + 0.01 SECONDARY-M (4.1 – RE)

TRD-FPS = –1.26** + 0.02 UNEMP-FPS + 0.004 DENSITY*** + 0.16 AGRI*** + 0.06 URBAN*** + 0.003 LITERACY-F –0.004 SECONDARY-F ... (4.2 – RE)

Determinants of TRA Workforce

TRA-UPSS = –2.51*** + 0.13 UNEMP** + 0.003 DENSITY*** + 0.12 AGRI** + 0.03 URBAN** + 0.02 LITERACY + 0.06 SECONDARY** ...(5.0 – RE)

TRA-MPS = –4.95*** + 0.05 UNEMP-MPS + 0.01 DENSITY + 0.31 AGRI** + 0.12 URBAN* + 0.01 LITERACY-M + 0.0 7 SECONDARY-M ...(5.1 – FE)

TRA-FPS = –1.24*** + 0.08 UNEMP-FPS*** + 0.002 DENSITY* –0.001 AGRI + 0.02 URBAN* + 0.003 LITERACY-F –0.01 SECONDARY-F ...(5.2 – FE)

Determinants of SVS Workforce

SVS-UPSS = 6.31**–0.17 UNEMP + 0.01 DENSITY + 0.08 AGRI + 0.002 URBAN –0.10 LITERACY** + 0.19 SECONDARY*** ...(6.0 – FE)

SVS-MPS = 13.89***–0.47 UNEMP-MPS***–0.003 DENSITY + 0.12 AGRI-0.15 URBAN-0.04 LITERACY-M + 0.04 SECONDARY-M ...(6.1 – FE)

SVS-FPS = –10.05 + 0.22 UNEMP-FPS*** + 0.03 DENSITY** + 0.32 AGRI + 0.34 URBAN* –0.17 LITERACY-F* + 0.28 SECONDARY-F ...(6.2 – FE)

From the estimated regression coefficients we thus find that for the rural non-farm sector as a whole, population density (as a 'push' factor in terms of land-man ratio, and a 'pull' factor through lowering of transaction costs) is acting as the most significant determinant. We also can observe that while unemployment rate is significant for the female workers and the subsidiary workforce, it is not an important determinant of growth in the male non-farm employment in the rural areas. Improvement on the human capital aspect, especially higher education, has a positive and significant effect on rural non-farm employment in India, but not for male and female principal workforce. For the MFG workforce we find that unemployment rate, population density and degree of urbanisation has positive and statistically significant impact on the UPSS and MPS workforce, but the female principal manufacturing workers are being influenced by only population density significantly. It is found that density of population and urbanisation also raises the demand for male construction workforce, while in the agricultural prosperous states the demand for female construction work is lower. Unemployment rate, population density and literacy rate in rural areas are also having significant positive impact on the MPS and UPSS in TRD activities, while agricultural prosperity and degree of urbanisation are helping the growth in TRD-FPS, along with density of population. For the growth in the TRA workforce we find that agricultural prosperity and urbanisation is creating demand for male workers. (The share of female TRA workforce is very low (and almost zero) in most of the states, and therefore nothing definite can be said about the regression analysis for TRA-FPS.) It can be expected that human capital could have a positive relationship with the SVS-sector employment. But the linear-formulation of the model is perhaps not much suitable for SVS sector, as the value of R-sq is found to be quite low. Still, the results show a negative relationship with the literacy rate and a positive relationship with the higher-education rate. For the male workers we find that SVS-sector jobs are negatively and significantly related with unemployment rate, while demand for the female workforce is increasing due to unemployment, density and urbanisation. Thus it might be the case that the secondary-passed population can get access to the better paid service-sector jobs, while most of the jobs are not requiring much involvement of human capital.

Thus on the whole we find that employment in the rural non-farm sector in India is increasing due to both distress-driven 'push' factors as well as growth-forces-driven 'pull' factors, but the impact varies across gender and sectors. Except for a few determinants for some sub-sectors, most of the relationships are showing the expected positive sign.

VI. Conclusion

For a vast country like India with lots of heterogeneity across its population over multiple dimensions, it is extremely difficult to pin down the exact causes and determinants of rural livelihood diversification and their impacts on the incidence of vulnerability of the poor rural households. Diversification of livelihoods enhances the incomes of the rural people as well as reduces the incidence of risk or vulnerability in the face of shocks or unknown events. As a coping strategy, diversification of livelihoods may be useful, but its success depends on a number of factors—both economic and social. While the literature has talked about push and/or full factors affecting diversification, there are scopes for the interplay of both these sets of factors. If one concentrates only one aspect of livelihood diversification, namely employment and income diversification, then all the contesting issues concerning rural livelihood and diversification thereof boils down to finding the nature of causality between rural non-farm employment and selected macroeconomic and development indicators in Indian states that contribute to our understanding of the phenomenon of livelihood diversification in rural areas. Our study pinpoints to the fact that among the various factors and determinants, the state-specific effects are not robust for all types of relationships postulated as classified into *push* as well as *pull* factors. We find that while unemployment rate is significant for the female workers and the subsidiary workforce, it is not an important determinant of growth in the male non-farm employment in the rural areas. Higher education, has a positive and significant effect on rural non-farm employment in India, but not for male and female principal workforce. For the manufacturing workforce we find that unemployment rate, population density and degree of urbanisation have positive and statistically significant impact on the UPSS and MPS workforce, but the female principal manufacturing workers are being influenced by only population density significantly. The diversification in income and employment patterns of rural population of India therefore connotes to the importance of economic and demographic factors which in turn depend on the variety of social and non-economic factors and their interactions. But the primary focus of policy of rural development in a country like India is to maintain stability of the relationship between such push and pull factors so as to ensure a sustainable pattern of livelihoods, and to insulate the people from the vulnerabilities generated in the development process through various shocks.

References

Acharya, S. and A. Mitra (2000). "The Potential of Rural Industries and Trade to Provide Decent Work Conditions: A Data Reconnaissance in India", *SAAT Working Papers*, International Labour Organization, New Delhi.

Ahluwalia, M.S. (1978). "Rural Poverty and Agricultural Performances in India", *Journal of Development Studies*, Vol. 14, No. 3, April.

Bhattacharya, B.B., N.R. Bhanumurthy and S. Sakthivel (2004). *Economic Reforms and Structural Changes in Employment: A Comparative Analysis of Gender-Specific Employment Behaviour in Organised and Informal Sector in India*, an unpublished report, Institute of Economic Growth, Delhi.

Central Statistical Organization (CSO). *Annual Series of Income* – various issues, New Delhi.

Chadha, G.K. (2001). "Impact of Economic Reforms on Rural Employment: No Smooth Sailing Anticipated." *Indian Journal of Agricultural Economics*, Vol. 56, No. 3, pp. 491-97.

Government of India (1994). *Report of the Technical Committee on DPAP and DDP*, Ministry of Rural Development, New Delhi.

Government of India (2001). *Report of the Task Force on Employment Opportunities*, Planning Commission, July 2001.

Government of India (2002). *Special Group on Targeting Ten Million Employment Opportunities Per Year*, Planning Commission, May 2002.

Government of India (2004). *Economic Survey 2003-04*, Economics Division, Ministry of Finance, GoI, New Delhi.

Jha, B. (2005). *Rural Non-farm Employment in India,* A Coordinated and

Consolidated Unpublished Report, submitted to Ministry of Agriculture, GoI, New Delhi.

Jha, Brajesh (2006). "Rural Non-Farm Employment in India: Macro-Trends, Micro-Evidences and Policy Options", *Working Paper*, Agricultural Economics Unit, Institute of Economic Growth, New Delhi.

Islam, Nurul (1997). "The Non-farm Sector and Rural Development: Review of Issues and Evidences", *FAED Paper No. 22*, IFPRI, Washington DC.

Islam, Nurul (2006). "Employment, Wages and Productivity in Indian Agriculture", *IEG Working Paper Series No. E/266/2006.*

Lanjouw, P. and A. Shariff (2002). "Rural Non-farm Employment in India: Access Impact and Poverty Impact", *Working Paper Series N. 81*, National Council of Applied Economic Research (NCAER), New Delhi.

Lewis, W.A., (1954). "Economic Development with Unlimited Supplies of Labour", *The Manchester School*, Vol. 22, No. 2, pp. 242-258.

Lipton, M. (1983). "Poverty, Undernutrition and Hunger", *World Bank Staff Working Paper No. 597*, Washington: World Bank.

Mahendra Dev, S. (2000). "Economic Reforms, Poverty, Income Distribution and Employment", *Economic and Political Weekly,* Vol. 35, No. 10 (March 4).

Mellor, John W. (1978) *The New Economics of Growth—A Strategy for India and the Developing World, A Twentieth Century Fund Study*, Ithaca: Cornell University Press.

National Sample Survey Organisation (NSSO, 1990). *Results of the Fourth Quinquennial Survey on Employment and Unemployment (All India), NSS Forty-third Round* (July 1987-June 1988), NSS Report no. 409, New Delhi.

National Sample Survey Organisation (NSSO, 1997). *Employment and Unemployment in India, 1993-94, NSS Fiftieth Round (July 1993-June 1994)*, NSS Report no. 409, New Delhi.

National Sample Survey Organisation (NSSO 2001). *Employment and Unemployment Situation in India, 1999-2000, NSS Fifty-fifth Round (July 1999-June 2000),* NSS Report no. 458, Key Results, Part-I, Part-II, New Delhi.

Papola, T.S. (1987). "Rural Industrialisation and Agricultural Growth: A Case Study in India", in Islam Rizwanul, (eds.), *Rural Industrialisation and Employment in Asia,* ILO/ARTEP, New Delhi.

Papola, T.S. (2005). "A Universal Programme is Feasible", *Economic and Political Weekly*, Vol. 40, No. 7 (February 12): 594-599.

Saith, A. (1991). "Development Strategies and the Rural Poor", *Journal of Peasant Studies* 17(2): 171-243.

Saleth, R.M. (1999). *Strategic Linkages in Rural Diversification: Empirical Analysis and Policy Issues*. New Delhi: Commonwealth Publishers.

Sen, Abhijit (2003). "Globalisation Growth and Inequality in South Asia—The Evidence from Rural India", in Jayati Ghosh and C.P. Chandrasekhar (eds.), *Work and Well-being in the Age of Finance*, New Delhi: Tulika Books.

Srivastava, Ravi (1997). "Poverty Reduction in India: Economic Growth, Human Development and Anti-poverty Programme", *A Background Paper for the World Bank.*

Uma Rani and Jeemol Unni (2004). "Unorganised and Organised Manufacturing in India—Potential for Employment Generating Growth", *Economic and Political Weekly*, Vol. 49, (October 9): 4568-4580.

Unni, J. (1997). "Non-Agricultural Employment, Livelihoods and Poverty in Rural India", *Working Paper No. 88*, Ahmedabad: Gujarat Institute of Development Research.

Vaidyanathan, A. (1986). "Labour Use in Rural India: A Study of Spatial and Temporal Variations", *Economic and Political Weekly*, Vol. 21, No. 52 (December 27): A130-A146.

Vaidyanathan, A. (1994). "Employment Situation: Some Emerging Perspectives", *Economic and Political Weekly*, Vol. 29, No. 50 (December 10): 3147-3156.

Visaria, P. and R. Basant (1994). "Non Agricultural Employment in India: Problems and Perspective", in P. Visaria and R. Basant (eds.), *Non-Agricultural Employment in India*, New Delhi: Sage Publications.

Vyas, V.S. and G. Mathai (1978). "Farm and Non-Farm Employment in Rural Areas: A Perspective for Planning", *Economic and Political Weekly*, Vol. 13, Nos. 6 and 7, (February annual number): 333-347.

2

Rural Livelihoods in India

Some Areas of Concern

Biswambhar Mandal

I. Introduction

"India lives in its villages"—this adage is as true today as it was when the country became independent in 1947. When one talks of socio-economic progress in India, what is mostly relevant is how the lives of the rural people have changed. As per the Census of India, 2011, Number of families residing in villages are 16,78,26,730 and in urban areas 7,88,65,937.

Around 69 per cent of the Indian population residing in villages. Out of the total of 1210.2 million populations in India, the size of rural population is 833.1 million. Majority of the rural inhabitant still find it difficult to ensure their basic amenities of life. Tackling rural poverty still remains a pressing challenge for rural India. The Government of India and various state governments have been implementing various programmes for rural uplift. However, rural poverty and unemployment still persist in the country and at the same time, rural poverty causes concern for the overall growth of our nation.

II. Livelihoods as a Concept

In everyday language "livelihood" refers to a "means of living". Asking someone "How do you earn your livelihood?" is the same as asking "What do you do for a living?" In development thinking, livelihood refers to the way people make a living, and analysing livelihood systems is the analysis of the factors involved in the way in which people make a living.

A person's livelihood refers to their "means of securing the necessities of life". Livelihood is defined as a set of economic activities, involving self-employment, and or wage employment by using one's endowments (both human and material) to generate adequate resources for meeting the requirements of the self and household on a sustainable basis with dignity. The activity is usually carried out repeatedly. For instance, a fisherman's livelihood depends on the availability and accessibility of fish.

Livelihoods are the means people use to support themselves, to survive and to prosper. Livelihoods are an outcome of how and why people organise to transform the environment to meet their needs through technology, labour, power, knowledge and social relations. Livelihoods are also shaped by broader economic and political systems within which they operate.

Conceptually, 'Livelihoods' denotes the means, activities, entitlements and assets by which people make a living. One can describe a 'livelihood' as a combination of the capabilities and resources people have (including social, human, financial, natural and material assets) and the activities they undertake in order to make a living and to attain their goals and aspirations.

A livelihood comprises the capabilities, assets (stores, resources, claims and access) and recovers from stress and shocks, maintain or enhance its capabilities and assets and provide sustainable livelihood opportunities for the next generation and which contributes net benefits to other livelihoods at the local and global levels and in the long and short run. (Chambers and Conway, 1992).

A 'livelihood' is sustainable when people cope with and recover from shocks and crises (e.g., seasonal, environmental and economic) and can maintain or enhance their capability and assets both now and in the future, while not undermining the natural resource base.

III. Rural Livelihood in India—An Overview

Rural livelihood is occupation as source of income and livelihood in the rural areas that include agricultural work and other allied rural employment such as labour, home industry etc. A rural livelihood is defined as, the capabilities, assets and activities that rural people require for a means of living. Of late, rural development has assumed global attention especially among the developing nations. It has great significance for a country like India where majority of the population live in rural areas. The present strategy of rural development in India mainly focuses on poverty alleviation, better livelihood opportunities, provision of basic amenities and infrastructure facilities through innovative programmes of wage and self-employment.

India is primarily an agriculture-based country. Agriculture contributes nearly one-fifth of the gross domestic product in India. Majority of population in rural India sustains on agriculture and linked occupations. Agriculture and allied activities that support the livelihoods of nearly 70 per cent of India's rural population, has lost its importance. In recent years, land based livelihoods of small and marginal farmers are increasingly becoming unsustainable. As their land has failed to support their family's food requirements they are forced to look at alternative means for supplementing their livelihoods. The rapid changes at the macro level that India witnessed since the early nineties has contributed to the instability of the livelihood systems of the poorer section of rural households. Searching jobs for the millions remain a challenge for rural India.

The agrarian economy in particular and the rural economy in general, has been in a state of crisis. Quite apart from the tragic phenomenon of lakhs of farmers being pushed into committing suicides—a phenomenon that has not abated much in the recent period—the rural economic crisis is clearly manifested in the slow growth and poor quality of employment as well as abysmal earnings from work during the reform period.

It is increasingly the case that rural workers are more foot loose than before, and there is considerable seasonal migration from rural to urban areas for short and medium term employment under a variety of arrangements. These distress migrants often lock their homes, take a few meager belongings and move across long distances. The children accompanying their parents are forced to drop out of school. Being away from their village, they do not belong to the places where they go and increasingly lose acceptance in their own villages. They are disconnected from their community, culture and traditions, unable to take part in festivals, fairs, religious and social functions, which are an integral part of their lives thus losing their sense of identity. The vulnerability of people who cross state boundaries is even greater as they find themselves increasingly at the mercy of their contractors. Dealing with emergencies, particularly back home is difficult, especially for those who go long distance.

Distress migrants find themselves with hardly any skills, assets or education. Earnings from migration arc at survival lcvcl and not enough to build assets. On the contrary, medical or other personal emergencies and the unsteady nature of work often push them further into debt. Those who own a few animals have to arrange that they are cared for or just end up selling them off at low prices – thus depleting their assets.

The work sites largely have no basic facilities like water, marketplace, schools, health centres, etc. Migrants are at the mercy of their employers for all their needs. Contractors retain control of labourers not only financially but also physically, forcing them to work even when they are sick or injured.

The slowing down of the economy as a result of the economic crisis is bound to impinge negatively on these employment opportunities in construction and in some service sector activities. Similarly, with export growth slowing down and may be, even turning negative on account of the recession in the developed capitalist countries, employment in both rural and urban areas will be affected. A significant part of India's exports consist of agricultural commodities and products of labour intensive sectors such as textiles, garments, leather products, artificial gems and jewellery and other handicrafts.

Let us consider the following Table 2.1 prepared on the basis of data published in the report of Census in India, 2011.

Table 2.1

Subjects	*Villages (%)*	*Towns (%)*	*Total (%)*
One roomed families	39.4	32.1	37.1
Distributed drinking water	17.9	62.0	32.0
Electricity	55.3	92.7	67.2
Sanitation facilities	30.7	81.4	46.9
Timber fuel for cooking	62.5	20.1	49.0
Uses of LPG/PNG in cooking	11.4	65.0	28.5
Banking services	54.4	67.8	58.7
Television	33.4	76.7	47.2
Computer	4.4	10.4	6.3
Telephone (Landline/Mobile)	54.3	82.0	63.2
Scooter/Motor Cycle/Moped	14.3	35.2	21.0
Motor Car/Jeep/Van	2.3	9.7	4.7

Source: Census in India, 2011.

IV. Global Crisis and Livelihoods Collapses in Rural India

Livelihood opportunities available to the people in villages are not satisfactory. Every year millions of poor families migrate in search of work. They are forced to migrate due to a livelihoods collapse in the villages. India ranked in 94th out of 118 countries in the Global Hunger Index. Understanding the livelihood systems of the poor is crucial to effective poverty reduction. Livelihoods of the poor can never be understood in any one-track logic—be it economic, social, technical, cultural or political. The livelihoods approach takes holistic consideration of things that the poor might be vulnerable to, assets and resources that help them thrive and survive, policies and institutions that impact their livelihoods, how the poor respond to threats and opportunities and what sort of outcomes the poor aspire to.

Financial liberalization served to both limit access to institutional credit for the peasantry and other small producers as well as raise the cost of credit through higher interest rates in the formal sector as well as through forcing increased reliance on high cost informal sector credit. Significant decline of purchasing power as well as a collapse of rural infrastructure impacting both supply and demand conditions in the rural economy negatively. These had severely negative implications not only in agriculture but also in such areas as education and health. The collapse of the public distribution system (PDS) in most parts of the country thanks to the resort to targeting worsened the rural economic crisis and increased the extent and depth of rural deprivation.

It is thus a greatly weakened and crisis-ridden rural economy that now faces the onslaught of the global economic crisis. Every single measure of rural well-being—whether of nutrition or of earnings from work or of assetlessness—testifies to the critical situation facing a large part of the rural population. It will of course not be independent of what policy measures are taken by government to deal with the crisis. So far, however, the government has shown little willingness to undertake the kind of massive programmes of investment in rural infrastructure and productive job creation that is critical to mitigating the impact of the crisis on the rural population. In fact, the government has proceeded in the direction of greater liberalization and opening up to foreign private capital, especially in the financial sector.

The global crisis will pose serious threats to the livelihood options facing the rural working people is clear. While government and media attention has been focused on the financial sector and on providing relief to the corporate sector, there has been little discussion of issues such as employment, food security and the impact on small and medium producers. It is these areas that we need to focus on. Employment for rural working people is an area of serious concern.

V. Government's Programmes and Livelihood Opportunities in Rural Areas

The Indian government has passed legislations and taken many programmes to benefit rural citizens. The benefits are inequitably distributed between the rural and urban areas. This rural-urban divide in accessing infrastructure services coupled with inability of civil society organizations to utilize the existing provisions has contributed to the slow growth of livelihood opportunities in rural areas. Table 2.2 shows a picture of 'divided India'.

Table 2.2: Difference in Rural-Urban (%)

	2001	*2011*	*Change*
Families having sanitation facilities	51.8	50.7	-1.1
Families having drinking water	44.4	39.8	-4.6
Families having banking facilities	19.4	13.3	-6.1
Families having electricity facilities	44.0	37.0	-7.0
Families having no property *	21.5	15.9	-6.8
Families having bathrooms	47.6	22.0	-25.6

Source: Census in India, 2011.

* The families who have no radio, television, computer, laptop, telephone, mobile, four wheelers, two wheelers and cycle.

The rapid changes at the macro level that India witnessed since the early nineties has contributed to the instability of the livelihood systems of the poorer section of both rural and urban households. While the benefits of globalisation process have largely accrued to the urban sector growth the rural sector has been left behind. Slowdown in agricultural growth and productivity, changing cropping patterns, increase in distress migration, changing consumption patterns, government policies favouring industrial houses, among others have seriously undermined the food and livelihood security of the poorer households. The widespread system of subcontracting that operates in non-farm sector employment especially in construction projects fudges responsibility and accountability so that it becomes very difficult for government officials to implement protective legislation.

VI. Coping Mechanisms of the Poor

A review of coping mechanisms reveals that a very small group of medium farmers is able to cope with adverse climatic conditions merely through the sale of available stocks. On the other end of the spectrum, landless labourers can only resort to seasonal migration due to lack of any productive assets or availability of alternative employment options in the village. Small/marginal farmers use a variety of adaptation options such as sale of cattle, shifts to other subsistence crops, wage labour, as well as seasonal migration. This range of options, however, constitutes only temporary coping measures. During adverse periods, farmers have implemented a range of livelihood and coping strategies to reduce their vulnerability ranging from appeasing the Lord Indra (the god of rain) to some social support system reduction of food consumption and change in the pattern of food consumption changing their occupation to households either sold or mortgaged their lands and household assets.

Options that enhance longer-term adaptive capacity (such as institutional credit, crop insurance, and use of drought-resistant varieties) are not used by farmers due to procedural complexities and stringent eligibility criteria, compounded by lack of awareness.

VII. Conclusion and Suggestions

Although concerted efforts have been initiated by the Government of India through several plans and measures to alleviate poverty in rural India, there still remains much more to be done to bring prosperity in the lives of the people in rural areas. At present, technology dissemination is uneven and slow in the rural areas.

In times of crisis, the small and medium enterprises not only find credit both expensive and difficult to access, but also face the problem that large enterprises to whom they supply their products do not pay them promptly. As far as agriculture is concerned, the problem of slowing down of exports will be compounded by an even greater deluge of cheap imports, given the absence of protection against imports by way of high tariffs or quantity restrictions. Without going into greater detail, it is safe to conclude that one key impact of the economic crisis on the rural economy will be a significant loss of employment opportunities. It follows that a key thrust in terms of mitigating the effects of the crisis on rural working people must be the demand for creation of productive employment on a large scale. An integrated, multidimensional and holistic approach to poverty eradication efforts is crucial to preserve and enhance the livelihoods of the poor.

References

Chambers, R. and Conway, G.R. (1992), "Sustainable Rural Livelihoods: Practical Concepts for the 21st Century", *Discussion Paper 296*, Institute of Development Studies, London.

Kingshuk Roy, Ganashakti, Kolkata, 19th March, 2012, p. 3.

Praduman Kumar, Mruthyunjaya, Madan M. Dey (2007), "Long-term Changes in Indian Food Basket and Nutrition", *Economic and Political Weekly*, September 1, 2007, pp. 3567-3572.

Sundaram, K. (2001), "Employment and Poverty in 1990s", *Economic and Political Weekly*, August 11-17, 2001.

www.icra-edu.org accessed on 12-4-13.

www. wiki.answers.com accessed on 22-2-2013.

www.soas.ac.uk/courseunits/c135.html accessed on 22-2-2013.

www.en.wikipedia.org accessed on 12-4-13.

3

Globalization and Rural Livelihoods

A Three-Sector Model

Soumik Banerjee, Shubhashrita Basu and *Ranjanendra Narayan Nag*

I. Introduction

With the effect of globalization reaching far and wide, and the life in big cities and metros being saturated, there has been an increased interest in the being and functioning of the rural community. This has specially been the case with the advent of the so-called developing nations of East and South Asia as big players in the global economy. Changes in agriculture pattern and land acquisitions have been the major aspects that have dotted the recent headlines and have affected rural livelihood the most. In this paper, we make an attempt to look into the various issues and perspectives of rural livelihood and analyze the effects of the development and displacement on the various sections of such a society.

In this chapter we construct a General Equilibrium Model to examine effects of globalization on factor prices, income distribution and sectorial composition of output which have profound bearing on rural livelihood. The model consists of 3-sectors that can apply to a large class of emerging market economies. The sectors under consideration are an import-competing industrial sector, a non-traded traditional agricultural sector and an export-oriented agricultural sector. The different comparative statics pertain to agricultural trade liberalization, tariff liberalization, a fall in foreign interest rate and technological progress in the agricultural sector. The results in this paper depend on existence of non-traded good, factor intensity rankings and multiple cross-effects embedded in a general equilibrium framework.

II. The Model

In this paper we construct a General Equilibrium Model to examine effects of globalization on factor prices, income distribution and sectorial composition of output which have profound bearing on rural livelihood. The model consists of 3-sectors that can apply to a large class of emerging market economies.

Notations Used

X: Import competing industrial sector (capital intensive)
Y: Traditional agricultural sector, non-traded (land intensive)
Z: Processed agricultural sector, agro industry (labour intensive)
w: Flexible wage rate in all the sectors
a_{Lx}: Coefficient of labour in sector X, i.e. labour per unit of X
a_{Ly}: Coefficient of labour in sector Y, i.e. labour per unit of Y
a_{Lz}: Coefficient of labour in sector Z, i.e. labour per unit of Z
a_{Kx}: Coefficient of capital in sector X, i.e. capital per unit of X
a_{Tx}: Coefficient of land in sector X, i.e. land per unit of X
a_{Ty}: Coefficient of land in sector Y, i.e. land per unit of Y
a_{Tz}: Coefficient of land in sector Z, i.e. land per unit of Z
r: Domestic return on capital
r^*: Foreign return on capital
R: Return on land
K_d: Domestic capital
K_f: Foreign capital
$K = K_d + K_f$
$\overline{L}$: Total endowment of labour
$\overline{T}$: Total endowment of land
t: Tariff rate
μ: Technology coefficient

Equation Structure

We assume that markets are competitive and price charged for the product equals average cost of production. For the sake of simplicity, we assume that factor coefficients are fixed. The model can be represented by the following equations:

Price System

$$P_x^*(1+t) = wa_{Lx} + ra_{Kx} + Ra_{Tx} \quad (1)$$

$$P_y = wa_{Ly} + Ra_{Ty} \quad (2)$$

$$P_z^* = wa_{Lz} + Ra_{Tz} \quad (3)$$

$$\frac{w}{P_y} \cdot \overline{L} = Y \quad (4)$$

Quantity System

$$\overline{L} = a_{Lx} \cdot X + a_{Ly} \cdot Y + a_{Lz} \cdot Z \quad (5)$$

$$\mu \cdot \overline{T} = a_{Tx} \cdot X = a_{Ty} \cdot Y + a_{Tz} \cdot Z \quad (6)$$

$$a_{Kx} \cdot X = K_d + K_f(r - r^*);\ K_f'(r) > 0 \quad (7)$$

Working of the Model

Here, *w*, *r*, *R*, P_y, *X*, *Y* and *Z* are the seven endogenous variables in question.

Equations (1), (2) and (3) represent zero profit condition for sector *X*, *Y* and *Z*. This follows from the assumption of competitive markets. Equations (5), (6) and (7) simply represent full employment of labour, capital and land respectively. Equation (4) shows equality between demand and supply functions of the non-traded agricultural sector.

We have seven equations and seven unknowns. From equations (2) and (3), we get *w* and *R* in terms of P_y (since P_z^* is given). Putting the values of *w* and *R* in equation (1), we get *r* in terms of P_y (since P_x^* is given). Putting the value of *w* in equation (4), we get P_y in terms of *Y*, given L¯. Now equation (7) gives us the value of *X*, given K_d and K_f. Once we know *X*, from equations (6) and (5) we can solve for the values of *Y* and *Z*. Once *Y* is known, we get the value of P_y and consequent values of *w*, *r* and *R*.

The equilibrium in *Y* sector is maintained by the condition $\frac{w}{P_y} \cdot \overline{L} = Y$. We assume for simplicity that workers consume only *Y* as food. Now, since P_y is endogenous the demand and supply factors for *Y* are determined by P_y. The Y sector being land intensive, if P_y rises, it leads to rise in rent (R) and fall in labour wage (w) as per the Stolper-Samuelson theorem. As a result $\frac{w}{P_y}$ falls which indicates a fall in the demand for Y. Thus we get a negatively-sloped demand curve for the Y sector.

Considering the supply side, a similar rise in P_y will cause w to fall and R to rise. However, the effect on r is obtained from equation (1) and is ambiguous. If r rises (falls), there is an inflow (outflow) of capital and hence by Rybzcynski's theorem, the X sector expands (contracts). Thus, the X sector will draw (release) land and labour and this may lead to either an expansion or a contraction in the Y sector accordingly. Hence, the supply curve of the Y sector may be positively or negatively sloped. However, in the latter case, the supply curve should be steeper than the demand curve for Walrasian stability.

The different cases are illustrated in the following figures–

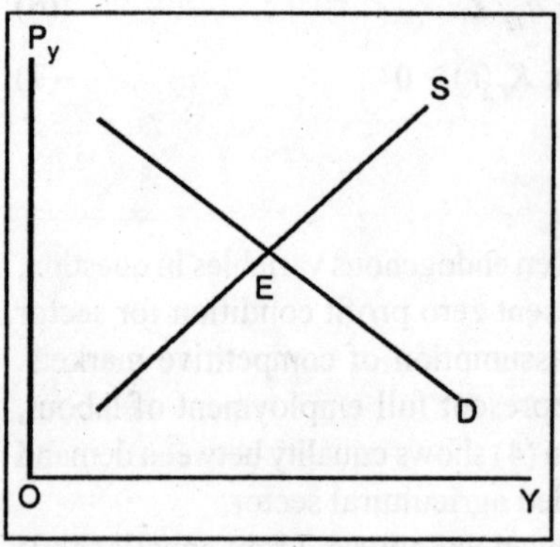

Fig. 3.1: The case of Positively sloped Supply Curve.

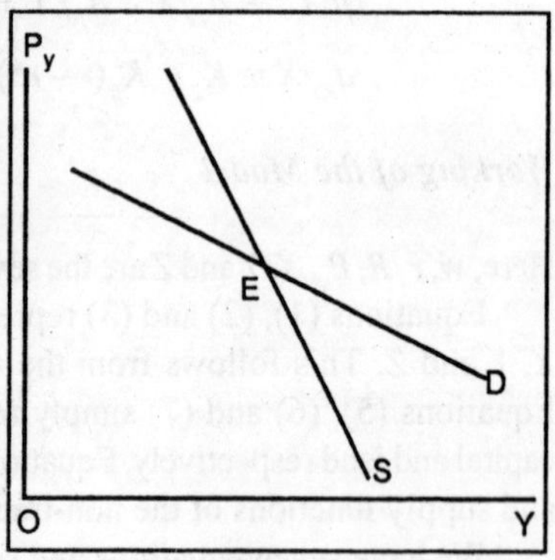

Fig. 3.2: The case of negatively sloped Supply Curve.

Differentiating equation (1) we get,

$$0 = a_{Lx}dw + a_{Kx}dr + a_{Tx}dR$$

$$\Rightarrow \quad 0 = \theta_{Lx}\hat{w} + \theta_{Kx}\hat{r} + \theta_{Tx}\hat{R} \quad \text{(1a)}$$

Differentiating equation (2) we get,

$$\hat{P}_y = \theta_{Ly}\widehat{W} + \theta_{Ty}\hat{R} \quad \text{(2a)}$$

Differentiating equation (3) we get,

$$0 = \theta_{Lz}\widehat{W} + \theta_{Tz}\hat{R} \tag{3a}$$

Here $0 < \theta_{ij} < 1 \ \forall \ i = \{L, K, T\}, j = \{x, y, z\}$

From equations (1a), (2a) and (3a) we get,

$$\begin{bmatrix} 0 \\ \hat{T}_y \\ 0 \end{bmatrix} = \begin{bmatrix} \theta_{Lx} & \theta_{Kx} & \theta_{Tx} \\ \theta_{Ly} & 0 & \theta_{Ty} \\ \theta_{Lz} & 0 & \theta_{Tz} \end{bmatrix} \begin{bmatrix} \widehat{W} \\ \hat{r} \\ \widehat{R} \end{bmatrix}$$

$$\begin{vmatrix} \theta_{Lx} & \theta_{Kx} & \theta_{Tx} \\ \theta_{Ly} & 0 & \theta_{Ty} \\ \theta_{Lz} & 0 & \theta_{Tz} \end{vmatrix} = \theta_{Kx}\left[\theta_{Lz}\theta_{Ty} - \theta_{Ty}\theta_{Ly}\right] > 0, \text{ given the factor intensities.}$$

Differentiating equation (4) we get,

$$\widehat{W} - \hat{P}_y = \hat{y} \tag{4a}$$

Taking $r - r^* = \alpha$ and differentiating equation (7) we get,

$$a_{Kx}dX = \frac{\partial K_f}{\partial \alpha} \cdot d\alpha$$

$$\Rightarrow \qquad \eta_{Kx}.\hat{X} = \frac{\partial K_f}{\partial \alpha}.\frac{\alpha}{K_f}.\frac{d\alpha}{\alpha}.\frac{K_f}{K_d + K_f}$$

$$\Rightarrow \qquad \eta_{Kx}\hat{X} = \varepsilon_K.\hat{\alpha}.\beta \tag{5a}$$

where ε_K is the elasticity of supply of foreign capital

$$\hat{\alpha} = \frac{d\alpha}{\alpha}$$

$$= \frac{dr - dr^*}{r - r^*}$$

Differentiating equation (5) we get,

$$\eta_{Lx}.\hat{X} + \eta_{Ly}.\hat{Y} + \eta_{Lz}.\hat{Z} = 0 \tag{6a}$$

Differentiating equation (6) we get,

$$a_{Tx}dX + a_{Ty}dY + a_{Tz}dZ = \overline{T}d\mu$$

$$\Rightarrow \qquad \eta_{Tx}\hat{X} + \eta_{Ty}\hat{Y} + \eta_{Tz}\hat{Z} = \frac{d\mu}{\mu} = \hat{\mu} \tag{7a}$$

Comparative Static Exercises

The following comparative static exercises give further insight into the functioning of the rural economy.

A. Fall in the foreign interest rate on capital, i.e., fall in *r**

A fall in the foreign interest rate on capital, i.e. fall in *r**, will result in inflow of foreign capital K_f. The *X* sector being capital intensive expands and thereby draws land and labour from the other two sectors. This might lead to three possible results—both *Y* and *Z* sectors contract, the *Y* sector contracts and the *Z* sector expands and the *Z* sector contracts and the *Y* sector expands.

From equation (5a) we get,

$$\frac{\partial\hat{X}}{\partial\hat{\alpha}} = \frac{\varepsilon_K\beta}{\eta_{Kx}} > 0 \text{ Since } \varepsilon_K > 0, 0 < \beta < 1 \text{ and } 0 < \eta Kx < 1$$

Hence, the X sector expands, but the effect on the *Y* and *Z* sector is ambiguous, as is shown in the following mathematical exercises.

Solving from equations (6a) and (7a) we get,

$$\eta_{Ty}\eta_{Ly}\hat{Y} + \eta_{Ty}\eta_{Lz}\hat{Z} = -\eta_{Lx}\hat{X}\eta_{Ty}$$
$$\eta_{Ly}\eta_{Ty}\hat{Y} + \eta_{Ly}\eta_{Tz}\hat{Z} = (\hat{\mu} - \eta_{Lx}\hat{X})\eta_{Ly}$$

$\hat{Z}(\eta_{Ty}\eta_{Lz} - \eta_{ly}\eta_{Tz}) = -\eta_{Ty}\eta_{Lx}\hat{X} + \eta_{Lx}\eta_{Ly}\hat{X} - \hat{\mu}\eta_{Ly}$ (By subtracting the 2nd equation from the 1st.)

$$\Rightarrow \quad \hat{Z} = \frac{\eta_{Lx}\hat{X}(\eta_{Ly} - \eta_{Ty}) - \hat{\mu}\eta_{Ly}}{(\eta_{Ty}\eta_{Lz} - \eta_{Ly}\eta_{Tz})} \quad \text{(a)}$$

$$\therefore \quad \frac{\partial\hat{Z}}{\partial\hat{X}} = \frac{\eta_{Lx}\hat{X}(\eta_{Ly} - \eta_{Ty})}{(\eta_{Ty}\eta_{Lz} - \eta_{Ly}\eta_{Tz})}$$

Now, as sector *Y* is more land intensive and sector *Z* is labour intensive, we have

$$\frac{\eta_{Ty}}{\eta_{Ly}} > \frac{\eta_{Tz}}{\eta_{Ly}}$$

$$\therefore \quad \eta_{Ty}\eta_{Lz} - \eta_{Ly}\eta_{Tz} > 0$$

Hence, $\frac{\partial \hat{Z}}{\partial \hat{X}} \gtrless 0$ according as $\eta_{Lx}(\eta_{Ly} - \eta_{Ty}) \gtrless 0$

$\because \quad 0 < \eta_{Lx} < 1$, therefore $\boxed{\eta_{Ly} \gtrless \eta_{ty}}$

Solving equations (6a) and (7a) we get,

$$\eta_{Tz}\eta_{Ly}\hat{Y} + \eta_{Tz}\eta_{Lz}\hat{Z} = -\eta_{Lx}\hat{X}\eta_{Tz}$$
$$\eta_{Lz}\eta_{Ty}\hat{Y} + \eta_{Lz}\eta_{Tz}\hat{Z} = (\hat{\mu} - \eta_{Lx}\hat{X})\eta_{Lz}$$

$\hat{Y}(\eta_{Tz}\eta_{Ly} - \eta_{Lz}\eta_{Ty}) = -\eta_{Lz}\eta_{Lx}\hat{X} + \eta_{Lz}\eta_{Tx}\hat{X} - \hat{\mu}\eta_{Ly}$ (By subtracting the 2nd equation from the 1st.)

$$\Rightarrow \quad \hat{Y} = \frac{\eta_{Lz}\hat{X}(\eta_{Tx} - \eta_{Lx}) - \hat{\mu}\eta_{Lz}}{(\eta_{Tz}\eta_{Ly} - \eta_{Lz}\eta_{Ty})} \tag{b}$$

$$\boxed{\therefore \frac{\partial \hat{Y}}{\partial \hat{X}} = \frac{\eta_{Lz}(\eta_{Tx} - \eta_{Lx})}{(\eta_{Tz}\eta_{Ly} - \eta_{Lz}\eta_{Ty})}}$$

Now, as sector *Y* is more land intensive and sector *Z* is labour intensive, we have

$$\frac{\eta_{Ty}}{\eta_{Ly}} > \frac{\eta_{Tz}}{\eta_{Lz}}$$

$$\therefore \quad \eta_{Ty}\eta_{Lz} - \eta_{Ly}\eta_{Tz} > 0$$

Hence, $\frac{\partial \hat{Y}}{\partial \hat{X}} \gtrless 0$ according as $\eta_{Lz}(\eta_{Tx} - \eta_{Lx}) \gtrless 0$

$\because \quad 0 < \eta_{Lz} < 1$, therefore $\boxed{\eta_{Tx} \gtrless \eta_{Lx}}$

B. The possibility of a Green Revolution, which can be attained through advancement in technology, i.e. a rise in μ:

Due to advancement in technology, there is an apparent rise in the availability of land, i.e. we can use the available land more optimally. The *Y* sector being land intensive, by Rybzcynski's theorem, it expands. As a result, P_y will fall and considering the H-O nugget between the *Y* and the *Z* sector, Stolper-Samuelson results show that *w* rises and *R* falls. Considering the effect on *r*, the effect on the *X* sector, i.e. whether it will expand or contract is ambiguous. However, we see that the *Z* sector always contracts, in accordance with Rybzcynski's theorem (as the *Z* sector uses land un-intensively).

From equation (b), we have $\hat{Y} = \dfrac{\eta_{Lz}\hat{X}(\eta_{Lx} - \eta_{Tx}) + \hat{\mu}\eta_{Lz}}{(\eta_{Lz}\eta_{Ty} - \eta_{Tz}\eta_{Ly})}$.

$$\boxed{\therefore \frac{\partial \hat{Y}}{\partial \hat{\mu}} = \frac{\eta_{Lz}}{(\eta_{Lz}\eta_{Ty} - \eta_{Tz}\eta_{Ly})} > 0}$$

From equation (4a), as $\hat{Y}$ rises, $\widehat{P_y}$ falls, given $\hat{w}$ is constant.

From equations (2a) and (3a), by the Stolper-Samuelson Theorem, we have

$$\hat{R} < \widehat{P_y} < \widehat{P_z^*} < \hat{w}$$

Now, $\widehat{P_z^*} = 0$

$\widehat{P_y} < 0$ and $\hat{w} > 0$. Hence $\dfrac{\hat{w}}{\widehat{P_y}}$ rises.

From equation (1a) we have,

$$\hat{r} = -\frac{\theta_{Lx}.\hat{w} + \theta_{Tx}\hat{R}}{\theta_{kx}}$$

$$\therefore \quad \frac{\partial \hat{r}}{\partial \hat{w}} = -\frac{\theta_{Lx}}{\theta_{Kx}} < 0 \text{ And } \frac{\partial \hat{r}}{\partial \hat{R}} = -\frac{\theta_{Tx}}{\theta_{Kx}} < 0$$

For *r* to rise/fall, $\left|\dfrac{\partial \hat{r}}{\partial \hat{w}}\right| \lesseqgtr \left|\dfrac{\partial \hat{r}}{\partial \hat{R}}\right|$

$$\Rightarrow -\frac{\theta_{Lx}}{\theta_{Kx}} \lesseqgtr \frac{\theta_{Tx}}{\theta_{Kx}}$$

$$\boxed{\Rightarrow \theta_{Tx} \lesseqgtr \theta_{Lx}}$$

From equation (a), we have $\hat{Z} = \dfrac{\eta_{Lx}\hat{X}(\eta_{Ly} - \eta_{Ty}) - \hat{\mu}\eta_{Ly}}{(\eta_{Ty}\eta_{Lz} - \eta_{Ly}\eta_{Tz})}$

$$\therefore \frac{\partial \hat{Z}}{\partial \hat{\mu}} = \frac{\eta_{Ly}}{(\eta_{Ly}\eta_{Tz} - \eta_{Ty}\eta_{Lz})} < 0$$

From our previous derivations we obtained the values of $\dfrac{\partial \hat{Y}}{\partial \hat{X}}$ and $\dfrac{\partial \hat{Y}}{\partial \hat{\mu}}$.

$$\therefore \quad \frac{\partial \hat{X}}{\partial \hat{Y}} \cdot \frac{\partial \hat{Y}}{\partial \hat{\mu}} = \frac{(\eta_{Tz}\eta_{Ly} - \eta_{Lz}\eta_{Ty})}{\eta_{Lz}(\eta_{Tx} - \eta_{Lx})} \cdot \frac{\eta_{Lz}}{\{-(\eta_{Tz}\eta_{Ly} - \eta_{Lz}\eta_{Ty})\}}$$

$$\Rightarrow \quad \frac{\partial \hat{X}}{\partial \hat{\mu}} = \frac{1}{(\eta_{Lx} - \eta_{Tx})}$$

$$\therefore \frac{\partial \widehat{X}}{\partial \widehat{\mu}} \gtrless 0 \text{ according as } \boxed{\eta_{Lx} \gtrless \eta_{Tx}}$$

C. Agricultural trade liberalization, i.e., increase in P_z*

Agricultural trade liberalization leads to opening up of the advanced agricultural sector and the terms-of-trade effect leads to a rise in P_z^*. Again considering the H-O nugget and applying Stolper-Samuclson results, we see that *w* rises and *R* falls. However, the effect on *r* is ambiguous and depending on the condition we derived earlier, we get results to be the same as in case *B*. Moreover, the change in P_y is also ambiguous.

Differentiating equation (3) we get,

$$\widehat{P_z^*} = \theta_{Lz}\hat{w} + \theta_{Tz}\hat{R} \tag{3a'}$$

From equations (2a) and (3a'), by the Stolper-Samuelson theorem, we get,

$$\hat{R} < \hat{P}_y < \widehat{P_z^*} < \hat{w}$$

$\hat{w}>0$; $\widehat{P_z^*}>0$; $\hat{R}<0$

From equation (2), $\hat{P}_y=\theta_{Ly}\hat{w}+\theta_{Ty}\hat{R}.$

$$\therefore \qquad \frac{\partial\widehat{P}_y}{\partial\hat{w}}=\theta_{Ly}>0 \text{ and } \frac{\partial\widehat{P}_y}{\partial\hat{R}}=\theta_{Ty}>0$$

If P_y rises or falls, $\left|\frac{\partial\widehat{P}_y}{\partial\hat{w}}\right| \gtrless \left|\frac{\partial\widehat{P}_y}{\partial\hat{w}}\right|$ accordingly.

Hence, $\boxed{\theta_{Ly}\gtrless\theta_{Ty}}$

Thus, effect on $\widehat{P}_y$ is ambiguous.

$\frac{\partial\hat{r}}{\partial\hat{w}}<0$ And $\frac{\partial\hat{r}}{\partial\hat{w}}<0$

For a rise in $\frac{\partial\hat{r}}{\partial\hat{w}}<\frac{\partial\hat{r}}{\partial\hat{R}}\Rightarrow\theta_{Lx}>\theta_{Tx}$

If r rises (falls), the X sector will expand (contract) as $\frac{\partial\hat{x}}{\partial\hat{\alpha}}>0$ and the effect on the Y and Z sector will be same (opposite) as in Case B.

D. Trade liberalization pertaining to fall in tariff rate, i.e., a fall in *t*

If t falls, $1+t$ falls, implying a fall in $\widehat{1+t}$. Consequently, $\hat{r}$ falls (following from the Stolper-Samuelson theorem). This implies that the inflow of foreign capital goes down, i.e. K_f falls. In that case, the X sector contracts. The consequent results are as have been analyzed in the previous cases.

From equation (1) we get,

$$a_{Lx}dw+a_{Kx}dr+a_{Tx}dR=P_x^*.dt$$

$$\Rightarrow \qquad \theta_{Lx}\hat{w}+\theta_{Kx}\hat{r}+\theta_{Tx}\widehat{R}=\frac{d(1+t)}{(1+t)}$$

$$\Rightarrow \qquad \theta_{Lx}\hat{w}+\theta_{Kx}\hat{r}+\theta_{Tx}\widehat{R}=\widehat{t+1}$$

$$\therefore \qquad \frac{\partial \hat{r}}{\partial \widehat{1+t}} = \theta_{Kx} > 0$$

III. Conclusion

Thus, we see that given the factor intensity assumptions, along with factor specificity and existence of the non-traded sector generate multiple cross-effects which drive comparative static results in this model. The results obtained from comparative static exercises shows the various facets of the effects of globalization on factor prices, income distribution and sectorial composition of output which have profound bearing on rural livelihood.

References

Jones Ronald W. and Sugata. Marjit (2003): "Economic Development, Trade and Wages", *German Economic Review*, Vol. 4, Issue 1, February.

Marjit, Sugata (2003): "Economic Reform and Informal Wage—A General Equilibrium Analysis", *Journal of Development Economics*, Vol. 72, Issue: 1, October.

4
Rural Livelihoods in India

Pritha Ghosh

I. India: Priorities for Agriculture and Rural Development

Although agriculture contributes only 21 per cent of India's GDP, its importance in the country's economic, social, and political fabric goes well beyond this indicator. The rural areas are still home to some 72 per cent of the India's 1.1 billion people, a large number of whom are poor. Most of the rural poor depend on rain-fed agriculture and fragile forests for their livelihoods.

The sharp rise in foodgrain production during India's Green Revolution of the 1970s enabled the country to achieve self-sufficiency in foodgrains and stave off the threat of famine. Agricultural intensification in the 1970s to 1980s saw an increased demand for rural labour that raised rural wages and, together with declining food prices, reduced rural poverty.

Sustained, although much slower, agricultural growth in the 1990s reduced rural poverty to 26.3 per cent by 1999/2000. Since then, however, the slowdown in agricultural growth has become a major cause for concern. India's rice yields are one-third of China's and about half of those in Vietnam and Indonesia. With the exception of sugarcane, potato and tea, the same is true for most other agricultural commodities.

The Government of India places high priority on reducing poverty by raising agricultural productivity. However, bold action from policymakers will be required to shift away from the existing subsidy-based regime that is no longer sustainable, to build a solid foundation for a highly productive, internationally competitive, and diversified agricultural sector. Prosperous 'Green Revolution' states of Punjab, Haryana and Uttar Pradesh have recently witnessed a slow-down in agricultural growth. Some of the factors hampering the revival of growth are:

- *Poor composition of public expenditures:* Public spending on agricultural subsidies is crowding out productivity-enhancing investments such as agricultural research and extension, as well as investments in rural infrastructure, and the health and education of the rural people. In 1999/2000, agricultural subsidies amounted to 3 per cent of GDP and were over 7 times the public investments in the sector.
- *Over-regulation of domestic agricultural trade:* While economic and trade reforms in the 1990s helped to improve the incentive framework, over-regulation of domestic trade has increased costs, price risks and uncertainty, undermining the sector's competitiveness.
- *Government interventions in labour, land, and credit markets:* More rapid growth of the rural non-farm sector is constrained by government interventions in factor markets—labour, land, and credit—and in output markets, such as the small-scale reservation of enterprises.
- Inadequate infrastructure and services in rural areas.

Weak Framework for Sustainable Water Management and Irrigation

- *Inequitable allocation of water:* Many states lack the incentives, policy, regulatory, and institutional framework for the efficient, sustainable, and equitable allocation of water.
- *Deteriorating irrigation infrastructure:* Public spending in irrigation is spread over many uncompleted projects. In addition, existing infrastructure has rapidly deteriorated as operations and maintenance is given lower priority.

Inadequate Access to Land and Finance

- *Stringent land regulations discourage rural investments:* While land distribution has become less skewed, land policy and regulations to increase security of tenure (including restrictions or bans on renting land or converting it to other uses) have had the unintended effect of reducing access by the landless and discouraging rural investments.

II. Issues and Challenges

Slow Down in Agricultural and Rural Non-Farm Growth

- *Computerization of land records has brought to light institutional weaknesses*: State government initiatives to computerize land records have reduced transaction costs and increased transparency, but also brought to light institutional weaknesses.
- *Rural poor have little access to credit*: While India has a wide network of rural finance institutions, many of the rural poor remain excluded, due to inefficiencies in the formal finance institutions, the weak regulatory framework, high transaction costs, and risks associated with lending to agriculture.
- *Weak Natural Resources Management*: One quarter of India's population depends on forests for at least part of their livelihoods.
- *A purely conservation approach to forests is ineffective*: Experience in India shows that a purely conservation approach to natural resources management does not work effectively and does little to reduce poverty.
- *Weak resource rights for forest communities*: The forest sector is also faced with weak resource rights and economic incentives for communities, an inefficient legal framework and participatory management, and poor access to markets.
- *Domestic Water*: The Ministry of Drinking Water and Sanitation administers the National Rural Drinking Water Programme (NRDWP), and the Total Sanitation Campaign through which support is extended to the states for implementing rural domestic water supply and sanitation schemes. Under the NRDWP powers to sanction individual projects is given to the states through their State Level Scheme Sanctioning Committees. Activities like, water quality monitoring and surveillance programme, management information system, IEC, Capacity and Communication Development Unit (CCDU) were brought under the umbrella of NRDWP. The achievement measured by habitations where the population is fully covered with adequate

(40 lpcd) and safe drinking water, as per information entered by States on the online monitoring system of the Ministry, is about 72 per cent of total rural habitations. The rest are either partially covered or have drinking water sources contaminated with chemical contamination. The achievement as estimated by independent studies like the NSSO 65th Round Survey of 2009-10 shows that about 90 per cent of rural households obtain their drinking water from improved sources. However coverage of piped water supply is still poor at 35 per cent as per IMIS. Issues like slippage from fully covered to partially covered due to depleting groundwater sources, contamination of sources, poor Operation and Maintenance, lack of adequate involvement by the community or Panchayats continue to dog the system, leading to poor service delivery. Therefore, the sector requires further strengthening on various aspects in order to successfully and effectively provide at rural households with safe and adequate domestic water supply available at all times.

III. Financial Challenges

Most Commitments Made in the Eleventh Plan Remain Unfulfilled

The Eleventh Five Year Plan had made commitments with the objective of strengthening women related legislations, institutional mechanisms and empowering women. However, as we track the performance made in this regard, the picture appears grim. The Eleventh Five Year Plan period had envisaged Swayamsiddha and Indira Gandhi Matritva Sahayog Yojana (IGMSY) as the main interventions. However, Swayamsiddha which aimed at empowerment of women through Self-Help Groups never really took off.

As opposed to the approved outlay of Rs. 500 crore for the scheme, only Rs. 78 crore was allocated. Moreover, in the last two years, no expenditure has been incurred in the scheme. The other major scheme envisaged in the Eleventh Plan, i.e. IGMSY, was also launched only in the latter part of the Plan period. Further, since it is a cash transfer scheme, it will need to be assessed before commenting on its implementation. The Eleventh Five Year Plan had also mentioned some very important measures such as setting up of a High Level Committee to review SHG related policies and programmes, a National Taskforce on violence against women in conflict zones and creating effective mechanisms for implementation of Protection of Women from Domestic Violence Act (PWDVA), 2005. However, no progress has been made in this direction. For instance, the Union Government has still not made allocations for implementation of PWDVA since its enactment in 2005.

IV. Problems of Regional Rural Banks (RRBs)

Regional Rural Banks play a vital role in the agriculture and rural development of India. The RRBs have more reached to the rural area of India, through their huge network. The success of rural credit in India largely depends on their financial strength. RRBs are key financing institutions at the rural level which shoulders responsibility of meeting credit needs of different types of agriculture credit in rural areas. At present, most of the regional rural banks are facing the problems of overdue, recovery, non-performing assets and other problems. Therefore, it is necessary to study financial performance of RRBs in India. This paper attempts to analyze the financial performance of RRBs in India during the period 2006-07 to 2010-2011.

Problems (Weakness) of RRBs

Although RRBs had a rapid expansion of branch network and increase in volume of business, these institutions went through a very difficult evolutionary process due to the following problems:

1. Very limited area of operations.
2. High risk due to exposure only to the target group.
3. Public perception that RRBs are poor man's banks.
4. Mounting losses due to non-viable level of operations in branches located at resource-poor areas.
5. Switch over to narrow investment banking as a turn-over strategy.
6. Heavy reliance on sponsor banks for investment avenues with low returns barring exceptions, step-motherly treatment from sponsor banks.
7. Chairman of RRBs under the direction of Regional Managers appointed as Board of Directors by sponsor banks.
8. Burden of government subsidy schemes and inadequate knowledge of customers leading to low quality assets.
9. Unionized staff with low commitment to profit orientation and functional efficiency.

10. Inadequate skills in treasury management for profit orientation.

IV. Failure of Some Aspects of Eleventh Five Yer Plan

Given that the Eleventh Plan focus was to make "growth faster and more inclusive", and that in this context efforts were also made to impart a "rights approach" in some major anti-poverty schemes, there should be a reminder of the long-haul nature of India's development promises. Like all previous plans, the Eleventh Plan was based on the understanding that the only way in which we can find meaningful solutions to the problems of mass poverty is through rapid economic growth. Rapid GDP growth and consequent rise in the state revenue made it possible to allocate larger resources for social sector expenditure. But the Eleventh Plan had also recognized that growth is not an end in itself—it must translate into better life for all citizens of our country. Chronic poverty continues because almost all past growth-mediated poverty reducing strategies have bypassed various historically marginalized groups and deprived regions. Persistent spatial backwardness and inequality have led to concentration of poverty in certain parts of the country, so there is a geographical dimension to poverty. Additionally, since poverty remains especially prevalent among certain occupational groups, there is a sociological dimension to its persistence. It summarizes the debates around the measurement of poverty in India and suggests that while there are differences with regard to measuring poverty, longitudinal tracking of households through panel data enables analysis of the dynamics of poverty. Poverty dynamics recognizes the existence of processes through which the poor either escape from poverty or fail to escape it and the non-poor either remain non-poor or become poor. Through analysis of a rural panel dataset covering about 3,000 households across the country it draws attention to the significant scale of incidence of chronic poverty; of non-poor households falling into poverty; and of a proportion of those who are poor managing to escape from it.

This issue is important in the context of the ongoing debate on food security. It is clear that the present Targeted Public Distribution System (TPDS) is leaky, inefficient, corruption-ridden and also hugely untargeted because very cheap grain is being distributed on the basis of a very faulty Below Poverty Line (BPL) identification process. Converting TPDS into law is difficult because the right to food cannot be targeted towards only the poor unless poverty can be legally defined and, this is impossible to do realistically. However, the alternative of making entitlements universal is also impossible if these are to involve sizeable quantities at very low prices. Therefore, we need to combine aspects of universal food security, say along lines of availability at prices close to Minimum Support Prices (MSP), with extra entitlements of either lower prices or cash transfers for those whose ability to access food at MSP is likely to be remain chronically limited because of their inability to access universal livelihood supports such as MGNREGA. These latter groups would have to be defined on the basis of individual characteristics rather than simply on basis of being "poor", and the research presented in this Report may be very useful for this purpose. Also, this research clearly shows that ill-health is a major driver into poverty and therefore limiting access to subsidized health care only to the pre-defined BPL will bypass many who will end up poor as a result. The design of what ought to be universal and what can be targeted in public healthcare can also therefore be guided by such findings.

Large-scale social safety net programmes such as India's Mahatma Gandhi National Rural Employment Guarantee Act (MGNREGA) are difficult to implement due to governance challenges related to elite capture, leakages, and corruption. The ability to identify how the governance challenges of programme implementation can be met requires detailed insights into the actual process of programme implementation, with clear views on the source of leakage and mismanagement, the sensitivity of programme implementation to the influence of different actors, local power structures and informal bureaucratic problems. MGNREGA is perhaps the most ambitious anti-poverty scheme launched anywhere in the world. However, the scheme has shown several anomalies when it comes to implementation in the right manner. It may be understood that the problems and challenges are from both, Government and public.

(A) Issues and Challenges Faced by the Government

(a) Poor Planning and Administrative Skill

The representatives of the Central and State governments, as well as NGOs, reviewed the MGNREGA in the month of April, 2011. What emerged was the comment that the annual budget of Rs. 40,000 crore could be better utilized with more effective planning. Thus far, the panchayats, barring those in Karnataka and, to some extent, in those in West Bengal, have no experience at all in planning large-scale programmes.

(b) Lack of Focus on Objectives

Though Schedule One of the MGNREG Act referred to conservation of natural resources such as rainwater, land, forests, this was not reflected in the works floated for the scheme. Under this scheme, contractors and machineries should not be used. But in some workplaces, contractors were allowed and machineries were involved. And the erring officials claim that the works were done as if they were completed by workers and not by machines.

(c) Lack of Adequate Manpower

Another issue is the deficiency of adequate administrative and technical manpower at the Block and Grama Panchayat (GP) Levels, especially at the level of programme officer, technical assistants, and Employment Guarantee Assistant Level etc. The lack of manpower has adversely affected the preparation of plans, scrutiny, approval, monitoring and measurement of works, and maintenance of the stipulated records at the Block and GP level. The CAG report points out that besides affecting the implementation of the scheme and the provision of employment, this also impacted adversely on transparency.

(d) Discrimination

MGNREGA has provided a unique opportunity to people from rural India to earn their own income without any discrimination of caste or gender. The most remarkable feature of MGNREGA is that it pays women the same as men, something that was virtually unimaginable in Rural India. However, cases of discrimination against women and people from backward groups are reported from several regions of the country. Some states such as Kerala and Andhra Pradesh have registered high percentage of women workers getting enrolled in the scheme whereas others have registered a very low percentage of women availing benefit under MGNREGA.

(e) Corruption and Irregularities

Statistics clearly indicate that the poverty alleviation programmes have had a minimal effect on poverty levels in India due to corruption. The actual funds that reach the beneficiaries are very little compared to the funds allocated for welfare schemes. Former Prime Minister, Rajiv Gandhi had once said that out of every 100 paisa allocated for public welfare only 14 paisa reaches the targeted people. Further concerns, include the fact that corruption of the local governments leads to the exclusion of specific sections of the society. Local governments have also been found to claim that more people have received job cards than people who actually work in order to generate more fund than needed, to be then embezzled by local officials.

(f) Lack of Safety Measures

Around one-third of the stipulated work force under MGNREGS is women. Therefore, Crèches have to be set up so as to enable women carrying their children to the work site to do their work without much apprehension about their children. It is seen at the workplace that women workers lay their children in cradles tied around tree branches. In the absence of this facility women may hesitate to come forward to demand for work. One of the objectives of the Scheme to strengthen women empowerment may go unrealized.

(g) Maoist Insurgency

Less than 9 per cent of households in the 60 districts most affected by Maoist militancy found the required 100 days of employment under the country's rural jobs programme in the year ended 31st March. The National average of households that have completed 100 days under the job guarantee plan last fiscal was also poor at 10.1 per cent compared with 8.8 per cent in the districts hit by the Maoist insurgency.

(B) Issues and Challenges Among the Pople

Following are the issues and challenges among the people covered under the Act:

(a) Inadequate Awareness

MGNREGA provides the rural poor a right to demand for work for 100 days in a financial year. But people's efforts to get jobs under this scheme have been stymied by the fact that Governments have done nothing to encourage people to register demands. The fact is that the national average for workdays generated under the scheme is less than half of the entitlement of 100 days per household, per year. Even in 2009-2010, a severe drought year, only 54 days of work per household were generated. In 2010-2011, this number decreased to 46.79 days. Due to lack of awareness about the provisions of the Act, People are unaware of their basic entitlements under MGNREGA such as Job Cards, Minimum Wage Amount, Unemployment Allowance. The receipt for the application which is the basic record for claiming unemployment allowance. There is a widespread ignorance about how to avail the unemployment allowance; sometimes even the officials deliberately do not give out this information as they fear punishment for not providing jobs and poor awareness not only leads to corruption but also to poor management of the scheme and thus true potential of the MGNREGA is not being realized.

(b) Non-Purposive Spending

MGNREGA has obviously, increased the earning capacity of the rural people. But the spending pattern of the workers assumes significance because there is hardly any saving out of the wage earned from MGNREGS. For example, payment to the workers under MGNREGA is made in cash in Tamil Nadu state instead of through banks or post office accounts. Raw cash in the hands leads to non-purposive spending. Lack of awareness on the impact of inflation and illiteracy level among the rural poor are the reasons for not saving part of their income from this scheme.

Large scale social security programmes like MGNREA are subjected to undergo several stumbling blocks. Government and NGOs must study the impact of MGNREGA in rural areas so as to ensure that this massive anti-poverty scheme is not getting diluted from its actual path and to see that the disparity in terms of socio-economic condition among people in rural and urban areas is reduced to considerable extent.

V. Integrated Rural Accessibility Planning and The "Shelf of Projects"

Gram Panchayats need to develop a five-year "Shelf of Projects" which involves the identification, ranking and programming of projects and other development activities. Projects should contribute to social and economic development in the area under the jurisdiction of the Gram Panchayat. In order to identify priority projects for improving rural accessibility, the Gram Panchayat needs to have an adequate ove view of access and infrastructure constraints hampering social and economic development. The activities that need to be carried out by the Gram Panchayat to produce the "Shelf of Projects" are grouped into three main categories:

- Data collection and mapping
- Describing the size and severity of the problems and analyzing the causes of the problems
- Identification, ranking and programming of projects.

India's Rural Markets: More Promising than Ever

For many businesses, India's rural markets hold the key to future growth. Companies that recognize this enormous opportunity are stepping up efforts to gain a strong foothold in these markets. Yet the high costs required to serve rural consumers make it difficult for companies to establish a profitable presence at scale.

The rural economy has rapidly transformed in the last decade and is now being led by manufacturing. Indeed, agriculture accounts for only about one-fourth of rural GDP compared to half a decade ago. About 55 per cent of manufacturing GDP is rural; nearly 75 per cent of new factories built in the last decade were in rural areas, and rural factories account for 70 per cent of all new manufacturing jobs. Industries in rural India has increased household purchasing power and income stability. Rural India accounts for about 50 per cent of India's GDP and nearly 70 per cent of India's population. This enormous development opportunity has been clear for a decade or more. However, only in recent years have these markets lived up to their promise. Per capita rural GDP has also experienced strong improvement over the past few years. Since 2000, it has grown faster than per capita urban GDP: 6.2 per cent Compound Annual Growth Rate (CAGR) versus 4.7 per cent. Between 2009 and 2012, rural consumption per person grew at 19 per cent per annum, two percentage points higher than its urban counterpart. In incremental terms, spending in rural India during these two years was US$ 69 billion, significantly higher than the US$ 55 billion spent by urban populations. As incomes rise, rural consumption shifts from necessities to discretionary goods and lifestyle products, including mobile phones, television sets and two-wheelers. Nearly 42 per cent of rural households owned a television in 2009-2010, up from 26 per cent five years earlier. Similarly, 14 per cent of rural households had a two-wheeler in 2009-2010, twice the penetration during 2004-2005. About one in every two rural households has a mobile phone today, even in India's poorest states such as Bihar and Orissa. Rural consumers have been trading up, and their consumption basket is beginning to mirror that of the urban consumer. Premium products are replacing entry-level versions, and commodities are giving way to branded products. Nielsen estimates that the fast moving consumer goods market in rural India will hit US$ 100 billion by 2025, up from US$ 12 billion currently. Moreover, the government's efforts to improve the efficiency of welfare programmes with cash transfers will further boost rural consumption; it plans to deposit US$ 570 billion in the accounts of 100 million poor families by 2014.

VI. Conclusion

A strong sense of local ownership and genuine participation in design, project implementation and monitoring and evaluation by both men and women are critical to successful implementation and sustainable benefits. Designs should build on local demand and initiatives. This requires that the stakeholders (i.e. the beneficiaries and local personnel) meaningfully participate and play a core role in the identification and design process. The idea should come from the community, belong to the community.

Political support and support by the authorities or authorized bodies is a key factor for the sustainability of impact of development projects. It is important to find the right level of support: local, regional, national or professional organizations. Programmes and projects are implemented within a wider policy environment. Government policies can have significant impact on the sustainability of development programmes or projects. The policy framework should be analyzed and taken into account during project design. Programmes and projects which 'fit' with Partner Government policies have much better prospects for sustainability as they are more likely to have high-level political and institutional support both during implementation and beyond. To promote sustainability of rural projects, the technology to be transferred must be selected on the basis of its appropriateness in terms of technical and financial criteria, plus social, gender and cultural acceptability.

References

Government of India (2006): *From Hariyali to Neeranchal*: Report of the Technical Committee on Watershed Programmes in India, Ministry of Rural Development.

Government of India (2007): *Report of the Working Group on Rainfed Areas for the 11th Five Year Plan*, Planning Commission.

Pal, Dipti Prakas and Debottam Chakroborty (2009): "Changes in Consumption Pattern in India", in Prankrishna Pal (Ed.), *Reforms and Structural Change in India*, Regal Publication, New Delhi.

www.nrega.nic.in.

www.downtoearth.org.in.

5
In Search of Rural Livelihoods in India

Asim K. Karmakar

I. Introduction

Most people living in India are engaged in an enormous struggle to secure a livelihood in the face of adverse social, economic and often political circumstances. Two points are central to an understanding of such struggles. Through detailed analysis of social relations in a particular historical context: between those with land and those without land, for example; between rich and poor households; between men and women; between rural households and the institutions of the market and the state, the circumstances of poverty and the reasons for poverty have to be understood. The second point pertains to the modes of livelihood that typically prevail both within households are highly diverse. Rural households may derive a part-livelihood from farming; a part-livelihood from migrant labour undertaken by absent household members in urban areas or other rural areas; and a part-livelihood from a variety of other activities, more or less informal. Various combinations of activities of this kind are often themselves subject to rapid change over time. For these two reasons, rural livelihoods are not at all easy to study. It is in this context, the chapter goes on to give a short picture of rural livelihoods in India.

II. A Short Literature Survey

Through exploration of 'agrarian structures and change' in three different regions of the world—Latin America, India and Saharan Africa—and through detailed analysis of 'making a living' H. Bernstein *et al.*, 1992 in their book *Rural Livelihoods: Crises and Responses* explored the vitally important processes of marginalization, dispossession, accumulation and differentiation that have affected rural communities and go far towards explaining poverty in the late twentieth century.

Two vignettes from the lives of poor people in very different rural areas are distinct for analysis of social relations and of understanding diversity of modes of livelihood. The first concerns a family of marginalized share-croppers in a Bangladesh village whose circumstances of the mid-1970s were graphically described in Hartmann and Boyce's moving book *A Quiet Violence* (1983). Despite hard work and constant struggle, Sharifa and Abu were forced to sell most of their own fragments of land and even to chop down fruit trees for sale as firewood in order to pay debts and buy a few days' supply of rice.

> We had to borrow money to eat. Sometimes neighbours would lend us money without interest, but we often had to sell our rice before the harvest. Moneylenders would pay us in advance, and take our rice at half the market price. No matter how hard we worked, we never had enough cash. We started selling things—our wooden bed, our cow, our plough. Then we began to sell our land bit by bit. Now, we have less than one dun left, and most of that is mortgaged to Mahmud Haji.
>
> (quoted in Bernstein *et al.*, 1992:19)

The second vignette is taken from Charles van Onselen's massive biography (1996) of a black South African, Karl Maine who strove throughout his long life to sustain a tenuous grip on land alienated to white settlers. Kas Maine (1894-1985) was a farmer who did not own land but engaged in many different share-cropping contracts with white landlords in the maize-growing region of the south-western Transvaal. Maine and his family experienced several hurdles the mounting exactions of landlords and the relentless politics of white supremacy. Eventually, they were evicted from the land altogether, so that he ended his life in a remote and dusty relocation camp in a former African 'homeland'. Kas Maine met those pressures with hard work, cunning and sometimes desperation. To supplement a livelihood constantly he engaged in many different activities in the informal economy: shoe and saddle-repairing, knitting and tailoring, traditional healing. He earned his livelihood within a difficult social and political environment. His wives, meanwhile, also strove to secure a small cash income through their own complementary activities: selling cow-dung, rearing pigs, brewing beer, occasional 'piece-jobs'.

So far as women are concerned globalization engulfed in recent years has exulted competition and export promotion as drivers of development, but these are also responsible for driving down wages and undermining labour rights. Pressures have intensified in the agricultural sector everywhere. Given the prominence of women in agriculture, the impacts will be significant for millions of females in the developing world. A recent UN publication summarizes the situation:

> Whereas these dynamics (of globalization) have in some ways brought benefits, in general, the largest proportion of rural women worldwide continues to face deteriorating health and work conditions, limited access to education and control over natural resources, insecure employment and low income. This situation is due to a variety of factors, including the growing competition on agricultural markets which increases the demand for flexible and cheap labour, growing pressure on and conflicts over natural resources, the diminishing support by governments for small-scale farms and the reallocation of economic resources in favour of large agro-enterprises.

In what follows, closely linked to the observation of diversity of modes of livelihood at any one time is the idea of diversification of livelihood over time. For example, 60-80 per cent of rural household income in the late 1990s was derived from non-farming sources, by comparison with an approximate 40 per cent in the 1980s (Bryceson, 1999). There were many different reasons for such changes: structural adjustment programmes, sharply worsening terms of agricultural trade, the collapse of meso-level infrastructures of support for small farmers, devalued currencies, new opportunities and necessities of cross-border smuggling and trade, etc. The literature on diversification, it causes and its implications, is reviewed by Ellis (1998). It is important to remember that it is not only poor households that are forced to diversify in order to make ends meet as best they can, richer households also diversify their economic activities. It is also important to note that migration for work elsewhere is one typical mode of diversification in the livelihoods of the rural poor that has arguably been inhibited by politicians and undervalued by policy-makers (de Haan, 1999).

Three questions arise out of recent valuable research work undertaken in the mid-1990s and the late 1990s. The first question is how, in view of the complexity of individual household trajectories of change that are illustrated in the two vignettes above, it is possible to derive defensible generalizations about the experience of large numbers of the rural poor over time. The second question is how to achieve a better understanding of the links and the tensions between different levels of analysis: the micro level of the household, the meso level of institutional intervention through local government, development agencies or regional markets, and the macro level of national policy-making. The third question, in the light both of prevalent neo-liberal policy prescriptions and of the reality of diversified rural livelihoods across a number of conventionally discrete economic sectors, is how policies are to be devised in practice that will have an effective impact upon the disparate livelihoods of the rural poor.

Third, academics are increasingly aware of the need to influence policy and action. This should include analysis of the effects of past policies; a commitment to changing 'mind-sets' amongst government officials, planners, donors, NGOs, etc.; the development of specific rationales for intervention at various levels; and procedures for monitoring and evaluation. The objectives of the prospective approach are better coordination of planning and implementation across sectoral boundaries; and building alternative conceptual frameworks for facilitating opportunities for improving livelihoods.

The sustainable (Rural) Livelihoods framework is one such that has come to dominate recent research. It combines, in effect, the circumspective, the retrospective and the prospective approaches outlined above. The term 'Sustainable Livelihoods' may be traced from the work of Robert Chambers and others, through a research programme undertaken by the Institute of Development Studies at Sussex, involving work in Bangladesh, Ethiopia and Mali in particular.

> A livelihood comprises the capabilities, assets (including both material and social resources) and activities required for a means of living. A livelihood is sustainable when it can cope with and recover from stresses and shocks and maintain or enhance its capabilities and assets both now and in the future, while not undermining the natural resource base.
>
> (DfID, 1999: Section 1.1)

Within a particular 'vulnerability context', defined for example by shifting seasonal constraints, short-time economic shocks and longer-term trends of change, people deploy five types of 'livelihood assets' or capital (the 'asset pentagon') in variable combinations, within circumstances influenced by institutional structures and processes, in order to pursue diverse 'livelihood strategies', with more or less measurable 'livelihood outcomes'. Two books, a series of flexible and sensible Sustainable Livelihoods Guidance sheets and a series of more specific working papers elaborate the framework and recent fruitful experience of its practical application (see, for example, Carney, 1998; Scoones, 1998; DfID, 1999, 2000). Further, some practitioners have developed out of their experience of working within the Sustainable Livelihoods paradigm a set of detailed guidelines on the proper conduct of an SL study in practice (for example, Khanya, 2000). The paradigm has a number of strengths and weaknesses, partly reviewed in Murray (2000). One problem is that fundamentally, it may be argued, capital is a social relation, not a 'thing': landlessness, for example, as shown vividly in the example of Sharifa and Abu above, should be understood not simply as a distinctive attitude of the rural poor but as an effect of the working out of unequal social relations over time.

III. Agriculture and Rural Livelihoods

The predominance of agriculture in supporting rural livelihoods makes it imperative for us to examine some of the major trends in the sector more closely. The most striking observation about the sector is the all-India decline in the population of cultivators between 2001 and 2011 from 127.3 million to 118.6 million. The population of agricultural workers, on the other hand, increased consistently from 74.6 million to 106.8 million and further to 144 million over the three census periods. The share of cultivators in total workers in rural areas came down from 40.2 per cent in 2001 to 33 per cent in 2011 and that of agricultural workers rose from 26 per cent to 30 per cent. The fall in the population of cultivators has been more pronounced in the case of Uttar Pradesh, Bihar, Madhya Pradesh, and Odisha and Tamil Nadu, which also registered absolute reduction in cultivators. It may be worth noting that some of these states report high incidence of indebtedness among farmers. At the same time, there has been a consistent increase in the number of and area under marginal operational holdings (<1 hectare). The percentage share of marginal holdings in all holdings increased from 62 per cent to 67 per cent between 2000-01 and 2010-11. But they accounted for only 22 per cent of the total area in 2010-11. This obviously suggests a decline in the average size of the holding. A typical marginal holding measured 0.38 hectare in 2010-11, 0.02 hectare less than its size a decade earlier. The total area under the smallest size class of operational holdings rose by 26 per cent between 1995-96 and 2010. In Odisha, the increase was substantial—81 per cent. Madhya Pradesh, Rajasthan, Maharashtra, and Gujarat also witnessed significant increase in the area under marginal holdings suggesting further fragmentation of agricultural land. The sustainability of these farms is a crucial factor that shapes the livelihood environment of rural areas. Some of the challenges faced by small and marginal farmers according to NCEUS (2008) in this context are imperfect markets for inputs/product leading to smaller value realizations; absence of access to credit markets or imperfect credit markets leading to suboptimal investment decisions or input applications; smaller access to suitable extension services regarding cultivation practices and technological know-how; poorer access to 'public goods' such as public irrigation, command area development, electricity grids; greater negative externalities from poor quality land and water management, etc. At the macro-level, the percentage share of agriculture to gross state domestic product (GSDP) across major states has declined steadily. Over the years 2004-05 to 2011-12 the decline has been more drastic in the case of states such as Punjab, Himachal Pradesh, Uttarakhand, Kerala, and Uttar Pradesh. States including Tamil Nadu, Maharashtra, Madhya Pradesh, Chhattisgarh, and Gujarat have witnessed modest decline in agricultural GSDP over the period. Apart from the structural transformation logic, i.e. the progressive movement of growing economies towards secondary and tertiary activities, there are also reasons that are specific to the agricultural sector such as deterioration of soil health and overexploitation of water resources. Lack of adequate capital investment in agriculture (irrigation works, command area development, land reclamation, afforestation and development of state farms, etc.) by the public sector has been identified as a major bottleneck in this regard. A recent media report quotes the government sources to point out that capital investment in agriculture and allied sectors has risen from 13.5 per cent of the GDP in 2004-05 to 20.1 per cent in 2010-11. If this is so, the effect of such investment will be seen in the years to come.

The states that rank high in number of micro, small, and medium enterprises (MSMEs) have all witnessed an absolute reduction in the population of cultivators.

IV. Changing Poverty Levels

The recent poverty estimates do help us understand the relative position of regions with respect to livelihood insecurity. As per these estimates in 2011-12, Chhattisgarh and Jharkhand are the poorest states in India with 40 and 37 per cent overall population below the poverty line. They also have the highest percentage of rural poor. Bihar, Odisha, Madhya Pradesh, and Uttar Pradesh are the other states with relatively higher incidence of poverty. Goa, Kerala, Himachal Pradesh, Punjab, and Andhra Pradesh have the lowest overall levels of poverty—less than 10 per cent. A recent study argues that the disparity in poverty at the sub-state level is more serious than the disparity between states. It finds that in both rural and urban sectors in almost all the states, some districts have higher intra-district inequality compared to the level of inter-state inequality. Through a detailed analysis of 20 major states, this study has brought about valuable insights as to how to identify 'pockets of impoverishment' by extending enquiries beyond the state level. The study highlights the high degree of variance in monthly per capita expenditure (MPCE).

V. Human Development Index

Livelihoods are not only about employment, enterprise, and income. Capability deprivation is a critically important consideration in understanding poverty and in preparing a public policy to promote livelihoods. The central argument behind the capability approach as propounded by Sen is that standard economic approaches to welfare—based on utility or access to resources—exclude a great deal of relevant information and provide unreliable guides to poverty and well-being. The solution to this problem is to view poverty and well-being in terms of human capabilities or opportunities to achieve positive freedoms, such as being able to live long, be well nourished, achieve literacy, take part in community life and achieve self-respect.

There are many different kinds of capabilities that are closely linked to human well-being. The HDI captures the importance of three critical human capabilities—achieving knowledge, longevity, and a decent standard of living. The HDI combines normalized measures of life expectancy, literacy, educational attainment, and GDP per capita for distinct regions.

VI. Conclusion and Policy Conclusions

The poor, vulnerable, and the marginalized people of this country look forward to responsive governments that at least make sincere attempts to address their life concerns. They expect that policies are timely made, made well, and most importantly executed well. The most important way to achieve this would be to conduct serious policy research, extensive deliberations on policy formations, serious pilots, and state-specific and region-specific strategies of scale-up, and then track policy implementation very closely on outputs and outcome levels. To make this happen, the most important intervention necessary is to conduct sweeping institutional reform, empowering local governments with authority and capacity. There is no country on earth that has progressed far without strong local governments, and there is no reason to believe India can be an exception.

The chapter attempts to compile some important informations relating to the overall context in which livelihoods, particularly rural livelihoods in India, need to be understood. The analysis of the major trends over the past two decades indicate that the livelihood base of rural population in the country has been transformed significantly due to the workings of a multitude of forces. An important aspect of this transformation is that the structure of the economy of almost all the states has shifted away from agriculture towards other sectors. While the shift has largely been towards services, some states such as Gujarat, Tamil Nadu, Punjab, Maharashtra, and Haryana also registered higher share of manufacturing income. These include some of the land consolidating states too. The challenges to livelihood diversification are particularly serious for the poorest states —Jharkhand, Chhattisgarh, Madhya Pradesh, Bihar, and Odisha—as they lag behind others in terms of human development achievements also. Initiatives to promote livelihoods in these states hence need to be anchored effectively on the goals of expansion of economic opportunities, alleviation of human poverty, improvement of capabilities, and reduction of inequalities.

Policy Implications

(i) Rural India needs special and renewed efforts at raising agricultural productivity, relieving debt distress, expanding agricultural credit, and increasing the coverage of extension activities. Other special groups in need of specially targeted assistance are women, children and disadvantaged castes.

(ii) Food security is critical: the PDS must be restored and improved.

(iii) Poverty is not just a matter of income deprivation: to address it, it would help to draw a district-wise map of India, with the colour red reserved for those districts displaying acute inadequacies in access to drinking water, energy for cooking, elementary health facilities, a school, and a road, and, on the basis of such a map, some efforts at infrastructural development must be initiated and sought to be implemented in a reasonable time-frame.

(iv) The plethora of anti-poverty employment schemes must be rationalized and streamlined.

Finally, as distinct from specific anti-poverty policy, strategies for the macro-economic desideratum of pro-poor growth must also be attended to.

References

Bagchi, D.K., Blaikie, P., Cameron, I., Chattopadhyay, M., Gyawali, N. and Seddon, D. (1998): "Conceptual and Methodological Challenges in the Study of Livelihood Trajectories: Case Studies in Eastern India and Western Nepal", *Journal of International Development* 10: 453-68.

Bernstein, H., Crow, B. and Johnson, H. (eds.) (1992): *Rural Livelihoods: Crises and Responses*, Oxford: Oxford University Press for the Open University.

Byrceson, D.F. (1999): "Sub-Saharan Africa Betwixt and Between: Rural Livelihood Practices and Policies", *Working Paper 43*, Leiden: Afrika-Studiecentrum.

Carney, D. (ed.) (1998): *Sustainable Rural Livelihoods: What Contribution Can We Make?*, London: Department for International Development.

Census of India (2011): *Primary Census Abstract.*

de Haan, A. (1999): "Livelihoods and Poverty: The Role of Migration—A Critical Review of the Literature", *Journal of Development Studies* 36(2): 1-47.

Department for International Development (DfID) (1999, 2000): *Sustainable Livelihoods Guidance Sheets.*

Ellis, F. (1998): "Household Strategies and Rural Livelihood Diversification", *Journal of Development Studies* 35(1): 1-38.

Ellis, F. (2000): *Rural Livelihoods and Diversity in Developing Countries*, Oxford: Oxford University Press.

Francis, E. (2000): *Making a Living: Changing Livelihoods in Rural Africa*, London: Routledge.

Government of India (2012): *Draft Twelfth Five-Year Plan (2012–17) Document*, Volume I, Faster, More Inclusive and Sustainable Growth, Planning Commission.

Government of India (2012): *Agricultural Statistics at a Glance 2012*, Directorate of Economics and Statistics, Department of Agriculture and Cooperation, Ministry of Agriculture.

Government of India (2013): *Economic Survey 2012–13*, Ministry of Finance.

Hartmann, B. and Boyce, J.K. (1983): *A Quiet Violence: View from a Bangladesh Village*, London: Zed Books.

Khanya (2000): "Guidelines for Undertaking a Regional/National Sustainable Rural Livelihoods Study", see www.khanya-mrc.co.za.

Murray, C. (2000): "Changing Livelihoods: the Free State, 1990s", *African Studies* 59(1): 115-42.

Scoones, I. (1998): "Sustainable Rural Livelihoods: A Framework for Analysis", *Working Paper 72*, University of Sussex: Institute of Development Studies.

van Onselen, C. (1996): *The Seed is Mine: The Life of Kas Maine, a South African Sharecropper, 1894-1985*, New York: Hill and Wang.

SECTION II
Determinants of Livelihoods

6

The Challenge of SHGs in Generation of Rural Sustainable Livelihood

Bridging the Gap Between "Shining India" and the Country

Sadhan Chandra Kar and *Surya Narayan Ray*

I. Introduction

> Sustainable Development is a process of development that "meets the needs of the present generations without compromising the ability of future generations to meet their own needs"
>
> —*World Commission on Environment and Development* (1987)

The above epoch-making definition of sustainable development, given in the 1987 seminal report entitled "Our Common Future" of the World Commission on Environment and Development, had highlighted the importance of sustainability in the development process. Srivastava (1998) had iterated that even in the Human Development Report (1994), released by the United Nations Development Programee, it was emphasised that "sustainable development is development that not only generates economic growth but distributes its benefits equitably; that generates environment rather than destroying it; that empowers people rather than marginalizing them. It gives priority to the poor, enlarging their choices and opportunities and providing their participation in decisions affecting them. It is development that is pro-poor, pro-nature, pro-jobs, pro-women and pro-children". Even after a quarter of a century of the Bruntland Commission Report, as mankind continues to leave their ever-enlarging carbon footprints in the world, the issue of sustainable development has now assumed immense global importance (Franchetti, 2012). In a country like India, the concept of sustainable development becomes hard to implement, as issues like poverty, employment, development and environmental degradation often arrive at cross-roads. These issues are not alien to India, as even the international communities have striven to develop the relationship between these variables since the 1970s (Nayak, 2008). However, unlike most other developing countries, nearly three-fourths of India's populace (73.8%) lives in the rural areas (Parmar *et al.*, 2013). The Father of the Nation, Mohandas Karamchand Gandhi, being a visionary was much ahead of his time, had once famously remarked way back in 1926 that "India's way is not Europe's. India is not Calcutta and Bombay. India lives in her seven hundred thousand villages" (worldviewer.com Inc, 2013). The importance of rural India can never be more relevant than today. Even as India came to be categorised as a Newly Industrialised Country by becoming a member of the elite G8+ 5 Group of countries, this second largest democracy cannot forget her teeming millions who are languishing as unemployed or underemployed in her rural backyard. In stark contrast to the "Shining India" image attached to being the tenth largest industrial nation in the world (Business Standard, 2011), 10.1 per cent of the rural labour force is still unemployed (Parmar *et al.*, 2013). In a first ever survey of its kind carried out by the Labour Bureau of the Government of India in 2010, it was estimated that only 63.5 per cent of the population is in the working age group of 15-59 years; and that not every member in the working age group are interested in joining the work force (Government of India, 2010). In the Indian context, the Labour Force Participation Rate is only 359 per 1000 persons. This essentially means that out of the 553.92 million rural population who are either employed or are interested in working, 10.1 per cent representing nearly 55.95 million rural population are still unemployed. These are colossal figures underline the unemployed rural human resource of modern India. Moreover, as the Labour Ministry data indicates, higher education and degrees are not helping rural job aspirants to get their coveted jobs (Ghosh, 2012). Moreover, the unemployment rate of females (14.6%) is much higher than the unemployment rate of males (8%), which is certainly a worrisome factor. So, the time has come to realize that a healthy Gross Domestic Product (GDP) growth of a "Shining India" must be integrated with the national objective of Financial Inclusion and Inclusive Growth, that is characterised by the generation of sustainable rural livelihood by the large number of Self Help Groups (SHGs) that are strewn across the landscape of rural India. This picture of the Indian rural landscape is well reflected in the Cooch Behar, a primarily rural district of West Bengal, which includes the Study Area of Dinhata.

Table 6.1: Ratios of Total workers, Cultivators, Agricultural Labourers and Non-Workers to the Population of Cooch Behar (1961-2001)

Year	*Population*	*Ratio of Cultivators to Population*	*Ratio of Agricultural Labourers to Population*	*Ratio of Total Workers to Population*	*Ratio of Non-Workers to Population*
1961	1019806	0.24	0.02	0.32	0.68
1971	1414183	0.19	0.04	0.28	0.72
1981	1771643	0.15	0.08	0.29	0.71
1991	2171145	0.25	0.15	0.31	0.69
2001	2256180	0.16	0.13	0.33	0.67

Source: Kar & Ray, 2012.

II. Importance of SHGs in Rural Sustainable Livelihood

> "A Self-Help Group (SHG) has an average size of about 15 people from a homogeneous class. They come together for addressing their common problems. They are encouraged to make voluntary thrift on a regular basis. They use this pooled resource to make small interest bearing loans to their members. The process helps them imbibe the essentials of financial intermediation including prioritisation of needs, setting terms and conditions, and accounts keeping. This gradually builds financial discipline in all of them. They also learn to handle resources of a size that is much beyond individual capacities of any of them. The SHG members begin to appreciate the fact that resources are limited and have a cost. Once the groups show this mature financial behaviour, banks are encouraged to make loans to the SHG in certain multiples of the accumulated savings of the SHG. The bank loans are given against group dynamics without any collateral and at market interest rates. The groups continue to decide the terms of loans to their own members. Since, the groups own accumulated savings are part and parcel of the aggregate loans made by the groups to their members,

peer pressure ensures timely repayments. Apart from financial help at the time of need, the group provides social security to its members"

—*National Bank for Agriculture and Rural Development* (2005)

The above concept note on SHGs provided by the National Bank for Agriculture and Rural Development (NABARD) in its Report entitled *Progress of SHG Bank Linkage in India-2005-06* gives the clearest picture of SHG and its importance to rural India. In a path-breaking study by the National Council of Applied Economic Research (NCAER) in 2010, it was revealed that the income disparity in India had increased after 1991, when the globalization process was officially kick started in the country. According to the NCAER (2010), during 1993-1994, the top 20 per cent of India's population had 36.7 per cent share of the national income, which has increased dramatically in 2009-2010, when the top 20 per cent of India's population had a whopping over 50 per cent share of the country's national income. Since the need of the hour is financial inclusion and inclusive growth of the poor, SHG has become an important tool as the major focus of SHGs is on the poor. The main steps by which SHGs help in generating sustainable rural livelihood are as follows:

1. Formation of SHGs among the rural poor;
2. Capacity building and skill training imparted by the SHGs;
3. Strengthening thrift and credit habit amongst members of the SHGs;
4. Provision of credit linkage of SHGs with banks and other financial institutions;
5. Provision of technology inputs for micro enterprises.

As envisaged in the United Nations Millennium Development Goals (UNMDG), it is of primary importance to realise sustained improvement in the living standards of the rural poor. According to recent National Sample Surveys, there has been an overall decline in the growth rate of employment especially in the agricultural sector—the primary sector contributing to a significant portion of the total employment in India. Overall, there has been a decrease in the rural employment opportunities, especially for women, in the agricultural sector. Secondly, only 13 per cent of the Small Scale enterprises, which has been the second largest employment provider to the Indian workforce after agriculture, is located in the rural economy and serving the rural community. In this backdrop, the M.S. Swaminathan Research Foundation (2004) had pointed out that it has become "essential to promote multiple livelihood opportunities in the rural sector especially among the socially and economically disadvantaged groups. The organized sector is not employment intensive and organized self-employment is the only opportunity in the future. Thus, there is an urgent need to refocus and develop a "New deal for the Self Employed" especially for the rural women, landless and the tribal .... an attempt to promote eco-entrepreneurship in rural areas to develop multiple livelihood systems among landless and marginal households through promoting Sustainable Self Help Group (SSHG) approach. Mobilization of women and men, group formation and federation of SSHGs, identification of enterprises with appropriate forward and backward linkages, capacity building to manage the enterprises as a successful business venture are the crucial aspects involved in developing a multiple livelihood systems among the rural men and women".

III. Objective of the Paper

The basic problem of our rural area is the problem of underemployment rather than unemployment. Various grass-root level studies has revealed that more than 60 per cent employed adults of the grass-root area economies have failed to make use of even 40 per cent of their labour power (Kar, 1992, 1986; Kar & Ray, 2006) in a complete agriculture-year. There is little opportunity to generate employment days by the agricultural sector for its surplus labour power, as has been discussed before. However, it has been observed that there has been some sort of marked distinctions between the first generation anti-poverty programmes and the consolidated anti-poverty programme which had been taken during the last year of the last century in the fold of the formation of SHGs. Since then it has been seen that the project of formation of SHGs has gained a lot of momentum particularly in the grass-root rural areas and this has enhanced the scope employment opportunities for the rural community. Not only that a comparison can be made among the rural poor who are in the SHG safety net and who have remained outside the safety net then a clear cut picture can emerge about the impact of the working of SHGs on employment. This is the main tenet of this write up.

IV. Study Area

To measure the impact of the working of SHGs on sustainable rural employment we have selected purposively the sub-divisional rural economy of Dinhata in the Cooch Behar District of North Bengal. Cooch Behar district in West Bengal is of paramount interest as it is the gateway to the North-East India as well as being located in a strategic position in close proximity to several international countries (Ray & Biswas, 2013). As such, the development of Cooch Behar is subject of national concern. The rationality behind the selection of this area economy of Dinhata in the Cooch Behar District is given below:

(i) Firstly, the highest number of SHGs has been formed in this area economy as compared to the other areas of the Cooch Behar district.

(ii) Secondly, this area economy has also been recorded highest number of SHGs that have been taken up the economic activities as compared to the other areas.

(iii) Thirdly, one of the authors has been living in this area since the 1960s and is thus well-acquainted with the area, its people and their language and the level of living.

V. Methodology

We have used both the random sampling and stratified random sampling without replacement for the selection of the Gram Panchayats (GPs) and for the selection of Self Help Groups (SHGs) respectively. First of all we have selected two GPs randomly from the all GPs of the sub-division. Then we have divided all the SHGs of these two GPs under four different stratums namely caste, religion, sex and education to find out the exact impact of the working of the SHGs on employment generation. Accordingly, all the SHGs of the two GPs are divided under these four stratums. Then we have picked up 4 SHGs from each stratum randomly to form our sample. Thus, we have taken 16 SHGs for the present study. Again we have taken 61 Below Poverty Line (BPL) households randomly from the same GPs to make a comparison about the nature of employment enjoyed by the SHG household members and the non-SHG household members.

A specially prepared SHG schedule has been used to collect information about the formation and functions of the SHGs. Another specially prepared employment schedule has been used to collect information about the employment of the SHG members, SHG household members and non-SHG household members.

VI. Sample Profile

Thus the 16 SHGs, 164 SHG households and 61 non-SHG households become the universe of this study. Most of the SHGs of our sample were formed with the initiation of the Non-Government Organizations (NGOs). The role either of the financial institutions or of the Govt. officials in the formation process of the SHGs is rather poor. All are given in Table 6.2. It can be seen from Table 6.2 that 53.33 per cent SHGs was formed by the NGOs. The role of the social workers ranks the second.

Table 6.2: Formation of the SHGs

Name of the Organization	*Percentage of SHGs*
Financial institutions	6.67
Govt. Officials	13.33
NGOs	53.33
Social workers	26.67
Total	100.00

Source: Primary Survey.

It is in order to find out the academic status of the leaders of the SHGs. Here we include the president, secretary and treasurer as leader and their academic background has been given in Table 6.3. It is very clear from Table 6.3 that the relatively educationally advanced poor people have come forward to fight against the threat of underemployment and unemployment as compared to the other poor people. One can also notice

Table 6.3: Academic Status of the Leaders

Academic Status	*Number of Persons*	*Percentage to Total*
Primary (up to class IV)	2	4.17
Middle School (class V-VIII)	20	41.67
High School (class IX-XII)	22	45.83
College and above	4	8.33
Total	48	100.00

Source: Primary Survey.

from the same table that nearly half of the leaders of our sample belong to the academic status group of high school level that is the education level which starts from class IX to class XII. In percentage this figure stands at 45.83 per cent. If we assemble the SHG leaders in the academic status group of class V to class XII, and then we see that more than 87 per cent leaders were belonging to this group. So as a whole the academic quality of the leaders of our sample SHGs is rather good.

There is no denying that the efficacy of the SHG very much depends on the education of the leaders and on the age structure of the SHG members. Again there is a common belief that higher the percentage of members of relatively lower age group higher will be the efficacy of the group and *vice versa*. However, there is no hard and fast rule regarding the lower and upper limit of age of the members at the time of their entry in the groups. We have distributed all the SHG members of our sample by five age groups. This is given in Table 6.4.

Table 6.4: Distribution of SHG Members by Age

Age Group	*No. of Members*	*Percentage to Total*
15—25	3	1.83
25—35	38	23.17
35—45	69	42.07
45—55	41	25.00
55 & above	13	7.93
Total	164	100.00

Source: Primary Survey.

We have also constructed two tables to exhibit the age distributional pattern of the SHG household members and non-SHG household members. All are given in Table 6.5 and Table 6.6 respectively. One can see from these tables that in comparison to the non-SHG households, the SHG member households have recorded relatively more percentage of younger members in their population structure. But in question of female-male ratio the non-SHG households have been enjoying a pro-female ratio than the SHG member households. The two calculated ratios are 0.94 and 0.85 respectively. However, the good female-male ratio doesn't necessarily signify the good choice that goes in favour of female child as our sample data speaks about that. If we have a look at the sex distribution of the children who have not yet been enjoyed their 5th birth day then we see that the incidence of female child is just double than male child among the households of the SHG members. But in case of non-SHG household

Table 6.5: Distribution of SHG Household Members by Age and Sex

Age Group	*Male*	*Percentage*	*Female*	*Percentage*	*Total*	*Percentage*
Up to 5	7	2.13	14	5.02	21	3.45
5-15	65	19.75	53	18.99	118	19.41
15-35	121	36.78	83	29.75	204	33.55
35-45	59	17.93	71	25.45	130	21.38
45-55	50	15.20	39	13.98	89	14.64
Above 55	27	8.21	19	6.81	46	7.57
Total	329	100.00	279	100.00	608	100.00

Source: Primary Survey.

Table 6.6: Distribution of Non-SHG Household Members by Age and Sex

Age Group	*Male*	*Percentage*	*Female*	*Percentage*	*Total*	*Percentage*
Up to 5	15	13.04	10	9.80	25	11.52
5-15	20	17.40	13	12.75	33	15.21
15-35	27	23.48	33	32.35	60	27.65
35-45	16	13.91	18	17.65	34	15.67
45-55	23	20.00	20	19.61	43	19.81
Above 55	14	12.17	8	7.84	22	10.14
Total	115	100.00	102	100.00	217	100.00

Source: Primary Survey.

members the incidence of male child still exceeds the incidence of the female child. Though it is a very small sample and also we are not in a position to make any inference about this demographic indication of favoured female child among the SHG household members, still it is a tiny indication that we want to mention here for further rigorous research on this issue.

At the same time it is also in order to assess about the quality of human resource of our sample in the light of the academic standard of both of the SHG household members and non-SHG households members. We have distributed all the SHG household members and non-SHG household members according to their academic standard in Tables 6.7 and 6.8, respectively. One notices from these two tables that there exists a significant difference in education level among the SHG household members and non-SHG household members. Firstly, more than half of the non-SHG household members were recorded themselves as illiterate, while the same for the SHG household members stands at 22.14 per cent. Secondly, if we consider that the education level from class V to class XII as the standard level, then we also see that 56.39 per cent of population of the SHG household members were belonging to this group, while the same for the non-SHG household members stands at only 27.38.

Table 6.7: Academic Status of the SHG Household Members

Education Level	*Male*	*Percentage*	*Female*	*Percentage*	*Total*	*Percentage*
Illiterate	63	19.15	67	25.97	130	22.14
Primary	60	18.24	41	15.89	101	17.21
Middle School	113	34.34	94	36.43	207	35.26
High School	73	22.19	51	19.77	124	21.13
College and above	20	6.08	5	1.94	25	4.26
Total	329	100.00	258	100.00	587	100.00

Source: Primary Survey.

Table 6.8: Academic Status of the non-SHG Household Members

Education Level	*Male*	*Percentage*	*Female*	*Percentage*	*Total*	*Percentage*
Illiterate	36	45.00	44	57.14	80	50.96
Primary	16	20.00	18	23.38	34	21.66
Middle School	24	30.00	15	19.48	39	24.84
High School	4	5.00	nil	nil	4	2.54
College and above	Nil	Nil	nil	nil	nil	nil
Total	80	100.00	77	100.00	157	100.00

Source: Primary Survey.

For the time constraint at present we are not in a position to present the incidence of age specific education among the members particularly among the teen age group household members of both SHG and non-SHG. However, an overview on the data permits us to say that the number of school going children of the SHG households exceeds that of the non-SHG households.

VII. Analysis of Primary and Secondary Occupations of SHGs

We have found ten broad groups of occupations as primary as well as secondary occupations among the SHG members, SHG household members and non-SHG household members of our sample area. They are:

(i) Farmers, those who are farming on own land (any amount) as well as on land taken on lease;

(ii) Agricultural labourers;
(iii) Village traders, including petty businessmen, shop keepers, selling cloths and processing of *chira* and *muri*;
(iv) Village artisans, including carpenters, Masons, tailors and village *Makers;*
(v) Concrete pole workers;
(vi) Rickshaw and van-pullers;
(vii) *Bidi* workers;
(viii) Mid-day meal Workers;
(ix) Service holders; and
(x) Private Tutors.

Now, we are in a position to distribute all the SHG members, SHG household members and non-SHG household members of our sample by primary and secondary occupations are under ten occupational heads.

VIIA. Distribution of SHG Members by Primary Occupation

We have stated earlier that the total number of SHG members is 164. Out of these 164 members, 118 members are engaged in different gainful occupations and the rest 46 members are not engaged themselves in any gainful occupation other than house works. They are all female members. We have distributed all these 118 members under ten broad occupational groups as given in Table 6.8. One thing that is clearly followed form this table that despite a decadal exercise of the working of the SHGs, non-agricultural base of this region remains in a nebulous negotiation. Still agricultural sector appears as the major employment providing sector in our sample. Exactly half of the SHG members are engaged directly in agricultural sector. Only 36.45 per cent SHG members are succeeded to engage themselves in the activities directly related to the SHG activities. Thus there is a long way still to go to make a socio-economic atmosphere where the SHG members mainly engaged in the activities related to only SHG activities. What is surprising is that none of our SHG members are showing any interest to initiate the very popular projects like goat farming, piggery, and poultry in their activities. Activity like sewing is not included in our sampling net.

VIIB. Ditribution of SHG Members by Secondary Occupation

Only 63 SHG members out of 118 gainfully employed members have

Table 6.9: Distribution of SHG members by Primary Occupation

Occupation	*Male*		*Female*		*Total*	
	No.	*P.C.*	*No.*	*P.C.*	*No.*	*P.C.*
Farmer	2	18.18	33	30.84	35	29.66
Agricultural Labouror	3	27.27	21	19.63	24	20.34
Village Traders	3	27.27	10	9.34	13	11.02
Village Artisans	2	18.18	1	0.93	3	2.54
Concrete pole Worker	—	—	4	3.74	4	3.40
Rickshaw/Van Puller	1	9.10	—	—	1	0.84
Bidi Worker	—	—	5	4.67	5	4.24
Mid-day Meal Worker	—	—	23	21.50	23	19.49
Service Holders	—	—	2	1.87	2	1.69
Private Tutors	—	—	8	7.48	8	6.78
Total	11	100.00	107	100.00	118	100.00

Source: Primary Survey.

succeeded to find out some sort of secondary occupation besides their primary occupation. The opportunity of secondary occupation arises mainly from the 100 days per capita per annum employment guarantee scheme of the Central Government and from the activities like mid-day meal cooking. These are given in Table 6.10.

Table 6.10: Distribution of SHG Members by Secondary Occupation

Occupation	*Male*		*Female*		*Total*	
	No.	*P.C.*	*No.*	*P.C.*	*No.*	*P.C.*
Farming	1	20.00	3	5.17	4	6.35
Agricultural Labourers	2	40.00	4	6.90	6	9.52
100 days Work	2	40.00	31	53.45	33	52.38
Mid-day Meal Cooking	—	—	20	34.48	20	31.75
Total	5	100.00	58	100.00	63	100.00

Source: Primary Survey.

VIIC. Distribution of SHG Household Members by Primary Occupations

We have had some idea about the nature of employment enjoyed by the SHG members of our sample in the previous paragraphs of this write up. Now we try to assess the impact of the working of the SHGs on employment generation considering the employed adult members of the SHG households who were engaged under ten occupational groups during the last year from the date of our survey. The number of employed adults that we have in the SHG households is 321. Out of these 321 employed adults the number of male employed adult is 204 and number of employed female adult is 117. Out of these 321 employed male and female adults, 21 male adults and 1 female adult remained absent during the time of our survey and reported that they have left the village for livelihood. So we have dealt with the 183 male employed adults and 116 female employed adults in our calculation. We have distributed all these male and female employed adults under our occupational groups in Table 6.11. This Table is to some extent a replica of Table 6.9. Whatever we get about the information in the case of the SHG members, here also we get more or less the same picture. Actually we are dealing with the very initiation phase of the working of the SHGs. So, the overall result regarding employment is rather same. However what is interesting is that 83 employed adults have found their jobs in the occupation directly or indirectly related to the working of the SHGs. In percentage form it stands at 27.76 per cent.

Table 6.11: Distribution of SHG Households Members by Primary Occupation

Occupation Group	*Male*		*Female*		*Total*	
	No.	*P.C.*	*No.*	*P.C.*	*No.*	*P.C.*
Farmer	44	24.04	34	29.31	78	26.09
Agricultural Labourer	60	32.80	23	19.83	83	27.76
Village Traders	22	12.02	9	7.76	31	10.37
Village Artisans	25	13.66	1	0.86	26	8.70
Concrete pole Worker	9	4.92	5	4.32	14	4.68
Rickshaw/Van Puller	10	5.46	—	—	10	3.34
Bidi worker	—	—	7	6.03	7	2.34
Mid-day Meal Worker	—	—	26	22.41	26	8.70
Service Holders	5	2.73	2	1.72	7	2.34
Private Tutors	8	4.37	9	7.76	17	5.68
Total	183	100.00	116	100.00	299	100.00

Source: Primary Survey.

VIID. Distribution of SHG Household Members by Secondary Occupations

There is no denying that the area that has been selected by us for the purpose of the present study is purely an agricultural area. There exists not even of a tiny cottage unit. We have seen some artisans, some pullers and some traders who are performing mainly the non-agricultural activities. Again there is no clear-cut distinction between the agricultural and non-agricultural activities. We have seen that some of the village artisans also perform some agricultural activities at the time of peak agricultural season either as farmer in the land owned by them or as agricultural labourer in the land owned by the others. Same is true for the other non-agricultural activities. As a result, the role of the secondary occupation is rather unimpressive in the sample. We have given a picture of secondary occupation enjoyed by the SHG household members in Table 6.12. One can see from this table that more than 70 per cent employed adults have been succeeded to add some employment days in their employment days basket through the 100 days work per capita per annum scheme. On the other hand, if we consider the working of the SHG then we see that activities related to SHG provide secondary employment to the tune of 10.85 employed adults of our sample.

Table 6.12: Distribution of SHG Household Members by Secondary Occupation

Occupation	*Male*		*Female*		*Total*	
	No.	*P.C.*	*No.*	*P.C.*	*No.*	*P.C.*
Farming	6	4.58	7	8.64	13	6.13
Agricultural Labourer	19	14.50	8	9.88	27	12.74
100 days Work	106	80.92	43	53.08	149	70.28
Mid-day Meal Cooking	—	—	23	28.40	23	10.85
Total	131	100.00	81	100.00	212	100.00

Source: Primary Survey.

VIII. Analysis of Non-SHG Household Members by Primary and Secondary Occupations

As in the previous section, here a similar analysis of the distribution of Non-SHG Household members by primary and secondary occupations that has been obtained through the primary survey has been analysed.

VIIIA. Distribution of Non-SHG Household Members by Primary Occupations

We have stated earlier in this write up that we have taken 61 BPL households who are not the member of any SHG. This is an attempt through which we try to make a comparison between the SHG household members and non-SHG household members to find out the differences in the nature and extent of employment enjoyed by these two groups of people. Accordingly, we have distributed all the employed adults of the non-SHG households by the eight occupational groups in Table 6.13. Here also we have excluded 8 male adults who left the village for livelihood during the last year from the date of our survey.

The occupational pattern of the employed adults of non-SHG household members again gives us a gloomy picture of employment situation of the grass-root rural area. Fortunately or unfortunately this is the ground reality. One can see two clear-cut occupations of non-SHG household members from Table 6.12. They are agricultural labourer and van-puller. The percentages of employed adults engaged in these two occupations are 51.76 per cent and 25.88 per cent respectively. Except these two occupations the other that need some mention is farming. The percentage of employed adults engaged in this occupation stands at 10.60 per cent.

Table 6.13: Distribution of Non-SHG Household Members by Primary Occupation

Occupation Group	*Male*		*Female*		*Total*	
	No.	*P.C.*	*No.*	*P.C.*	*No.*	*P.C.*
Farmer	5	7.35	4	23.53	9	10.60
Agricultural Labourer	36	52.94	8	47.06	44	51.76
Village Traders	3	4.41	—	—	3	3.53
Village Artisans	2	2.94	—	—	2	2.35
Rickshaw/Van Puller	22	32.35	—	—	22	25.88
Bidi Worker	—	—	3	17.65	3	3.53
Mid-day Meal Helper	—	—	2	11.76	2	2.35
Total	68	100.00	17	100.00	85	100.00

Source: Primary Survey.

VIIIB. Distribution of Non-SHG Household Members by Secondary Occupations

We have 85 employed adults in the non-SHG households. Out of these 85 employed adults 45 employed adults were succeeded to add some working days to their total working days. This simply means that only 27.38 employed adults were succeeded to enjoy the benefit of secondary occupation. But in the case of the SHG household members this percentage figure remains at 56.39. This higher percentage is mainly because of the fact that the SHG household members were better informed about the working of the 100 days work as they were in regular connection with the local Gram Panchayat officials and thus easily enrolled their names more in number than the other poor non-SHG household members. Information about the non-SHG household members by secondary occupation are given in Table 5.14. What is important to say here in the case of secondary occupation is that while out of 212 employed adults of the SHG household members 149 employed adults were benefited from the 100 days work scheme, but the same for the non-SHG household members stands at 21 out of 45 employed adults. If we express these in percentage form then the two percentage figures become 70.28 per cent and 46.67 per cent respectively.

Table 6.14: Distribution of Non-SHG Household Members by Secondary Occupation

Occupation	*Male*		*Female*		*Total*	
	No.	*P.C.*	*No.*	*P.C.*	*No.*	*P.C.*
Farming	6	15.79	1	14.28	7	15.55
Agricultural Labourers	14	36.84	3	42.86	17	37.78
100 days Work	18	47.37	3	42.86	21	46.67
Total	38	100.00	7	100.00	45	100.00

Source: Primary Survey.

IXA. Incidence of Employment

Now, we are in a position to present the incidence of employment among the employable adults of both of the SHG household members and non-SHG household members on the basis of the data given in the previous tables. To find out the number of employable adults we simply consider the population of the age group 15-55 on the initial assumption that all of them are ready to offer their labour power if opportunity opens before

Table 6.15: Incidence of Employment

Category	*No. of Employable Adults*	*No. of Employed Adults*	*Percentage*
SHG household Members	423	299	70.68
Non-SHG household Members	137	85	62.04
Total	560	384	68.57

Source: Primary Survey.

them. On the basis of this assumption and of the data given in the previous tables we construct Table 6.15 to find out the incidence of employment.

Thus, we can say that the incidence of employment among the SHG household members is rather high as compare to that of the non-SHG household members. Here the difference between the two proportions is significant statistically at 5 per cent level of significance.

IXB. Employment Days through Primary Occupation

Incidence of employment and its impact on employment days both are equally important in any analysis regarding employment. We have already discussed about the incidence of employment in the previous paragraphs. Now we try to present the impact of the incidence of employment on employment days on the basis of the occupational groups as given at the beginning of this section. As we have seen in the preceding paragraphs that the number of employed adults in the SHG households and that of the Non-SHG are 299 and 85 respectively. We have distributed all the employed adults of the SHG household members and that of the non-SHG household members on the basis of their primary occupations in Tables 6.10 and 6.12 respectively. Now, we examine the mean employment as enjoyed by the employed adults through all of their primary occupations during the last year from the date of our survey. These are given in Tables 6.15 and 6.16 respectively for the employed adults of SHG and Non-SHG household members. One can see from these tables that the mean employment enjoyed by these two groups of employed adults are 208 man days and 190 man days respectively. Thus on an average the SHG household members are enjoyed 17 man days of employment per capita per annum more than that of the non-SHG household members. We have also observed a lot of differences in the mean employments under different occupations. For the employed adults of the SHG household members the mean man days of employment varies from 160 to 330 man days. On the other hand, for the employed adults of the Non-SHG households it ranges from 97 man days to 307 man days. All are given in Tables 6.16 and 6.17 respectively.

Now, it is in order to find out the number of employed adults who are in full employment during the last year from the date of our survey. Here we use three definitions of full employment. If we consider 330 man days as full employment man days then 7 employed adults of the SHG household members are succeeded to maintain the full employment level. However, if we assume 240 man days as full employment man

Table 6.16: Employment days Enjoyed by the SHG Household Members through Primary Occupation

Occupation	*Persons employed in Primary Occupation*		*Mean Employment Through Primary Occupation*	*Total Employment days*	
	Number	*Percentage*		*Number*	*Percentage*
Farming	78	26.09	201	15678	25.26
Agricultural Labour	83	27.76	186	15438	24.87
Village Traders	31	10.37	247	7657	12.33
Village Artisans	26	8.70	211	5486	8.84
Concrete pole Work	14	4.68	160	2240	3.61
Rickshaw/Van Puller	10	3.34	311	3110	5.01
Bidi Rolling	7	2.34	240	1680	2.70
Mid-day Meal Cooking	26	8.70	205	5330	8.59
Service	7	2.34	330	2310	3.72
Private Tuition	17	5.68	185	3145	5.07
Total	299	100.00	208	62192	100.00

Source: Primary Survey.

Table 6.17: Employment Days Enjoyed by the Non-SHG Household Members through Primary Occupation

Occupation	*Persons employed in Primary Occupation*		*Mean Employment Through Primary Occupation*	*Total Employment*	
	Number	*Percentage*		*Number*	*Percentage*
Farming	9	10.60	97	873	5.41
Agricultural Labour	44	51.76	171	7524	46.61
Village Traders	3	3.53	198	594	3.68
Village Artisans	2	2.35	187	374	2.31
Rickshaw/Van Puller	22	25.88	266	5852	36.25
Bidi Rolling	3	3.53	234	702	4.35
Mid-day Meal Helper	2	2.35	112	224	1.39
Total	85	100.00	190	16143	100.00

Source: Primary Survey.

days then 55 employed adults of this group remain in full employment. If however, we reduce further the number of man days to 180, then we see that 230 employed adults of this group remain in full employment. All these are given in Table 6.16.

Again from the Table 6.17 we can also calculate the number of employed adults who are in full employment according to our three definitions. One can see from this table that none one of this group is in full employment if we assume 330 man days as full employment man days. If we reduce the figure to 240 then only 12 employed adults will be in full employment. If we further reduce the number of full employment days to 180 then 57 employed adults will be in full employment. In percentage form this has been given in Table 6.18 which is self-explanatory.

Table 6.18: Employed Adults in Full Employment

No. of Full Employment Days	No. of Adults in		P.C. of Adults in	
	SHG	Non-SHG	SHG	Non-SHG
330	7	Nil	2.34	Nil
240	55	12	18.39	14.12
180	230	57	76.92	67.06

Source: Primary Survey.

The mean employment enjoyed by the members of the SHG households is 207. The same for the members of the Non-SHG households is 190. The difference between the two means is significant apparently. The null hypothesis that there is no significant difference between the mean employments of the two groups is rejected and the calculated Z value is greater than the table value at 5 per cent level of significant.

IXC. Good and Bad Employment

We define elsewhere the term good employment as the employment for more than 150 days and bad employment as employment for less than 150 days in a complete agricultural year in analyzing the rural employment (Kar, 1993, 2002, 2007). On the basis of this definition we have distributed all the employed adults of SHG households and that of the non-SHG households of our sample in Table 6.19. One can see from this table that about 69 per cent employed adults of the SHG households are in good employment during the last year according to our definition. The same for the non-SHG households is 45.88 per cent. Apparently we have a significant difference in good employment among the SHG and non-SHG household adults. On the other hand, 31.10 per cent employed adults of the SHG households and 54.12 per cent employed adults of the non-SHG households were in bad employment during the last year. Thus, the total number of employed adults who are in bad employment of our sample stands at 139. Roughly, we can say that 36.20 per cent employed adults are remaining underemployed in our sample area during the last year from the date of our survey.

Table 6.19: Good and Bad Employment in Primary Occupation

Nature of Employment	*SHG Household Members in*		*Non-SHG Household Members in*	
	No.	*P.C.*	*No.*	*P.C.*
Good Employment	206	68.90	39	45.88
Bad employment	93	31.10	46	54.12
Total	299	100.00	85	100.00

Source: Primary Survey.

X. Findings and Conclusions

XA. Some Findings

1. The role of the NGOs in the formation of the SHGs is still significant even after the implementation of the second generation anti-poverty programmes.
2. The role of the Government officials as well as that of the financial institutions still needs to be rigorous explored in this regard.
3. Although educationally advanced portion of the rural poor population comes forward in the formation of the SHGs, still we have observed a positive impact of the working of the SHGs on the education of the children in the households of the SHGs as compared to the households of the non-SHGs.
4. Still agriculture and allied activities played an important role in the generation of employment in this sample area.
5. Less than 40 per cent employed adults of the SHG households have succeeded in finding employment for themselves in the activities related to the SHG activities.
6. On an average the members of the SHGs of our sample are better informed with the information that related to the employment generated on the part of the Central Government under various anti-poverty schemes, particularly in 100 days employment schemes.
7. We have also have an impression from Table 6.15 that the members of the SHG households are succeeded to find more

employment as compared to the members of the non-SHG households.

8. If we have a look on the mean man days of employment then we see as a whole that SHG household members have enjoyed annually 18 more man days of employment than the non-SHG household members.
9. We have seen a significant difference in the incidence of employment among the employed adult women of the SHG households and non-SHG households. While, more that 60 per cent employable adult women of the SHG households are in employment during the last year, but the same for the other group is only 24 per cent.
10. Both apparently and statistically significant number of employed adults of the SHG households are in good employment than that of the employed adults of the non-SHG households.

XB. Conclusions

Thus on the basis of the above presentations and findings now we are in a position to make the conclusion that the working of the SHG in the area economy under our study has some positive impact on the expansion of the opportunity of employment among the employed adults. Apparently, one can say that 18 days more employment enjoyed by the employed adults of the SHG households than that of the employed adults of the non-SHG households is not so significant but if we consider these employment days in value term then we see on an average the employed adults of the SHG households have enjoyed more wage income worth of Rs. 2700 per capita per annum as compared to the employed adults of the non-SHGs. Finally, what is more important to say here is that the working of the SHGs has no doubt increased the employment opportunity among the employable female adults in the grass-root rural area economy. As Ray (2012, 2013), had pointed out, the working of SHGs in India is inextricably linked with women empowerment. Finally, it is on this positive note and with the immortal words of the Nobel laureate Mohammed Yunus who had revolutionized the way the world thought about SHGs and microfinance with his Grameen bank model, that we end this chapter:

> "If the poor are to get a chance to lift themselves out of poverty, it's up to us to remove the institutional barriers we've created around them. We must remove the absurd rules and laws we

have made that treat the poor as minorities. And we must come up with new ways to recognize a person by his or her own worth, not by artificially measuring sticks imposed by a biased system".

(Mohammed Yunus, 2009)

References

Basu, P. and Srivastava, P. (2005): "Scaling up Microfinance for India's Rural Poor", *World Bank Policy Research Working Paper*, Geneva: World Bank.

Business Standard (2007): "India among Top 10 Industrial Nations," *International Yearbook of Industrial Statistics-2011*, March 30, New Delhi: Business Standard.

Dasgupta R. (2005): "Microfinance in India: Empirical Evidence, Alternative Models and Policy Imperatives", *Economic and Political Weekly*, 40(12).

Dasgupta, R. (2006): "An Architectural Plan for a Micro Finance Institutional Net Worth", *Economic and Political Weekly*, 41(11).

Franchetti, M.J. (2012): *Carbon Footprint Analysis: Concepts, Methods, Implementation, and Case Studies*, Florida: CRC Press.

Ghosh, R.A. (2012): "Unemployment Rate is Higher amongst Highly Educated Rural Indians", *DNA Analysis*, September 18, http:/www.dnaindia.com (accessed on 13 June 2013).

Government of India (2010): *Report on Employment and Unemployment Survey (2009-10)*, Ministry of Labour and Employment, Chandigarh: Labour Bureau.

Harper, M. (1998): *Profit for Poor*, Oxford University Press, Oxford.

Hulme, D. and Mosley, P. (1996): *Finance against poverty*, Routledge, London.

Jayaraman, R. (2002): "Role of Self Help Groups in Fisherwomen Development in India", Paper presented at the *Coastal Zone Asia Pacific Conference*, 12-16 May, 2002, Bangkok, Thailand.

Kar, S.C. (1992): *Surveying Rural Economies: For Rural Development Planning*, Kolkata: Academic Enterprise.

Kar, S.C. and Sarkar, P.C. (1986): "The Question of Further Lowering the Ceiling of Rural Land in West Bengal—A Case Study", *Indian Journal of Agricultural Economics*, 41.

Kar, S.C. and Ray, S.N. (2006): "Social Security of Labour in the Informal Sector: A Case Study of Cooch Behar District", Paper presented at *Second Global Labour Forum*, New Delhi: Institute of Human Development.

Kar, S.C. and Ray, S.N. (2012): "Myths and Realities of Human Resource Management: A Study on Cooch Behar District", *Resource Management: Human and Natural, Perspective on North-East Region*, Kolkata: Readers Service.

Khandker, S.R. (1999): *Fighting Poverty with Micro Credit: Experience in Bangladesh*, Oxford University Press, New York.

Mahajan, V. (2005): "From Micro Credit to Livelihood Finance", *Economic and Political Weekly*, 40(41).

Morduch, J. (1999): "The Microfinance Promise", *Journal of Economic Literature*, 37(4).

National Bank for Agriculture and Rural Development (2005): *Progress of SHG Bank Linkage in India-2005-06*, Press Release on March 31, 2006, www.nabard.org/pdf/introduction05-06.pdf, accessed on 13th July, 2013.

National Council of Applied Economic Research (2010): "NCAER Annual Report 2009-2010", *NCAER*, New Delhi.

Nayak, K.B. (2008): *Sustainable Development: An Alternative Approach in Rabindranath Tagore's Vision*, Serials Publications, New Delhi.

Parmar, D.K., Jain, A.K., and Modi, V.K. (2013): "Status and Causes of Rural Unemployment in India, Research Paper", *International Journal of Scientific Research*, 2(1).

M.S. Swminathan Research Foundation (2004): *Ecoenterprises for Sustainable Livelihoods: Decentralised Production of Trichoderma viride—a Biofungicide for Crop Protection: Elayathendral Women's Self-Help Group, S. Pudur, Kannivadi, Dinndigul District*, JRD Tata Ecotechnology Centre, M.S. Swaminathan Research Foundation, Chennai.

Ray, S.N. (2012): "The Microfinance Institutions (Development and Regulation) Bill, 2011 and Women Empowerment: Some Key Issues, "*Microfinance and Women's Empowerment in India*", Naba Ballygunge Mahavidyalaya, Kolkata.

Ray, S.N. (2013): "Exclusion of Women in the Micro Finance Institutions (Development and Regulation) Bill, 2011", *Financial Inclusion, Self-help Groups (SHGs) and Women Empowerment*, New Century Publications, New Delhi.

Ray, S.N. and Biswas, A.B. (2013): "Movements in Cooch Behar", Paper to be published in *East-Indian Journal of Social Sciences*, Alipurduar, Prolegomena.

Rhyne, E. (2001): *Mainstreaming Microfinance*, Kumarian Press, Connecticut.

Rutherford, S. (2000): *The poor and their money*, Oxford University Press, Delhi

Sinha, F. (2005): "Access, Use and Contribution of Microfinance in India: Findings from a National Survey", *Economic and Political Weekly*, 40(17).

Srivastava, S.P. (1998): *Development Debates: Critical Perspectives*, Rawat Publications, Jaipur and New Delhi.

United Nations Development Programme (1994): "Human Development Report", *UNDP*, Geneva.

WorldViewer.com Inc. (2013): "Quotations", *Epigrams from Gandhiji-V*, T-2-256, http://www.mahatma.com, accessed on 13 July, 2013.

World Commission on Environment and Development (1987): *Our Common Future*, Oxford University Press, Oxford.

Yunus, M. (2009): *Lifting People Worldwide Out of Poverty*, Knowledge@ Wharton, Pennsylvania.

7

Poverty Eradication Through NRLM

The Changed Face of Rural Livelihoods in West Bengal, India

Debasis Mukhopadhyay

I. Introduction

India's strong economic growth has consistently sought to include the rural poor, who are concentrated in areas where rainfed agriculture is the main economic activity. However, poverty persists because of limited and inequitable access to productive resources, such as land, water, improved inputs and technologies and microfinance, as well as vulnerability to drought and other natural disasters. Low levels of literacy and skills conspire to keep people in the poverty trap, preventing them from claiming their basic rights or from embarking on new activities to earn income or build assets.

The Ministry of Rural Development (MoRD) has made a substantial contribution to improving rural livelihoods in India. This has been mainly achieved by supporting programmes led by state governments in Andhra Pradesh, Orissa, Madhya Pradesh and West Bengal. However, the reduction of rural poverty through livelihoods promotion has been a unifying goal.

These programmes focus on some of the poorest and most remote districts in these states and particularly target women and socially excluded tribal and caste groups.

The rural livelihoods approach places people at the centre of development, and programmes based on this approach help men and women build assets and develop their skills so that they can access new opportunities for income generation and employment. Most rural people depend on natural resources and agriculture for their livelihoods and these supported programmes pay particular attention to the sustainable management of water, land and forests. Particular packages of support are directed to the landless and to marginal farmers so they also have opportunities to benefit. Robust institutions and reliable services are essential to increase people's participation in development. Rural livelihoods programmes have supported the formation of self-help groups and producer groups and have significantly increased access to microfinance on fair terms, to veterinary and crop advisory services, to inputs such as improved seeds and to markets. A capacity building programme at all levels—from State to village—is inherent to the success of the programmes. Working through state governments has enabled lessons learned to be efficiently captured and rapidly scaled up. It goes on to consider some of the new challenges and opportunities facing rural India including converging different rural development schemes for greater development effectiveness, tackling persistent food insecurity and adaptation to climate change.

The rural livelihoods approach places people at the centre of development, and focuses on building assets and skills so that women and men can access new opportunities for income generation and employment. Supportive policies, robust institutions, and regulatory and incentive structures that both encourage growth and protect the most vulnerable, are essential to improving livelihoods. At the same time, reliable services—such as micro-finance, veterinary and crop advice—and access to agricultural inputs and markets, are necessary to ensure that improvements are sustained. People's participation, capacity building, technical innovation and service delivery are central to all our rural livelihoods programmes. However, several programme models have evolved, responding in part to the priorities of our state government partners. In the late 1990s, our main emphasis was on the rainfed farming projects in eastern India and western India, managed by the NGO, Gram Vikas Trust, and on forestry projects. These projects resulted in improved livelihoods, capacity and services in participating villages. Some of the lessons learned were influential in subsequent programmes but the lack of formal institutionalization in government systems hampered widespread uptake.

II. The SGSY

The Swarnjayanti Gram Swarozgar Yojana (SGSY) Scheme, a Centrally Sponsored Scheme implemented in all states except Delhi and Chandigarh since 1999, is primarily designed to promote self-employment oriented income generating activities for the BPL households in the rural areas. Woven around the mechanism of Self-Help Groups (SHGs), the SGSY has been designed to break the financial, technical and market constraints that the individual BPL households face to cross the threshold of poverty line. The main components of the scheme include: (i) formation of SHGs of rural poor households; (ii) capacity building training for managing the SHGs and skill training to take up micro-enterprises; (iii) strengthening thrift and credit in SHGs by providing revolving fund support; (iv) credit linkage with banks/other financial institutions and back ended subsidy for eligible SHGs/members to take up micro enterprises; (v) Provision of support for marketing and infrastructure creation to strengthen the forward and backward linkages; and (vi) technology inputs for micro enterprises. In addition, 15 per cent of the total SGSY allocation is earmarked for special SGSY projects in the nature of pioneer/innovative projects capable of triggering growth impulses.

Several evaluation studies have shown that the scheme is relatively successful in alleviating rural poverty wherever systematic mobilization of the poor into SHGs, their capacity building and skill development was taken up in a process-intensive manner. An overview of the implementation of the scheme in the country over the last ten years throws up a mixed picture. Dedicated administrative structures created in Andhra Pradesh, Kerala, Tamil Nadu etc. for taking up these tasks have immensely contributed to the success of SHG movement there. The robust network of SHGs and their federations in these states have enabled the poor to access substantial institutional credit and overcome some of the critical technical and market constraints they would otherwise have to face. But elsewhere in the country, the progress of the scheme has been rather slow. In terms of coverage of rural BPL households in the SHGs, it has taken more than 10 years to create 17 lakh SHGs and in order to complete the coverage of the remaining BPL households in rural areas, another 28 lakh SHGs need to be formed, which is clearly a tall order in the light of not only the resource availability but more importantly the delivery systems in place in different states. Further, the fact that only 22 per cent of the SHGs were able to access bank credit for income generating activities including micro enterprises, reflects the need for augmenting credit absorption capacity of SHGs through systematic capacity in skill building and sustained technical, marketing and even placement support, besides streamlining the credit delivery system for making available adequate and timely credit at reasonable rates.

Poverty is complex, and multi-dimensional in nature. The Ministry has visualized this and accordingly prepared a strategic framework by bringing a chapter entitled "Poverty Eradication in India by 2015—Rural Household Centered Strategy". This chapter indicates main areas of concern of poverty such as lack/inadequate access to natural resources (land, forest, water), over dependence, low productivity due to inadequate use of technology, and deficient infrastructure, unemployment and underemployment in agriculture. Further, the changing local requirements and the inability of rural people engaged in traditional occupations/crafts to upgrade their skill accordingly, non-availability and inaccessibility to basic social infrastructure such as education, health, and drinking water, and sanitation, physical infrastructure such as road, power, storage, communication, low coverage due to non-availability of adequate funds for rural development. Besides availability of funds, strong and efficient governance structure and other factors as mentioned below are equally important to implement the programmes in a time bound manner to realize their visible impact.

- Increasing the awareness of programmes and access of rural poor to avail the benefits.
- Social mobilization for collective action and economies of scale.
- Replication of successful experiments on mass scale.
- Introduction of appropriate technologies and involvement of experts.
- Removing the design defects of various schemes and programmes based on earlier experiences.
- Availability of timely and adequate credit at low cost.
- Emphasis on strengthening forward and backward linkages.
- Setting up of dedicated, motivated and professional implementation structure.
- Proper targeting through suitable poverty mapping mechanism.
- Transparency and accountability of implementing structure.
- Coordination with other Ministries and convergence of their programmes.

Given the overarching objective of reduction of rural poverty in a focused and time bound manner, the following are the inter related tasks that assume significance:

(i) Strengthening IEC activities and mobilization of all the poor households into functionally effective SHGs and their federations;
(ii) Availability of necessary institutional mechanism for capacity building, credit, marketing etc.;
(iii) Building their capacities and skills for gainful and sustainable self-employment;
(iv) Enhancing their access to bank credit at reasonable rates and other financial, technical and marketing services;
(v) Coordination with banks to improve the reach of rural poor and also having better bank linkages;
(vi) Provisioning of adequate resources to achieve the intended targets;
(vii) Infrastructure and other necessary arrangements for facilitating economic activities/enterprises taken up by rural poor;
(viii) Dedicated implementation structure equipped with professionals at various levels to strengthen the delivery mechanism; and
(ix) Dedicated MIS for transparency and convergence.

Rationale for Restructuring of the Programme

The need for restructuring the SGSY has arisen on account of feedback provided and recommendations made by various studies including those conducted by National Institute of Rural Development (NIRD), Hyderabad, Bankers Institute of Rural Development (BIRD), Lucknow, Centre for Management Development, Thiruvananthapuram etc. and reports of the Steering Committee constituted by the Planning Commission for the 11th Plan. Further, the Ministry of Rural Development (MoRD), Government of India (GoI) has accepted the recommendation of the Committee on Credit Related Issues under SGSY (Prof. Radhakrishna Committee) to create a National Rural Livelihoods Mission (NRLM) to provide greater focus and momentum for poverty reduction to achieve the Millennium Development Goal (MDG) by 2015 through rapid increase in the coverage of rural poor households under self-employment. In addition to self-employment, the Mission will also help in enhancing their capabilities and facilitate access to other entitlements such as wage employment and food security and benefits of Indira Awas Yojana (IAY), drinking water, land improvement, education, and health and risk mitigation through convergence and coordination mechanism. National Rural Livelihoods Mission was launched from 2009-10 to facilitate effective implementation of the restructured SGSY scheme in a mission mode.

Meanwhile three major developments have taken place in the recent years which have had major impact on the rural economy especially the rural poor, i.e. (i) the economy experienced a robust growth; (ii) National Rural Employment Guarantee Scheme (NREGS) emerged as a major programme to provide additional income to the rural poor; and (iii) various initiatives taken under the National Skill Development Mission (NSDM).

Taking these developments into account and in order to achieve the objective of the 11th Plan of broad based inclusive growth, strategy paper of the Ministry envisages a four pronged strategy to attack rural poverty comprising (i) generation of self-employment in credit linked micro enterprises and salaried employment through demand driven skill development; (ii) wage employment under National Rural Employment Guarantee Scheme; (iii) payment of pension to elderly and vulnerable sections under National Social Assistance Programme; and (iv) income generation and social security programmes of other Ministries of Government of India. Flowing from above, the restructuring of SGSY as National Rural Livelihood Mission has been conceived as a cornerstone of national poverty reduction strategy.

SGSY: Main Weaknesses

Results of evaluation of the SGSY, (Planning Commission, 2005: Mid-Term Appraisal of 10th Five Year Plan 2002-07, pp. 238-242) show inadequate infrastructure and insufficient capacity building as main constraints. Most of the factors responsible for its poor performance relate to weaknesses in delivery systems. The following are the gaps/weaknesses thrown up in the last ten years of implementation of the scheme by the Ministry or reported as the findings/recommendations of various studies, committees working groups etc.:

Uneven spread in formation of SHGs (weak in the poverty pockets of the country). In the southern part of the country the pace of formation of SHGs as compared to the BPL population in these states is remarkable. On the other hand, the pace of formation in northern and in eastern states is not very encouraging. In the northern and in eastern states, the rural

BPL population is about 63 per cent of the total country's rural BPL population but only 40 per cent of total SHGs have been formed in these States. In the southern states there is only 11 per cent rural BPL population of the country but more than 33 per cent of total SHGs have been formed in these states.

The attrition rate is very high, i.e. less number of SHGs are passing to Grade-I level (65%), from Grade-I to Grade-II (29% of total SHGs) and from Grade-II to finally entering in the Micro Enterprise level (23% of total SHGs). Thus, only 23 per cent of total SHGs formed are entering in the Micro-enterprise level. The main reasons for high attrition rate are inadequate availability of funds, lower credit availability, low level of education and skill, lack of beneficiaries owned umbrella organization at various levels, inaccessibility to financial institutions and non-availability of multiple doses of credit ensuring long-term handholding.

Issues concerning access to Credit: Poor need financial assistance to meet their consumption needs, working capital requirement for their exiting occupations and to purchase new income generating assets. On the demand side, there is need for capacity building and training to enhance the credit absorption capacity and establish their creditworthiness. On the supply side, the weakness is largely due to inaccessibility of existing banking facilities due to sparsely spread of bank branches in the rural areas, lack of staff in rural banks, and lack of interest/awareness on the part of bankers. In addition, the banking system and its procedures are too complex and as such not suited to the rural poor.

Lack of capacity building and training: This occurs due to, (i) Inadequate institutional infrastructure, (ii) lack of trainers, (iii) limited capacity of existing institution and their inaccessibility to rural poor due to entry level barriers, high costs and distant locations, and (iv) lack of umbrella organization for implementation.

Lack of SHGs Federations at various levels: People-led and people-centred organization such as federal structure encompassing federations of rural BPL SHGs from village up to the district level are necessary to strengthen their voice, bargaining power and reduce their dependency on external agencies. In most of the states very few SHGs have been federated at various levels in the country.

Inadequate Risk Mitigation: Risk coverage for the beneficiaries either for life or property/assets and health has been almost negligible. Risk coverage for life property and health, at least in some rudimentary form is essential to prevent upward mobile swarozgaris from slipping back into poverty due to loss of any of these factors.

Dedicated Implementation Structure: Inadequate Manpower in the DRDAs, lack professionals to implement the complex and process oriented programme and existing staff overburdened with number of schemes. Due to this no follow-up under SGSY for various activities and thus weak delivery mechanism.

Lack of Convergence: Under NRLM special emphasis will be on convergence with programmes of the Ministry of Rural Development as well as of other Ministries to overcome the constraints faced by rural poor to achieve optimum results in terms of maximizing the livelihood opportunities to the rural poor and their entitlements such as wage employment and food security and benefits of Indira Awas Yojana (IAY), drinking water, land improvement, education, and health and risk mitigation.

Grievance Redressal Mechanism: Majority of the rural poor belong to disadvantaged social groups such as SC/ST, OBC and Minorities. They are not familiar with formal systems and face all type of deprivations due to lack of proper system to address their grievances.

Lack of Transparency and Accountability: This acts as barrier to reach the targeted groups and enhances the chances of coverage of in-eligible groups under the programme. Due to non-availability detailed information of SHGs, their activities and products and ignorance about their entitlements, the rural poor are not able to get the desired benefit of the scheme. There is need for capturing all the information starting from the formation of SHGs till the SHGs reach at the micro enterprise stage and fund flow mechanism, availability of credit and other financial transactions through a dedicated MIS. Table 7.1 and Table 7.2 reports physical progress under SGSY since inception and utilization of funds, credit and subsidy under SGSY in 2007-08.

In West Bengal

The SGSY aims at alleviating rural poverty by facilitating creation of self-employment opportunities for the poor. Organizing the poor, particularly the poor woman, in SHGs has been given priority under this scheme. The primary objectives of the groups are:

- To mobilize savings of the individual members;
- To ensure availability of need-based financial services to them; and
- To take up income-generating activities.

Table 7.1: Physical Progress under SGSY since Inception

(thousands)

Years	*SHGs Formed*	*No. of SHGs Passed Grade I*	*No. of SHGs Passed Grade II*	*SHGs Taking up economic activities*	*SHGs Swarozgaris assisted*	*Individual swarozgaris assisted*
1999-2000	292	125		29	35	586
2000-01	223	214	74	26	319	687
2001-02	434	176	54	31	365	573
2002-03	399	190	95	36	414	412
2003-04	392	205	91	51	578	320
2004-05	266	220	106	68	789	327
2005-06	276	211	92	80	873	278
2006-07	246	222	156	138	1472	220
2007-08	306	251	117	181	1154	254
2008-09 (Oct. 2008)	298	201	62	46	557	117
Total	3134	2014	948	685	6869	3772

Source: Ministry of Rural Development, Government of India, 2008.

Table 7.2: Utilization of Funds, Credit and Subsidy under SGSY in 2007-08

	West Bengal	*All India*
Funds utilized (Rs. Cr.)	126.5	1951.2
Total funds available (Rs. Cr.)	153.2	2427.6
Share of utilization of funds	6.5	100.0
% utilization to total funds	82.6	80.4
Share of total credit disbursed	1.6	100.0
% of credit disbursed to target	17.2	73.7
Share of total subsidy disbursed	2.1	100.0
Share of total investment disbursed	1.7	100.0
Credit subsidy ratio	1.58	2.14
Share of rural poor (2004-05)	7.8	100.0
Credit per rural poor (Rs.)	24.9	124.9
Credit/assisted SHG (Rs.)	6098	57634

Source: Ministry of Rural Development, Government of India.

When the groups seek to undertake economic activities, SGSY assistance is provided to them in the form of bank credit and subsidy.

According to the guidelines of SGSY, after the formation of a group, the members would rely on their own savings, with the Government providing training and infrastructural support. After around six months, the SHGs are graded first by the banks and Government officials for judging the eligibility for providing access to bank credit. Those found eligible are allowed to open cash credit account in a bank, part of which is contributed by the Government and do not bear any interest. In order to increase the credit limit, the Rural Development Cell (DRDC) places a revolving fund in the account. The credit limit set by the bank is determined by the quantum of the revolving fund and the group's own savings. The money in the cash credit account can be withdrawn for consumption or for taking up micro enterprises. The SHGs, which pass the first grading become eligible for scheme based lending after being graded for the second time. Only grade I groups with six months experience are supposed to be graded for the second time.

Table 7.3 shows that during 2002-03 to 2011-12, progress was achieved not only in the formation of groups but group savings also increased by about forty times.

Table 7.3: Performance and Progress of SHGs under SGSY

Year	*No. of SHGs formed Since inception*	*Savings (Rs. Crore) (Cumulative)*	*No. of SHGs Passed Grade I (cumulative)*	*No. of SHGs Passed Grade II (year-wise)*	*No. of SHGs Having access to cash credit Account (cumulative)*	*Cash credit Drawn (crore) (During the year)*	*No. of SHGs Who took up economic activities and received credit and subsidy*
2002-03	58708	13.47	27129	2004	14648	28.28	462
2008-09	257307	238.98	199098	15294	158034	114.98	4403
2009-10	292430	322.76	241333	18601	198664	232.21	5849
2010-11	331344	521.38	272612	18092	230584	278.04	6167
2011-12	350811	554.11	295610	15431	246700	178.91	4695

Source: Department of Panchayats and Rural Development, Government of West Bengal.

A major problem in the implementation of SGSY is inadequate banking infrastructure and poor delivery of credit related services. Around 938 GPs, out of the total of 3354 GPs, do not have banks within their geographical areas. Out of these 938 GPs, 246 GPs have been identified as having no bank branches within a radius of about 15 kms. and 265 GPs have no branches within a radius of 10 kms. while the remaining GPs have no banking facility within a radius of 5 kms. Even where they exist, their performance with regard to delivery of credit related services has not been satisfactory. Taking up grading exercises, time has been a chronic problem. Delay also occurs in opening cash credit accounts by the banks even after the groups passed Grade-I. Delay also takes place in sanctioning micro-enterprise project proposals submitted by Grade II passed groups.

Table 7.4: Year-wise Status of Credit Linkage through Project Based Lending

Year	No. of groups Linked to projects	Amount disbursed (Credit)	(lakh) Subsidy	(Rupees) Total	Credit subsidy Ratio
2002-03	462	4105.6	2108.5	6214.1	1.95
2003-04	1177	3516.2	2116.9	5633.1	1.66
2004-05	1861	3339.0	2278.8	5617.8	1.47
2005-06	1514	2252.4	1615.0	3867.4	1.39
2006-07	2513	3161.1	2254.2	5415.3	1.40
2007-08	3167	4310.6	2733.8	7044.4	1.58
2008-09	4403	6192.9	3959.8	10152.7	1.56
2009-10	5849	8688.5	5400.1	14088.5	1.61
2010-11	6167	9595.9	5989.8	15353.2	1.69
2011-12	4695	7491.9	4432.6	11924.6	1.69

Source: Department of Panchayats and Rural Development, Government of West Bengal.

Most of the SGSY groups have been formed by women belonging to the families below the poverty line. It is natural that they take more time to absorb project-linked credit. It proves that this type of organization is more acceptable to woman. The status of women led SHGs are shown in Table 7.5.

Table 7.5: Status of Women led SHGs

Year	No.of women SHGs formed since inception in 1.4.99	No. of women SHGs took economic activities during the current year
2010-11	282008	15489
2011-12	298682	8981

Training and nurturing of groups is a major component of the State's SGSY programme. Towards this end, the State Govt. has taken various steps. In 2010-11, 5,57,978 Swarojgaris were trained as compared to 5,93,866 during 2009-10, around 24.66 per cent of them belonged to the minority community, 29.61 per cent belonged to Scheduled Castes and 6.89 per cent belonged to Scheduled Tribes.

The State Government provides non-credit inputs to the SHGs so that they can take up income generating schemes. For instance, Grade-I passed SHGs have been made eligible to obtain lease of Government fisheries. Tanks excavated under different employment generation schemes are also given on lease to SHGs. The Panchayats give land to SHGs for raising nurseries. Inputs for agriculture like seeds, fertilizers have also been given to SHGs for carrying out cultivation of crops. Other inputs like chicks, piglets, fingerlings have been provided to SHGs for taking up income generating activities in animal husbandary and fishery sectors. In a few districts like Burdwan, Uttar Dinajpur etc. many SHGs have taken up dehusking of paddy in an organized way for supplying rice to FCI.

In aggregate, about 14 lakh groups have been formed in the state. The membership of SHG is about 1 crore 40 lakh, out of which 90 per cent are women. The flow of institutional finance for SHGs is the area of concern. The department of SHG and Self-Employment has streamlined the flow of institutional finance to SHGs. The banks have been asked to earmark a day in a week for SHGs to facilitate sanction of their loan in time and some banks have started to act in this direction. The State Government has announced an interest subsidy scheme known as "The West Bengal Swanirvar Sahayak Prakalpo" with effect from 1.4.2009. According to this scheme all SHGs under bank linkage programme including SHGs promoted by Primary Agricultural Societies and other Co-operative agencies and SHGs undertaking group based projects schemes under SGSY and SJSRY will have to bear at the rate of 4 per cent interest only on their loans and the rest of the interest not exceeding 7 per cent will be subsidized by the State Government Approximately Rs. 4.84 crore was released on this account.

Number of SHGs formed under major Schemes or financial institutions up to 31.12.2012 is shown in Table 7.6:

Table 7.6: Number of Government Schemes in Groups

Schemes	*No. of Groups*
SGSY Groups	262541
NABARD Groups	708117
SIDBI Groups	309746
SJSRY- Thrift and Credit Groups	34586

Source: Department of SHG and Self-Employment, Government of West Bengal.

In 2010, SGSY restructured into National Rural Livelihoods Mission (NRLM). These programmes showed that investing in self-managed institutions of the poor and aggregating those institutions beyond the community level yields impressive returns for poverty reduction.

III. The National Rural Livelihood Mission (NRLM)

Largest poverty reduction initiative—largest programme for women in

the world—goal of reaching nearly 70 million rural households—launched in 12 states accounting for 85 per cent of rural poor households in India—GoI to invest 5.1 billion US dollar till 2017—World Bank committing 1 billion US dollar through NRLP—largest single investment in a poverty reduction programme.

Mission Objective

The central objective of the Mission is to reduce poverty among rural BPL through promotion of diversified and gainful self-employment and wage employment opportunities to provide appreciable increase in income on sustainable basis. In the long run, it will ensure broad based inclusive growth and reduce disparities by spreading out the benefits from the islands of growth across the regions, sectors and communities.

Mission, Outputs and Outcomes

The Mission has been designed to achieve the following 'Outputs' and 'Outcomes' by 2016-17 as shown in Table 7.7.

Strategy

To achieve the above objectives, the Mission will adopt the following interrelated strategies:

(i) **Universal Mobilization of BPL Households:** Mobilization of all the rural BPL households into functionally effective, self-managed and self-governed institutions of the poor *viz.,* Self-Help Groups (SHGs);

(ii) **Federations/People's Institution:** Promotion of people's institutions by facilitating federation of SHGs at village block and district level such that the rural poor are able to overcome the financial, technical, infrastructural, marketing and other constraints and risks that inhibit their growth and also in order to strengthen their voice and bargaining power and reduce their dependence on external agencies, in a time bound manner;

(iii) **Capacity Building and Training:** Provisions have been made for sustained capacity building and orientation training of the SHGs and their federations through using multi-pronged approach. Involving optimal use of the existing infrastructure

Table 7.7: Output and Outcome Targets for the NRLM: 2016-17

(In Lakh)

Sl. No.	*Outputs/Outcome Indicators*	*Target for Remaining Period of 11th Plan*	*Tentative Target for 12th Plan*	*Total Target by 2016-17*	*No. of BPL families*
I.	**Outputs***				
1.	Total number of new BPL SHGs to be formed	12.25	15.75**	28	280
2.	No. of SHGs to be provided revolving fund support	12.25	15.75	28	280
3.	No. of SHGs to be provided Capital subsidy	5.25	10.75	16	160
4.	No. of SHGs to be provided interest subsidy	10	12	22	220
5.	No. of Rural BPL youth to be provided skill development training	15	60	75	75
II.	**Outcomes**				
1.	No. of SHGs to be entering at Micro enterprise level	5.25	10.75	16	160
2.	No. of Rural BPL youth to be provided placement support	15	60	75	75

Note: Each SHG having on an average 10 members (one from each family).

* Subject to availability of resources and cooperation from other stakeholders.

** Tentative timeline for achieving the target is 2014-15 (Universalization of SHGs).

facilities at the district as well as the block levels such as Polytechnics, Krishi Vigyan Kendras, Jan Shikshan Sansthans (JSSs), Khadi and Village Industries Boards, State Institutes of Rural development, Extension Training Centres and other Departmental facilities available in that area.

Setting up of dedicated training institutes for rural poor, i.e., 500 Rural Self Employment Training Institutes (RSETIs) one in each district of the country through replication of successful RUDSETI model.

Dedicated structure for training and capacity building at districts and State level involving professionals as envisaged under the National Rural Livelihood Mission (NRLM).

Public Private Partnerships with NGOs, Voluntary Organizations etc.

Training of large number of trainers who would further train people down below. This would lead to a cascading effect and benefit the poor people right at the lowest level.

Creating a cadre of service providers, Community Resource Persons (CRPs) and Master Craftsmen and utilizing their services for training of SHG beneficiaries;

(iv) **Pro-Poor Financial Services:** Provision of pro-poor financial services including provision of interest subsidy for ensuring that NRLM beneficiaries can get loans from commercial banks at the rate of interest at which farmers are getting agricultural loan at 6 per cent rate of interest.

(v) **Marketing and Infrastructure Support:** Provision of marketing support through engagement of professionals at various levels for drawing up marketing strategies and involvement of private/NGO partnerships for diversifying and sustaining self-employment activities and support for meeting the critical gaps in the existing infrastructure;

(vi) **Convergence:** Promotion of convergence with programmes of different ministries in order to achieve synergy and maximizing livelihood opportunities for rural BPL poor by dovetailing of funds for focused application. To mitigate the risk factor in case of life, assets, health etc., the requisite convergence will be put in place with respective programmes like Aam Admi Bima Yojana, Rashtria Swasthya Bima Yojana etc.;

(vii) **Sensitive Support Organizational Structure:** Promotion of professionally competent but dedicated sensitive support umbrella organizations at the National, State level and units for managing and supporting all the activities of the restructured SGSY, henceforth to be known as the National Rural Livelihood Mission (NRLM), dedicated implementation structure at the district and sub-district level (which will catalyze mobilization and institution building, capacity building and skill development and placement, access to pro-poor financial services, infrastructure and marketing support for promotion of micro enterprises, risk mitigation activities, convergence with other scheme activities for technical, financial and other inputs, monitoring and evaluation of the programme etc.);

(viii) **Support for upscaling Skill Development and Placement and Innovative Projects:** Promotion of placement based skill development activities to diversify and provide elastic sources of income to the rural youth and other innovative pilot projects, using the services of premier national and state level institutions including reputed NGOs and corporations;

(ix) **Demand Driven Approach:** Institution of a need based and demand-driven approach to the allocation of funds among the various components of the programme on the basis of specific and time bound state action plans and targets for poverty elimination through self-employment and skill-based wage employment, built on the structure of people's institutions in a phased manner; and

(x) **Transparent Systems:** Institution of transparent systems such as social auditing and concurrent evaluation as well as a comprehensive MIS.

Mission Structure

Three-Tiers

The Rural Livelihoods Mission will have a three-tier interdependent structure. At the apex of the structure will be the National Rural Livelihoods Mission, under the Ministry of Rural Development, GoI. At the State level, there will be an umbrella organization under the State Department of Rural Development/Department which is responsible for implementing self-employment/rural livelihoods promotion programmes. The State level Mission with dedicated professionals and domain experts under the State department of Rural Department will be guided financially, technically and supported by the NRLM on need basis. The National and the State Mission will have a symbiotic relationship. They will have mutual access to the knowledge and services in the area of rural livelihoods.

At the district level, there will be a dedicated unit to implement NRLM under the overall guidance of the State Mission suitably linked to the District Rural Development Agencies (DRDAs). The district units will be guided by the State organization in planning and implementation of livelihood promotion activities including implementation of NRLM in close coordination with the DRDAs. Thus, the three tiers of the Livelihoods Mission will be closely interlinked and be guided by the common objective of promoting sustainable livelihoods of the poor and work for the eradication of rural poverty.

The Functions of the NRLM

(i) Facilitate establishment of state level umbrella agencies by the state governments for providing institutional support for poverty elimination programmes;

(ii) Support state level umbrella organizations in the design and implementation of pro-poor programmes;

(iii) Provide professional and technical support and guidance to the state agencies by seeking out and disseminating pro-poor technologies and institutional innovations through research and development and forging linkages between the state agencies and the national centres of excellence;

(iv) Liaise with other Missions/departments to explore areas for convergent action and facilitate such convergence to enhance the capabilities and facilitate access to other entitlements such as wage employment, food security, education, health, etc.;

(v) Explore and facilitate partnerships between National/State Rural Livelihoods Missions and public, private, NGOs and Co-operative sector partners, for diversifying and sustaining the livelihoods of the poor;

(vi) Undertake/commission studies to assess emerging self-employment/skill based employment opportunities and disseminate the information to the State agencies;

(vii) Study best practices in self-employment/micro enterprise activities across the country and support their replication in other parts of the country through workshops, cross-learning visits and exchange programmes;

(viii) Develop capacity building and training modules for functionaries of the peoples institutions as well as the state agencies and district units, and other stakeholders participating in the poverty elimination programmes;

(ix) Facilitate analysis and dissemination of the impact of changing economic policies on the poor and play policy advocacy role;

(x) Act as information warehouse on rural poverty statistics by accessing information from multiple sources;

(xi) Identify shortcomings in programme design and implementation and facilitate debates/discussions thereof by experts for finding innovative and workable solutions and their dissemination to the state agencies;

(xii) Promote institution of comprehensive monitoring and learning systems at the state agencies and district units, including web enabled MIS and community monitoring systems; and

(xiii) Identify high quality institutions in livelihoods education and training and facilitate linkage of the state organizations with missions with such institutions for capacity building of professionals.

State Level Mission of NRLM

A state level Mission with induction of professional and domain experts will be constituted by all State Governments to oversee the implementation of the Mission and other poverty eradication programmes in the states, wherever such organizations do not exist. The State Mission will set up separate entity under overall charge of Secretary/Principal Secretary of RD Department for implementing the Mission in the state.

The State Management Team

A Project Management Team will be constituted at the state level under the leadership of the Chief Executive Officer of the agency, drawn from the state government, equivalent in rank to Secretary to the State Government. The State Management Team will be assisted by highly competent technical experts to be appointed on contractual basis with specific terms of reference, for the implementation of the Mission/ restructured SGSY and other poverty alleviation programmes.

The state team will include experts in the areas of social mobilization, institution building, capacity building and training, micro-finance development, marketing and micro enterprises like forest produce based livelihoods, fisheries based livelihoods, value chain analysis, skill development and placement support, gender aspects of poverty, communication, monitoring and evaluation.

Apart from providing critical inputs required for the promotion of people's institutions and the implementation of the Mission's programmes, the state team will have the responsibility to ensure collaboration among various line departments of the state government to facilitate implementation and convergence of activities for deriving optimal benefits from NRLM and other programmes. The team will use the services of national and state institutions functioning in the district in the implementation of different components of the Mission's programmes and will also ensure proper coordination with the DRDAs.

District Level Units

At the district level, a dedicated unit suitably linked to DRDA will be set up by all the states. The district level units will be responsible for implementing the Mission's programmes in the district following the guidelines. The district level unit will be the implementation arm of the DRDA under the overall supervision of the state agency and as such it will not be an independent society or entity.

The district unit will facilitate setting up of block level programme units and put up personnel having expertise in social mobilization/ institution building, livelihood promotion and SHG bookkeeping/ accounting. The district unit could consider outsourcing the entire tasks of Mission in a block level to an experienced NGO with good track record in SHG promotion. The district unit will interface with district administration and line departments, banks, NGOs, PRIs and corporate agencies. The district unit will facilitate the formation of district and block level federations in the light of their economic viability and technical feasibility. The major task of the district unit will be to train the block level personnel in the core areas of social mobilization, institution and capacity building, microfinance and livelihoods. It will also undertake regular monitoring and review of the performance of the block level unit.

Block Level Unit

The principal role of block level unit will be mobilization of all BPL households into the SHG fold and build their capacities. The units will also be responsible for building village level and block level federations of SHGs depending upon their economic viability which will undertake the bigger tasks of negotiating with the financial and marketing institutions as well as the PRIs. To accelerate the process of social mobilization, the block level unit may divide the block into clusters and place each cluster under the charge of a coordinator and master bookkeeper. Eventually, the block level federations will replace the block level units over a period and perform all the activities that the block level mission units will initially perform. Thus, the people's institutions are expected to takeover the entire implementation responsibility of sustaining all activities after the Mission.

Role of Panchayati Raj Institutions

Panchayati Raj Institutions (PRIs) will be actively involved in the following activities of the Mission:

- In the identification and mobilization of BPL households into SHGs, with priority being given to the SC and ST households especially primitive tribal groups, poorest of the poor households, women headed households and households engaged in declining occupations;
- In facilitating federation of SHGs at the village/gram panchayat level/block level and providing basic facilities for the effective functioning of such federations in terms of providing accommodation for federation office and such other basic facilities;
- For giving priority to the demands of the SHGs and their federations in the annual plans/activities of the PRIs by making suitable financial allocations;
- In entrusting execution of panchayat activities including civil works to SHGs and their federations on a priority basis;
- To lease out panchayat resources such as fishing ponds/tanks, common property resources, market yards, buildings and other properties to the SHGs and their federations for proper management and maintenance;
- In entrusting responsibility for collection of panchayat revenues including house property tax to the SHGs for a small fee;
- Entrusting management and maintenance of select civic amenities to the SHGs; and
- In any other activity which could be taken up by the members of the SHGs or their federations.

Area of Operation of NRLM

NRLM programmes will be implemented in all rural districts of different states excluding the districts in Delhi and Chandigarh. However, the GC, based on the latest available data is empowered to include or exclude the districts for the implementation of various components of the Mission.

Mechanism of Funds Flow

It is envisaged that the State Governments will transit into the NRLM mode only in a phased manner. Till such time the States do not transit into NRLM mode, the SGSY activities will continue to be implemented as per current guidelines/norms and fund releases will be made to DRDAs as per existing procedures. The revised norms of SGSY will be applicable to the States having the commitment to fulfill the following within the stipulated time period:

(i) State level agencies and the district level units are set up,
(ii) Full complement of professional staff has been trained and placed, and
(iii) State level poverty reduction strategy has been formulated.

Funds for implementing the Mission's programmes will be directly released separately to the state level agency and the DRDAs on the basis of the detailed district-wise annual action plans submitted by the state agencies and approved by the EC of the National Mission, but within the overall allocation indicated for each state on the basis of the poverty ratio. The funds to state level agencies will be transferred to meet expenditure on: (i) establishing and running the dedicated state/district/sub-district level agency; (ii) organizing state level skill development and placement services (covering more than one district); and (iii) other activities such as technical services, concurrent evaluation and such other activities.

The funds to DRDAs will be transferred to meet the expenditures on: (i) subsidy to SHGs. (ii) infrastructure and marketing (district level and sub-district level), (iii) corpus for federations, (iv) interest subsidy, (v) training and capacity building of all stakeholders, and (vi) engagement of NGO facilitators. The funds to district units will be released where full complement of professional staff has been placed and district poverty reduction plans have been formulated. In other cases, the exiting procedure of fund release will be followed.

Funds will be released in two installments based on the progress report and submission of utilization certificates by the district units under intimation to the state level agency. The State level agency will compile and consolidate expenditure details, physical progress and other details and submit to National Mission periodically. MoRD will release 75 per cent of the approved amount to the State Government/DRDA and the State government will release the balance amount of 25 per cent. In respect of north-eastern states, J&K, Himachal Pradesh and Uttrakhand, the GoI and state share will be in the proportion of 90:10, respectively.

As far as possible, e-banking will be used for transfer of funds to the state level agencies and to the districts. The state level agency will maintain a separate budget and prescribed accounting system for the Mission activities both at the state and district level. The district units will adhere to the accounting system and financial guidelines prescribed by the state agencies. The block units will be directed by the district units to follow similar systems and guidelines to ensure transparency and accountability.

Monitoring of NRLM

The National Livelihood Mission will have a strong mechanism of Monitoring and Evaluation with the involvement of the state level agency and dedicated district level units. The Monitoring and Learning (M&L) specialists at the Mission and state agency levels will coordinate concurrent monitoring of the Mission activities. At the district level, the Monitoring and Learning specialist will undertake monitoring of the physical and financial targets of various Mission interventions, adopting the formats designed by the National Mission for this purpose. In addition, the district level M&L specialist will be responsible for instituting community monitoring systems including a system of self-monitoring by the SHGs and their federations.

At the state agency level, the activities of the Mission will be monitored by a committee headed by the Chief Executive Officer with members drawn from the Departments of Rural Development, Panchayati Raj, NABARD, District federations and select professional experts and NGOs. The M&L specialist at the state agency will act as the member-convener of the committee and will furnish the committee information on the progress of the Mission activities. The proceedings of the committee will be placed before the EC of the State Agency.

At the National Level, the activities of the Mission will be monitored by a committee headed by the Mission Director (Joint Secretary/ Additional Secretary in the MoRD) with members drawn from the Planning Commission, NABARD, Ministry of Finance and reputed national research institutions. The M&L specialists at the National Mission Team will act as the Convener of the committee and furnish the required information to the committee. The proceedings of the committee will be placed before the EC of the National Mission Society.

Reporting System in NRLM

The district units and the state agencies will ensure the submission of monthly and quarterly progress reports to the National Mission by 10th of every month. Similarly, the quarterly report will be sent to the Mission within 15 days after the end of the quarter. The annual progress report will be submitted before April 15th of the following financial year by each district unit and state agency. The formats for reporting will be prescribed by the National Mission.

Evaluation Process under NRLM

The State Agencies will undertake a Base Line Survey (BLS) to assess the extent of social mobilization, progress of people's institutions, extent of self-employment and skill-based wage employment activities undertaken and their impact in different districts. If necessary, the state agencies will commission independent studies for this purpose. In addition, the state teams will undertake/commission concurrent evaluation to assess the performance of the Mission activities. There will be a Mid-Mission Evaluation study by an independent agency to assess the performance and shortcomings so as to take the remedial measures and corrective action.

An Impact Evaluation Study at the national and state levels will also be undertaken through independent agencies towards the end of the Mission to assess the impact of various activities on self-employment, skill-based wage employment, income generation and poverty elimination.

A comprehensive web-enabled MIS system will be positioned to capture the progress of the project in near real-time mode. The system will capture information from the block, district and state levels. Specialized software and reporting structures will be developed for this purpose.

Criteria for Identification of Beneficiaries and Safeguards

All the Mission activities are meant for the BPL households. Therefore, the state agencies and the district units will target only BPL households in all Mission activities starting with social mobilization, SHG formation, federation building, capacity and skill building, pro-poor financial services, technical and marketing support and skill-based wage employment. However, the district units will particularly focus on the vulnerable groups among the rural BPL households such as the SCs, the STs, the women-headed households and households living vulnerable circumstances. In the sanction of financial assistance for the Mission, the safeguards in force shall continue to be followed. Accordingly, the SCs and the STs will account for a minimum of 50 per cent, women for 40 per cent, minorities 15 per cent and disabled for 3 per cent of the total members assisted in a year. The assistance will not only include capital subsidy but also the newly introduced interest subsidy. Even in respect of subsidy to SHGs towards revolving fund and towards corpus for federations, preference will be given to the SHGs and federations with a predominant presence of the SCs and the STs.

Procedure for Approval and Implementation of Projects by NRLM

The Department of Rural Development, Government of India will communicate the tentative annual outlay to each State/District, for approved Mission activities. The dedicated district units will prepare the annul action plan keeping in view the extent of social mobilization and institution building completed and potential for promoting self-employment and skill-based wage employment activities and submit the district plan to the state level agency. The state agencies will be required to prepare a state action plan based on the district annual action plans and the overall outlay indicated by the MoRD.

The state agencies could engage the in-house team of experts or alternatively outsource to technical consultants for preparing the annual action plans. The state level agencies will submit the detailed state action plan indicating the state level and district level components under training, infrastructure and monitoring and skill development to MoRD. The EC of the National Mission will examine the state action plan and will be within its powers to recommend changes if necessary and approve the same in the light of overall national objectives, outlays and priorities.

Convergence for Technical and Other Inputs

Under NRLM special emphasis will be given on convergence with other programmes of the Ministry of Rural Development as well as of other Ministries to achieve optimum results.

National Rural Employment Guarantee Scheme (NREGS) is one of the flagship programmes of Ministry of Rural Development with focus on wage employment, development of natural resources and creation of community assets and livelihood opportunities for rural poor. Under NRLM, convergence with NREGS will be one of the important activities such as formation of SHGs at NREGS work site, mobilization of savings, etc. Further, the land belonging to BPL people will be developed through NREGS and receive further value addition provision of technical inputs and credit under NRLM. This will help in enhancement of productivity and sustained income to rural poor. It is also proposed to tap various livelihood opportunities generated in different processes of NREGS and other programmes like IAY, Drinking Water and Sanitation, Watershed Management, and PMGSY etc. for SHGs and rural poor. This will be done through training and skill development of SHGs and generating awareness among implementing agencies, PRIs and other stakeholders about benefits of convergence. Similar efforts will also be undertaken for convergence of SGSY with programmes of Ministries Panchayati Raj Institutions, Human Resource Development, M/o Health and Family Welfare, Textiles, Agriculture and Department of Women and Child Development etc.

Transparency and Accountability

Transparency and accountability will be integral parts of the programme. To ensure this a dedicated MIS will be put in place for capturing all the information starting from the formation of SHGs till the SHGs reach at the micro-enterprise stage. The fund flow mechanism availability of credit and other financial transactions will also be captured through this MIS. In addition to this periodic review through evaluation studies and social auditing involving third parties will also be conducted.

Brief of NRLM

NRLM will have multipronged approach to strengthen livelihoods of the rural poor by promoting SHGs, improving existing occupations, providing skill development and placement and other activities thereof. The training and capacity building, deployment of multidisciplinary experts and other initiatives will enhance the creditworthiness of the rural poor. The services of craft persons, community resource persons etc will be utilized as TOT for capacity building and training under NRLM. The periodic interaction of Mission with Public Sector Banks and other financial institutions to enhance the reach of rural poor to the un-banked areas will ensure their financial inclusion. Further, poor have multiple livelihoods and they need multipronged approach to strengthen it. The existing strategy of social mobilization of poor, their organization into SHGs, training and capacity building, credit linkage for micro-enterprise for self-employment will continued to be one of the main components of NRLM. Emphasis will be on convergence with various schemes of Rural Development along with other line departments/ministries to strengthen the exiting occupations of the rural poor, ensure their participation as beneficiary of emerging opportunities as a result of various schemes for sustainable livelihood and also introducing newer technologies in their enterprises. The multidisciplinary domain experts at various levels will coordinate with all the stakeholders for benefiting the poor in risk mitigation, food security, training and capacity building, micro-financing, infrastructure development and better marketing linkages for getting appropriate prices for their products. People owned and people centred organization by federating SHGs will act as facilitators for strengthening the SHGs and thereby benefiting the rural poor. In addition skill development and placement will be the subset of the redesigned programme for deploying the rural BPL poor in the sun-rising sectors of the economy. The Mission will make concerted efforts to train rural BPL to provide last tier implementation personnel as service providers, lok sevaks, etc. to local bodies to implement to programmes efficiently and effectively.

IV. Conclusion

Thus, we conclude that the new focus on NRLM from SGSY is a move where the later is primarily designed to promote self-employment oriented income generating activities for the BPL households in the rural areas. Woven around the mechanism of Self-Help Groups (SHGs), the SGSY has been designed to break the financial, technical and market constraints that the individual BPL households face to cross the threshold of poverty line. Whereas the former will have multipronged approach to strengthen livelihoods of the rural poor by promoting SHGs, improving existing occupations, providing skill development and placement and other activities thereof. The training and capacity building, deployment of multidisciplinary experts and other initiatives will enhance the credit-worthiness of the rural poor. Whether NRLM is more effective than SGSY in eradicating rural poverty or not only time can say. Let us hope for the best.

References

AIAMED (2000): *Good Practices of NGOs in Setting Up Alternative Development Financial Institutions*, AIAMED, New Delhi.

AIMS (2000): *Learning from Clients: Assessment Tools for Microfinance*

Practitioners, the Small Enterprise Education and Promotion (SEEP) Network, Washington, DC.

APMAS (2001): "The Study of SHG Movement in Cuddapah District" (http://www.apmas.org).

Ankuram-Sangamam-Poram (2000): *Making a Difference: Where It Matters Most*, Approach Paper, Hyderabad.

Arunachalam, Ramesh (1999): *Alternative Technologies in the Indian Micro-Finance Industry: A Study for Action Aid,* Bangalore.

ASSEFA (n.d.), Mid Term Assessment of Women's Development Programme (mimeo), Chennai.

BIRD, (2001), "Sustainable Microfinance Challenges Facing MFIs", Report of a workshop organised by SIDBI and BIRD, Lucknow, 15-17 January.

BASIX (1999), Case Studies on Select Micro-Finance Institutions in India, IFAD, July.

Bhat, M.K. (2000): "SHGs: Delivery Mechanism or Empowerment Tool?" Paper presented at the Workshop on Best Practices in Group Dynamics and Micro Credit, 15-17 February, Manesar, Gurgaon.

Basu, Kishanjit and Krishan Jindal (eds.), (2000): *Micro-finance: Emerging Challenges*, Tata McGraw-Hill, New Delhi.

Biswas, Soumen (n.d.), Expanding NGO-SHG-Bank Linkage Across the Country—Some Issues and Recommendations (mimeo), PRADAN.

Bosch, Ellie and Pieter Damen (2000): *Self Help Groups Landscape (Draft)*, I/C Consult, The Hague, The Netherlands.

Bosch, Ellie (2001): *SHG Development in India: Some Issues Relating to Quality and Sustainability*, I/C Consult, The Hague, The Netherlands.

Bouman, F. (1995), "Rotating and Accumulating Savings and Credit Associations: A Development Perspective", *World Development*, 23: 30, pp. 371-84.

Dadhich, C.L. Lessons from the Micro-Credit Experience of India, www.aproacha.th.com

Das, Biswaroop (2001): "Role and Impact of Microfinance on Poor", *Friends of Women's World Banking*, India, Ahmedabad.

Department for International Development (1998): *India—Credit and Savings for Household Enterprise (CASHE)*, Project Document (Draft), November.

Department of Women and Child Development and Gender Equality Fund, CIDA (2000): *Best Practices in Group Dynamics and Micro-Credit*, Report of a Workshop, 15-17 February, Manesar, Gurgaon.

Dichter, Tom (1999): "Case Studies in Microfinance: Non-government Organizations in Microfinance: Past, Present and Future—An Essay". http://www.esd.worldbank.org/html/esd/agr/sbp/end/ngo.htm

Fernandez, Aloysius Prakash (1994): *The MYRADA Experience: Alternate Management Systems for Savings and Credit of the Rural Poor*, MYRADA, Bangalore.

Fernandez, Aloysius Prakash (1999): "Is Micro-Credit heading toward a Macro Mess?" *Search Bulletin,* Jan.-March.

Fernandez, Aloysius Prakash (2000): "Putting Institutions First Even in Microcredit", Paper presented at the Workshop on Best Practices in Group Dynamics and Micro-Credit, 15-17 February, Manesar, Gurgaon.

FWWB, Annual Report 2000-2001.

FWWB (1999), *India's Emerging Federations of Women's Savings and Credit Groups*, Ahmedabad.

Gain, Raji and P. Satish (1995), "A Micro Study on Group Dynamics and Group Functioning", Lucknow, Bankers Institute of Rural Development.

Gittinger, J. Price, (1984): *Economic Analysis of Agricultural Projects*, The Johns Hopkins University Press, Baltimore.

Government of West Bengal: *Economic Review (2010-11; 2011-12)*, Department of Statistics.

Government of India: *Economic Survey (2010-11; 2011-12; 2012-13)*; Ministry of Finance.

Government of Andhra Pradesh (2001), "Swarnajayanti Gram Swarozgar Yojana (SGSY) and the Role of Self-Help Groups (SHGs)", Paper presented at the National Conference for Ministers of Rural Development, Hyderabad: June 23-24.

Government of India, Swarnajayanti Gram Swarozgar Yojana—Guidelines, New Delhi: Ministry of Rural Development.

Harper Malcolm, "Self-help groups and Grameen Bank groups: What are the differences"? Chapter-7.

Harper, Malcolm (1998), *Profit for the Poor—Cases in Micro-Finance*, Oxford and IBH Publishing Co. Pvt. Ltd., New Delhi.

Harper, Malcolm (2002), '*Indian' Self-Help Groups and Bangladesh Grameen Bank Groups: A Comparative Analysis*, Discussion Paper, Friends of Women's World Banking India, Ahmedabad.

Harper, Malcolm, Ezekiel, Esipisu, A.K. Mohanty and D.S.K. Rao (1998), *The New Middlewomen—Profitable Banking Through On-Lending Groups*, Oxford & IBH Publishing Co. Pvt. Ltd., New Delhi.

Hishigsuren, Gaamaa (2000), *Holistic Approach to Development*, Practitioner-led Assessment of ASA, ASA, Tamil Nadu.

Hoff, K. and J.E. Stiglitz (1993), "Imperfect Information and Rural Credit Markets: Puzzles and Policy Perspectives", in K. Hoff *et al.* (eds.) The Economics of Rural Organisation, World Bank/Oxford University Press, Oxford, Chs. 1 and 2.

Holy Cross Social Service Centre (1997), *Self-Help Group—A Breakthrough into the Culture of Silence: An Innovative Experiment in Women's Thrift and Credit*, Hazaribagh, Bihar.

Hulme, David (2000), "Impact Assessment Methodologies for Microfinance: Theory, Experience and Better Practice", *World Development*, Vol. 28, No. 1, pp. 79-98.

Hulme, David and Paul Moseley (1996), *Finance Against Poverty*, Vols. 1 and 2, Routledge, London and New York.

ICCO, On the Road to Justice—ICCO Policy Plan 2001-2005.

Innovations in Microfinance Products and Mechanisms in India (2000), South Asian Network of Microfinance Initiatives, Dhaka.

International Monetary Fund (IMF), (2001), "India: recent economic developments and selected issues", IMF Country Report No. 01/181.

Jayaraman, B. (2001), *Micro-Finance—Retrospect and Prospects*, Occasional Paper No. 20, NABARD, Mumbai.

Johnson, Susan and Ben Rogaly (1997), *Microfinance and Poverty Reduction*, Oxfam and Action Aid, U.K.

Joshi, Vijay and I.M.D. Little, 1996. *India's Economic Reforms: 1991-2001* (Oxford, Clarendon Press).

Kamesan, Vepa (2003), "Indian Economic Scenario—yesterday-today-tomorrow". Inaugural Address at seminar on Banking-Agriculture-Industry-IT-New Hopes–New challenges organized by Telugu Vaibhavam at Hyderabad, Sep. 16.

Karmakar, K.G (1999), *Rural Credit and Self-help Groups—Micro-finance Needs and Concepts in India*, Sage, New Delhi.

Kilby P., T. Kidder N. Nayar, M. Leach and N. Mule (2000), Report of Phase 1 of the Oxfam Development Finance Institution Feasibility Study and Review of Oxfam Interventions in Micro-Finance, Oxfam, January.

Krishnaiah, P. (2003), *Poverty Reduction: Self-Help Group Strategy*, UBSPD, New Delhi, p. 180.

Mahajan, Vijay and G. Nagasri (1999), "Building Sustainable Microfinance Institutions in India", Paper presented at Seminar on New Development Finance, Frankfurt, September.

Mahajan, Vijay (2002), Microfinance Policy: Review and Prospective Suggestions, Presentation to the Sa-Dhan Subgroup on Policy, January.

Mahajan, Vijay, Bharati Gupta Ramola and Mathew Titus (2000), "Dhakka-Starting Microfinance in India" in K. Basu and K. Jindal (eds.), Microfinance: Emerging Challenges, Tata McGraw-Hill, New Delhi.

Mayoux, Linda (1998), Women's Empowerment and Micro-Finance Programmes: Approaches, Evidence and Ways Forward, DPP Working Paper No. 41.

Morgan, A. (1995), "Adult Change and Development: Learning and Peoples" Lives' in D. Sewart (ed.) One World Many Voices: Quality in Open and Distance Learning,

Reserve Bank of India Bulletin: Various Issues (March 2000-August 2012).

Sabharwal, Gita (2003): "From Margin to the Mainstream: Micro-finance Programmes and Women Empowerment: The Bangladesh Experience", http://www.gdre.org

The M-CRIL Report, 2000 (2001): *Micro-Credit Ratings and Guarantees India Ltd.*, Gurgaon, Haryana.

Tankha Ajay, (2002), "Self-Help Groups as Financial Intermediaries in India: Cost of Promotion, Sustainability and Impact", A Study prepared for ICCO & Cordaid, The Netherlands.

Tesoriero Frank (2005): "Strengthening communities through women's self help groups in South India", *Oxford University Press and Community Development Journal.*

Z. Husain, Mukherjee D. and Dutta M. (2012): "Self-Help Groups and Empowerment of Women: Self Selection or Actual Benefits?" *Journal of International Development.*

8

Impact of MGNREGA on the Rural Livelihoods of West Bengal

Debjani Ray

I. Introduction

For inclusive growth rural India must flourish along with its urban counterpart. Development of rural sector is crucially dependent on the progress of agriculture and allied sector and employment opportunities of the rural people.

Since its inception the problem of poverty and unemployment has been considered as the biggest challenge to development planning in India. Instead of mitigating reforms in India intensified the problem. Both male and female unemployment rates in rural India have gone up in 2004-05 as compared to 1993-94. The male unemployment rate by current daily status has gone up by 2.4 percentage points, while the female unemployment rate has gone up by 3.1 percentage points (NSS 61st round). A decline in the level of employment adversely affects the purchasing power and thereby the process of demand creation hampers. In this backdrop NREGA came into force from 2006 promising to provide for the livelihood security of rural households. The NREG Act is theoretically a demand driven legislation where rural people can get work on demand and also have a say in deciding what kind of developmental works are to be undertaken locally. Thus, democratic decentralisation and sustainable community development are the twin planks on which NREGA is premised. Provision of works and creation of durable assets are the economic mechanism of the NREGA. Both these objectives have important socio-economic implications in terms of livelihood in rural India. Successful implementation of the NREGA can achieve the twin objectives of employment generation in the rural India, and at the same time address the issue of falling agricultural productivity through the creation of proper infrastructure. As an immediate effect, wages earned through NREGA can become a source of great respite for the large masses of rural population in terms of maintaining the minimum levels of foodgrain consumption. On a long run perspective, durable assets created through NREGA related works can help in raising agricultural productivity. Works like land development, minor/micro-irrigation, construction of ponds, etc., are important complementary inputs for agricultural activities. The NREGA Act was notified on September 7, 2005 and was launched on February 2, 2006. It was renamed as the Mahatma Gandhi National Rural Employment Guarantee Act (MGNREGA) on October 2, 2009. It was extended to an additional 130 rural districts in financial year 2007-08. The remaining 266 districts have been notified under the MGNREGA with effect from April 1st 2008. The NREGA covers the entire country with the exception of districts that have a hundred per cent urban population. The erstwhile programmes of the Sampoorna Gramin Rozgar Yojana (SGRY) and the National Food for Work Programme (NFFWP) have been subsumed under NREGS. NREGA makes a paradigm shift from all previous wage employment programmes because of its following unique features:

1. NREGA provides a legal guarantee of wage employment.
2. It is a demand-driven programme where provision of work is triggered by the demand for work by wage-seekers.
3. It has legal provisions for allowances and compensation in case of failure to provide work on demand and delays in payment of work undertaken. Work is to be made available to anyone who demands it within 15 days of receiving an application to work, failing which the state governments are liable to pay an unemployment allowance.
4. It incentivises states to provide employment as 100 per cent of the unskilled labour cost and 75 per cent of the material cost of the programme is borne by the Government of India (GoI).
5. Unlike the earlier wage employment programmes that were allocation-based MGNREGA is demand driven and transfer of resources from Govt of India to states is based on the demand for employment in each of the states. This provides an additional

incentive for the states to leverage the Act to meet the employment needs of the poor.

II. Objectives of the Study

The objective of the study is to evaluate the district-wise performance of NREGA for the improvement of rural livelihood in West Bengal during the financial year 2011-12.

In West Bengal the proportion of population living in the rural area is 66.11 per cent according to the 2011 population census and 28 per cent of the rural population live below the poverty line.

NREGA has implemented in the following 10 districts of West Bengal–Jalpaiguri, Uttar Dinajpur, Dakshin Dinajpur, Malda, Murshidabad, South 24 Parganas, Paschim Midnapur, Bankura, Purulia, Birbhum in phase 1. Eight more districts—Cooch Bihar, Darjeeling G.H.C., Siliguri MP, Nadia, North 24 Parganas, Hoogly, Purba Midnapur, Burdwan was included in the second phase. Howrah was included in the last phase.

III. Data Source

Publicly available websites concerning NREGA, NREGA implementation status report from the Ministry of Panchayat and Rural Development and 2011 Census report are taken into account for the study. Author's calculation from this data are used for the detailed analysis.

Since, the main objectives of MGNREGA are provision of demand based employment and productive asset creation, both of them have important socio-economic implications in terms of livelihood strategies in rural areas. These are important instruments to achieve inclusive growth as well as sustainable development.

From the district-wise implementation status report it is evident that people who applied but job card not issued amounts to 80,447. Although it is less than one (0.73) per cent of the total job cards issued in the whole year, the number of people who are denied job card is quite significant. Out of five districts where job card denial took place, Hoogly with 60,711 people is ahead with a vast margin with others. Here the significance of NREGA to improve the rural livelihood gets the real jolt. The reason behind it needs proper intervention. From Table 8.1, it is clear that 5185 (0.11% of total persons demanded jobs) persons who demanded employment are not provided with. Since by name NREGA is demand

Table 8.1: Districtwise Implementation Status Report under NREGA during 2011-12

Sl. No.	*Name of the District*	*Application registered*	*Job card issued*	*Applied but job card not issued*	*Household demand for employment*	*Household provided employment*	*Excess demand for employment*
1.	Jalpaiguri	6,48,097	6,44,948	3,149	3,85,508	3,85,251	257
2.	Uttar Dinajpur	4,47,592	4,47,592	0	56,796	56,796	0
3.	Dakshin Dinajpur	2,73,871	2,73,871	0	74,579	70,977	3,402
4.	Malda	5,81,890	5,76,073	5,817	1,64,024	1,64,024	0
5.	Murshidabad	1,042,246	1,042,246	0	3,98,696	3,98,696	0
6.	South 24 Parganas	8,04,864	8,04,864	0	1,96,762	1,96,493	269
7.	Paschim Midnapur	8,54,132	8,54,132	0	4,24,521	4,24,444	77
8.	Bankura	5,72,565	5,72,565	0	2,32,866	2,32,866	0
9.	Purulia	4,49,234	4,47,542	1,692	1,52,214	1,52,214	0
10.	Birbhum	6,60,075	6,60,075	0	2,633	3,42,633	0
11.	Cooch Behar	6,01,9595	5,92,881	9078	3,13,247	3,13,247	0
12.	Darjeeling G.H.C.	1,25,734	1,25,734	0	87,900	87,362	538
13.	Siliguri MP	85,478	85,478	0	41,886	41,886	0
14.	Nadia	7,08,215	7,08,215	0	2,02,974	2,02,974	0
15.	North 24 Parganas	6,94,697	6,94,697	0	5,137	3,35,137	0
16.	Hoogly	6,94,697	6,33,986	6071	4,33,144	4,32,705	439
17.	Purba Midnapur	6,55,984	6,55,984	0	2,69,834	2,69,831	3
18.	Burdwan	9,85,953	9,85,953	0	3,78,240	3,78,240	0
19.	Howrah	2,27,907	2,27,907	0	71,941	71,941	0
Grand total		11,115,160	34,713	80,447	45,62,902	45,57,717	5185

Source: District-wise Financial and Physical Progess Report under NREGA during 2011-12.

driven employment guarantee scheme not a single person should be devoid of employment. Unemployment allowance given or not cannot be known from the website.

IV. Number of Days Provided for Employment

The most important criterion of the NREGA for improving the rural livelihood is the number of days the household receive employment on demand. NREGA gives legal guarantee for 100 days of wage employment in a year. But in reality the number of days household provided employment is far below the target of 100 days throughout India.

Moreover, the average person days generated per employed household shows a declining trend in the past two financial years. It declined from 54 days in 2009-10 to 47 days in 2010-11 and to 42 days in 2011-12.

Table 8.2 shows the average person days per household for the country, from FY 2008-09 to FY 2011-12 and the corresponding figures for West Bengal in order to have some idea about their relative positions.

Table 8.2: Average person days generated through MGNREGA in different years

	2008-09	*2009-10*	*2010-11*	*2011-12*
India	48	54	47	42
WB	26	45	31	34

Source: MGNREGA Sameeksha and Monthly Progress Report of the Programme.

The primary objective of the Act is to enhance livelihood security of the people in rural areas by providing 100 days of guaranteed wage employment in a financial year to every rural household whose adult member volunteer to do unskilled manual work. One of the important goals of the scheme is to build up a strong social safety net for the vulnerable groups by providing a fall back employment source when other employment alternatives are scarce or inadequate.

Table 8.3 shows the achievement of 100 days of work under NREGA during 2011-12 in different districts of West Bengal.

Although the basic objective of NREGA is to provide 100 days' work in a financial year with the aim of improvement of rural livelihood through provision of productive employment to rural households demanding work, achievement of 100 days' work under NREGA during 2011-12 in different districts of West Bengal is negligible. In West Bengal, 85,251 families completed 100 days of work during the year. Only 1.87 per cent of families that provided employment completed 100 days of work on the average. Birbhum tops the list with 6.42 per cent and Cooch Behar is at the bottom with 0.10 per cent.

According to some researchers one possible reason for low employment generation is the lack of demand for employment. The persons who worked fewer days generally have some alternative source of income. It is true that for the total population the average person days may turn out to be small if only a small proportion of the total population complete 100 days of work while large portion works few days due to their low demand for MGNREGA work.

Table 8.3: District-wise Implementation Status Report under NREGA during 2011-12

Sl. No.	*Name of the district*	*Household provided employment (a)*	*Number of families completed 100 days' work(b)*	*% of families that provided employment completed 100 days' work (b/a)*100*	*Rank*
1.	Jalpaiguri	3,85,251	2098	0.54	16
2.	U Dinajpur	56,796	578	1.01	9
3.	Dakshin Dinajpur	70,977	276	0.39	17
4.	Malda	1,64,024	3,813	2.32	7
5.	Murshidabad	3,98,696	2,301	0.58	15
6.	South 24Pgs	1,96,493	4,577	2.33	6
7.	Paschim Midnapur	4,24,444	3,963	0.93	10.5
8.	Bankura	2,32,866	8,133	3.49	3
9.	Purulia	1,52,214	5,099	3.35	4
10.	Birbhum	3,42,633	21,990	6.42	1
11.	Cooch Behar	3,13,247	325	0.10	19
12.	Darjeeling G.H.C.	87,362	4,321	4.95	2
13.	Siliguri MP	41,886	127	0.30	18
14.	Nadia	2,02,974	1,603	0.79	13
15.	North 24Pgs	3,35,137	9,860	2.94	5
16.	Hoogly	4,32,705	9,689	2.24	8
17.	Purba Midnapur	2,69,831	2,485	0.92	12
18.	Burdwan	3,78,240	3,500	0.93	10.5
19.	Howrah	71,941	513	0.71	14
	Grand Total	45,57,717	85,251	1.87	

Source: Websites concerning NREGA.

V. Women Participation under NREGA

Various provisions under the Act aim to ensure women empowerment through equitable and easy access to work, decent working condition and equal payment of wages.

In West Bengal, participation of women in MGNREGA is low compared to the national average for all the years 2006-2012 but there has been a gradual increase in participation rate over the period mentioned in Table 8.4 depicts women participation in the different districts of West Bengal under NREGS during the financial year 2011-12.

Women participation in West Bengal is 33.92 per cent. Participation of women is highest in Siliguri MP (53.13%) followed by Darjeeling G.H.C. (49.44%) and lowest (13.85%) in Murshidabad.

Table 8.4: Women person days as a percentage of total person days generated in different financial years

	FY 2006-07	*FY 2007-08*	*FY 2008-09*	*FY 2009-10*	*FY 2010-11*	*FY 2011-12*
India	40	43	48	48	48	47
West Bengal	18	17	27	33	34	32

Source: MGNREGA SAMEEKSHA.

NREGS is a landmark in rural employment generation programmes undertaken by the Government of India. By looking at the data given in the table we are sure about it. On an average 1502.25 lakh persondays (cumulative) have been generated during 2011-12. Burdwan tops the list with 189.99 lakh persondays. Birbhum (170.81), Hoogly (135.80), Paschim Midnapur (117.38), North 24 Parganas (115.20), Bankura (106.88) are the districts where through the scheme improvement of rural livelihood takes place.

In West Bengal, average persondays generatd per family is 33 days. It is quite below the national average which is 43 days in 2011-12. In some districts its performance is not at all satisfactory. What is the real reason behind it—insufficient demand because of its temporary nature, unmet demand due to paucity of funds, improper planning and implementation needs to be investigated in detail. The factors behind district-wise variations must be pointed and thereby taken care of. A pertinent question in this context is whether the demand for employment as well as provision of employment is related to rural poverty.

There occurs a shocking disparity of available fund per GP between different districts. Howrah with Rs. 26.72 lakh is at the bottom and Birbhum with Rs. 182.91 lakh ranks highest among districts. What really accounts for this huge gap—paucity of demand, supply bottleneck planning authority cries out for proper investigation. Reasonable enough expenditure per gram panchayat also varies from Rs. 21.43 lakh in Howrah to Rs. 182.86 lakh in Birbhum.

Now, we examine the relation between percentage of expenditure to available funds and percentage of works completion out of total works.

Table 8.8 presents an interesting picture. Naturally, there should be one-to-one correspondence between percentage of expenditure to available fund and percentage of works completion rate out of total works. But the observed relation tells a different story. In nine out of ten districts, the relationship is reverse, i.e. districts with higher percentage of

Table 8.5: Women Participation in different districts under NREGA during financial year 2011-12

Sl. No.	*Name*	*Percentage of women person days in total person days*	*Rank*
1.	Jalpaiguri	41.02	6
2.	Uttar Dinajpur	33.66	9
3.	Dakshin Dinajpur	25.90	13
4.	Malda	33.60	10
5.	Murshidabad	13.85	18
6.	South 24 Parganas	17.99	17
7.	Paschim Midnapur	30.70	11
8.	Bankura	36.57	7
9.	Purulia	42.55	5
10.	Birbhum	22.78	15
11.	Cooch Behar	23.94	14
12.	Darjeeling G.H.C.	49.44	2
13.	Siliguri MP	53.13	1
14.	Nadia	29.38	12
15.	North 24 Parganas	33.06	10
16.	Hoogly	34.48	8
17.	Purba Midnapur	48.64	3
18.	Burdwan	46.59	4
19.	Howrah	20.23	16
	Grand total	33.92	

Source: Website concerning NREGA.

expenditure to available funds end up with lower work completion rate. Uttar Dinajpur provides the case how proper planning and ideal implementation of available funds does produce desired results. A good planning authority makes it to the top (86.40%) in the work completion area with least possible expenditure (83.79%) to available funds.

This observation can open a new hope about NREGA in fulfilling the twin objective of provision of fall back employment along with creation of durable assets in the way that with limited resources judicious planning can produce better results in creating infrastructure which can in turn create employment opportunities other than NREGA. In this way implementation of NREGA generates positive externalities for the improvement of rural livelihood in West Bengal.

Progress of work undertaken – The objective of the various unskilled works undertaken by the programme is to develop infrastructural base of rural areas. These works include: 1. Water conservation and water harvesting (digging new ponds, percolation tanks, dams, etc.); 2. Drought proofing (afforestation/tree plantation); 3. Micro-irrigation works (minor irrigation canals); 4. Provision of irrigation facility to land owned by

Table 8.6: Person days Generated under NREGA during 2011-12

Sl. No.	*Name*	*Person days generated (cumulative) (in lakh person days)*	*Rank according to person days generated (cumulative)*	*Person generated per family*	*Rank according to person days generated per family*
1.	Jalpaiguri	101.01	7	26	10
2.	Uttar Dinajpur	20.44	16	36	5
3.	Dakshin Dinajpur	15.48	17	22	12
4.	Malda	54.15	12	33	7
5.	Murshidabad	84.74	9	21	13
6.	South 24 Pgs	70.14	10	36	5
7.	Paschim Midnapur	117.38	4	28	9
8.	Bankura	106.88	6	46	3
9.	Purulia	68.60	11	45	4
10.	Birbhum	170.81	2	50	2
11.	Cooch Behar	43.99	15	14	15
12.	Darjeeling G.H.C.	46.72	14	53	1
13.	Siliguri MP	7.66	19	18	14
14.	Nadia	50.01	13	25	11
15.	North 24 Parganas	115.20	5	34	6
16.	Hoogly	135.80	3	31	8
17.	Purba Midnapur	87.89	8	33	7
18.	Burdwan	189.99	1	50	2
19.	Howrah	15.37	18	21	13
	Grand Total	1502.25		33	

Source: website concerning NREGA.

SC/ST; 5. Renovation of traditional water bodies (de-silting of tanks/ ponds, canals, welis, etc.); 6. Land development (plantation, land levelling etc.); 7. Flood control and protection (Drainage in water-logged areas); 8. Rural connectivity (construction of concrete roads to facilitate easier travel); and 9. Any other activity approved by Ministry of Rural Development.

These works have both short and long term implications for rural development. In the short run the NREGA activities address the problem of rural unemployment, conserve rural natural resource base and protect environmental pollution and degradation. On a long run perspectives, creation of durable assets can help in raising agricultural productivity and in bringing sustainable improvement in rural livelihood.

During FY 2011-12 in West Bengal, total number of works taken was 327857. Of these 183581 works are completed and the remaining 144276 works are ongoing. Thus work completion rate was 56 per cent. Although work completion rate by itself is not a criterion to assess the

Table 8.7: District-wise Financial Status Report during 2011-12

Sl. No.	*Name*	*Number of gram panchyat (GP) in the district*	*Available fund per GP during the year (Rs. in lakh) (rank in bracket)*	*Expenditure per GP during the year (Rs. in lakh) (rank in bracket)*
1.	Siliguri MP	22	68 (14)	64.87 (13)
2.	Dakshin Dinajpur	65	51.47 (17)	45.86 (15)
3.	Uttar Dinajpur	98	53.18 (16)	44.56 (16)
4.	Darjeeling G.H.C.	112	105.32 (7)	100.58 (7)
5.	Cooch Behar	128	79.47 (11)	68.55 (11)
6.	Jalpaiguri	146	142.36 (2)	131.98 (3)
7.	Maldah	146	78 (12)	76.66 (10)
8.	Howrah	157	26.72 (19)	21.43 (19)
9.	Birbhum	167	182.91 (1)	182.86 (1)
10.	Purulia	170	80.85 (9)	75.27 (10)
11.	Nadia	187	57.24 (15)	53.15 (14)
12.	Bankura	190	119.06 (5)	113.65 (6)
13.	North 24 Parganas	200	137.62 (3)	135.44 (2)
14.	Hoogly	207	115.75 (6)	126.09 (5)
15.	Purba Midnapur	223	80.44 (10)	78.57 (8)
16.	Murshidabad	254	68.18 (13)	65.29 (12)
17.	Burdwan	277	134.31 (4)	127.84 (4)
18.	Paschim Midnapur	290	88.29 (8)	78.18 (9)
19.	South 24 Parganas	312	47.32 (18)	41.71 (17)
	Total	3351		

Source: District-wise financial progress report under NREGA during 2011-12, Author's calculation from the report.

quality of work, it is an important parameter to evaluate the progress of the scheme in creating assets for the development of rural infrastructure. For the state as a whole, different types of works undertaken in different districts of West Bengal, their completion rate is shown in Table 8.9.

Uttar Dinajpur with overall work completion rate of 86.40 per cent stood ahead of all closely followed by Howrah (83.69). Howrah performs best in all the works undertaken such as rural connectivity, flood control, water conservation and water harvesting, drought proofing, micro irrigation followed by Birbhum and then Siliguri MP. Cooch Behar stands at the bottom in all the sectors except drought proofing.

Main Findings

1. Demand and provision of employment has increased overtime. It implies that people's interest to join the programme has increased. This tendency may be interpreted as a decline in the

Table 8.8: District-wise Financial and Physical Progress Report under NREGA during 2011-12

Sl. No.	*Name*	*Percentage of expenditure to available fund (Rs. in lakh) [rank in bracket]*	*Percentage of work completion out of total works (works completed + works in progress) [rank in bracket]*
1.	Siliguri MP	95.40 (9)	70.87 (8)
2.	Dakshin Dinajpur	89.09 (14)	42.47 (16)
3.	Uttar Dinajpur	83.79 (18)	86.40 (1)
4.	Darjeeling G.H.C.	95.50 (7)	48.22 (14)
5.	Cooch Behar	86.26 (17)	26.40 (19)
6.	Jalpaiguri	92.71 (13)	68.83 (9)
7.	Maldah	98.27 (4)	72.81 (7)
8.	Howrah	80.18 (19)	83.69 (2)
9.	Birbhum	99.97 (2)	78.02 (5)
10.	Purulia	93.10 (11)	73.87 (6)
11.	Nadia	92.84 (12)	83.15 (3)
12.	Bankura	95.45 (8)	78.68 (4)
13.	North 24 Parganas	98.41 (3)	52.04 (12)
14.	Hooghly	108.94 (1)	41.97 (17)
15.	Purba Midnapur	97.68 (5)	49.02 (13)
16.	Murshidabad	95.75 (6)	61.70 (10)
17.	Burdwan	95.18 (10)	28.98 (18)
18.	Paschim Midnapur	88.55 (15)	55.63 (11)
19.	South 24 Parganas	88.15 (16)	45.83 (15)

Source: Author's calculation from the District-wise Financial Progress Report under NREGA during 2011-12.

rate of migration from the village which is one of the objectives of NREGA.

2. Average persondays generated in the state is far below the target of 100 days. A very small percentage of the households who provided employment, completed 100 days of work. As it is a demand driven programme, the small number of persondays may imply low demand for work. It needs in depth study about the reasons behind low demand.
3. Women have a greater take in the scheme due to favourable time schedule, proximity of the work site, employment on demand, additional source of income.
4. Works completion rate is 56 per cent. But whether there is sustainable asset creation is a questionable issue.
5. The nature of impediments in the implementation of NREGA can be broadly classified as lack of proper awareness, insufficient resources and wage payment as the crux of the problem, lack of

Table 8.9: Progress Report on performance indicated asset created through percentage of different types of works completed out of the total works done under NREGA during 2011-12 in different districts of West Bengal

Sl. No.	*Name*	*Rural connectivity (Rank)*	*Flood control (Rank)*	*Water conserva-tion and water harvesting (Rank)*	*Drought proofing (Rank)*	*Micro Irrigation (Rank)*	*Total works Completed out of total works undertaken (works completed+ work in progress) {Rank}*
1.	Jalpaiguri	65(3)	42.33(11)	62.85(3)	39.50(10)	44.40(9)	68.83(9)
2.	Uttar Dinajpur	50.10(5)	40.00(13)	49.69(6)	56.12(4)	40.00(11)	86.40(1)
3.	Dakshin Dinajpur	18.50(18)	50.00(7)	16.85(18)	13.88(18)	30.73(14)	42.47(17)
4.	Maldah	39.16(12)	43.05(8)	49.46(8)	50.78(8)	47.12(5)	72.80(8)
5.	Murshidabad	24.75(17)	18.99(18)	23.23(17)	36.31(12)	11.14(19)	61.69(10)
6.	South 24 Parganas	25(16)	33.61(14)	24.80(15)	13.79(19)	27.63(16)	45.84(15)
7.	Paschim Midnapur	28.18(14)	28.87(15)	29.89(13)	22.52(17)	29.63(15)	55.63(12)
8.	Bankura	42(10)	42.73(9)	45.50(10)	32.51(14)	59.03(4)	78.68(4)
9.	Purulia	40.76(11)	70.00(4)	49.49(7)	22.98(16)	44.61(8)	73.89(6)
10.	Birbhum	73.81(2)	79.52(2)	69.93(2)	78(2)	82.78(2)	78.02(5)
11.	Cooch Behar	16.47(19)	11.76(19)	9.705(19)	36.05(13)	14.81(18)	26.40(19)
12.	Darjeeling G.H.C.	26.79(15)	23.20(17)	23.81(16)	40.23(9)	23.52(17)	48.22(14)
13.	Siliguri MP	59.67(4)	76.74(3)	60.00(4)	76.76(3)	77.6(3)	70.87(7)
14.	Nadia	49.70(6)	59.28(5)	51.69(5)	51.09(7)	45.73(7)	83.15(3)
15.	North 24 Parganas	48(7)	26.15(16)	47.77(9)	38.09(11)	41.26(10)	52.04(13)
16.	Hoogly	47.67(8)	50.70(6)	41.47(11)	52.48(6)	39.09(13)	42.58(16)
17.	Purba Midnapur	42.64(9)	42.68(10)	38.00(12)	53.56(5)	46.59(6)	49.02(13)
18.	Burdwan	29.63(13)	41.39(12)	27.20(4)	30.20(15)	39.77(12)	28.97(18)
19.	Howrah	81.87(1)	82.73(1)	91.67(1)	85.47(1)	84.81(1)	83.69(2)
	Total						55.99

Source: Author's calculation from Monthly Progress Report on Performance Indicated asset created FY 2011-12.

proper planning for the creation of durable assets to build rural infrastructure.

(A) Lack of awareness about various provisions of the Act proved to be major impediments in its implementation. Majority of the villagers are unaware of the fact that NREGA was an Act not a scheme.

(B) Insufficient resources are also a major problem for proper and effective implementation of the Act. This is so because to attain the desired 100 days of guaranteed wage employment to all of those who demand it, much more allocation of funds is needed that has been allocated so far.

(C) Determination of wage by task rate system is not clear to workers. Also the main source of corruption is to be found in the wage payments that are made. The modus operandi for this is fudging of muster rolls by filling in false information either regarding the names of workers or number of days or both. To get rid of this leakage, the government has adopted the system of payments through the bank or post office.

VI. Conclusion

The enactment and implementation of a right-based MGNREGA has undoubtedly marked a paradigm shift from the existing wage employment programmes. This is primarily to be achieved by taking up project-oriented activities covering works on water conservation/harvesting, drought/flood control, plantation, land development, rural connectivity, etc. The need of the hour is to improve quality of assets created and to bring about synergy between MGNREGA and agriculture and allied rural livelihoods. This endeavour will not only uplift the under privileged and socially and economically vulnerable, but also support in making the agriculture a viable occupation.

References

Government of India (2012): *Draft Twelfth Five-Year Plan (2012-17) Document*, Volume I, Faster, More Inclusive and Sustainable Growth, Planning Commission.

Government of India (2013): *Economic Survey 2013-14*, Ministry of Finance.

Government of India (2013): *Mahatma Gandhi National Rural Employment Guarantee Programme*.

Government of India (2013): *Report to the People*, Ministry of Rural Development, Department of Rural Development, New Delhi.

9

Food and Livelihood Security in Rural West Bengal

An Experience

Uttam Haldar

Background

Despite economic growth, green revolution, government employment generation programme the rural livelihood in India is enamored with poverty and hunger.

High economic growth in India during post-reforms period is reflected in Annual growth rate of GNI_{FC} at 2004-05 in plan period, 3.4 per cent (4th plan), 4.9 per cent (5th plan), 5.9 per cent (6th plan), 5.6 per cent (7th plan), 6.6 per cent (8th plan), 5.7 per cent (9th plan), 7.6 per cent (10th plan), 8.0 per cent (11th plan)

To solve the acute food crisis in post-independence period, Government of India gives importance to attain self-sufficiency in food-grain and to increase purchasing power of all section of people through distribution of land and non-land asset, employment generation etc. To attain self-sufficiency in foodgrain Government of India introduced new and improved method of cultivation which contains HYV seeds, chemical fertilizer, pesticides, insecticides and deep-tube-well irrigation. Now, India becomes more or less self-sufficient in cereals mainly in rice and wheat but deficit in pulses and oilseeds. It enhanced capacity to cope with inter-year fluctuation in production. After remaining a food deficit country for about two decades after independence, India became largely self-sufficient

Table 9.1: India's Foodgrains Stock and Net Import (Million Tonne)

	1951	*1961*	*1971*	*1981*	*1991*	*2000*	*2001*	*2002*	*2003*	*2004*	*2005*	*2006*	*2007*	*2008*	*2009*	*2010*
Procurement	3.8	0.5	8.9	13.0	19.6	35.6	42.6	40.3	34.5	41.1	41.5	37.0	35.8	54.2	60.5	56.1
Pds ss	8.0	4.0	7.8	13.0	20.8	13.0	13.2	18.2	23.2	28.3	31.0	31.8	32.8	34.7	47.3	43.7
Buffer stock	–4.2	–3.5	1.1	00.0	–1.2	22.6	29.4	22.1	11.3	12.8	10.5	5.2	3.0	19.5	19.2	12.4
Net import	4.8	3.5	2.0	0.5	–0.6	–1.4	–4.5	–8.5	–7.1	–7.7	–7.2	–3.8	–7.0	–14.4	–7.2	–4.7

Source: Food security: Mohan Das (Deputy Director, NSSO) and Amlan Biswas (senior investigator, NSSO) Kalodhavni, Jan. 2005, pp. 15 and http://indiabudget.nic.in pp. 25-26

in foodgrains production at the macro level. Surplus stock of foodgrains and foodgrains export/import are two major indicators to claim attainment of self-sufficiency (Table 9.1). (A.K. Giri, 2006, Dev, S. Mahendra *et al.* (2009), Golait, Ramesh *et al.* (2006), P. Nasurudden *et al.* (2006).

To eradicate poverty and to earn livelihood, time to time Government of India introduced different employment generation programmes such as IRDP (1967-77), NREP (1980), RLEGP (1983), SEEUY (1983-84), SEPUP (1986), JRY (1989), NRY (1989), PMRY (1993-94), EAS (1993), REGP (1995), SJSRY (1997), SGSY (1999), IAY (1999-2000), PMGY (1999-2000), PMGSY (2000), SGRY (2001), NFFWP (2004), NREGS (2006), MGNREGS (2006), NREGA (2005), MGNREGA (2009). As a result poverty has been reduced. As per Tendulkar Committee recommendations, anyone earning Rs. 672.8 monthly that is earning Rs. 22.42 per day in the rural area and Rs. 859.6 monthly or Rs. 28.35 per day in the urban area is lie above the poverty line at the national level. Whereas in West Bengal the poverty line estimated as Rs. 643.2 in rural and Rs. 830.6 in urban areas (though World Bank criterion of poverty line is $1.25 per day). According to this estimate 29.8 per cent of the Indian population alone was under the BPL in 2009-10 which was 37.2 per cent in 2004-05, whereas in West Bengal, BPL population declined from 34.2 per cent in 2004-05 to 26.7 per cent in 2009-2010.

In all-India level Head Count Ratio (HCR) has declined by 7.3 percentage points from 37.2 per cent in 2004-05 to 29.8 per cent in 2009-10, with rural poverty declining by 8.0 percentage points from 41.8 per cent to 33.8 per cent and urban poverty declining by 4.8 percentage points from 25.7 per cent to 20.9 per cent.

(*Source*: http://planningcommission.nic.in/news/press_pov1903.pdf)

Existence of chronic food insecurity at micro level in many parts of India is illustrated in various studies. The Global Hunger Index 2009 ranks India at the bottom with 65th position (out of 84 countries) with a GHI of 23.90 and which the index characterizes as "alarming" food security situation such as about 50 per cent of Indian children under three years of age are malnourished, India has largest number of malnourished children in the world. One-third of India's adult population has a body mass index of less than 18.5. (IFPRI, U.B.I. 2009).

National family and health survey 3 (NFHS-3) reported that average percentage of undernourished children under five years for 26 sub-Saharan African countries was 25 per cent about half of the Indian average of 46 per cent. Weight and height of Indians have not shown significant improvement. 21.5 per cent babies in India born with low weight, a problem begins at womb. Child malnutrition is higher in rural areas compared to urban areas implying a lower food intake and a majority of socially marginalized people live in rural areas. Highest percentage of underweight and stunted children was recorded for STs followed by SCs, among religious group is Muslim.

Data on calorie intake as revealed by various round of National Sample Survey Organization (NSSO) shows that average per capita calorie intake is declining in India both in Rural and Urban areas over four decades.

Table 9.2: Per-Capita Intake of calories in India, 1972-73 to 2009-2010

	Kcal/day	
	Rural	*Urban*
1972-73 (27th round)	2266	2107
1983 (38th rcund)	2221	2089
1993-94 (50th round)	2153	2071
1999-2000 (55th round)	2149	2156
2004-05 (61st round)	2047	2020
2009-10 (66th round)	2020	1946
Percentage change between 1972-73 and 2009-10	–10.9	–9.5

Source: NSS 66th round, computed from p. 70.

High economic growth, declining of poverty, increasing of buffer stock and export of foodgrain shows India's progress on food and livelihood security. The bright picture of food and livelihood security shall be blunt when we noticed that average per-capita intake of calories has declined. Side by side the decrease in percentage share of cereal (major and cheapest source of energy) on Monthly Per Capita Expenditure (MPCE) and monthly per capita consumption of cereal in absolute term (Kg) both in rural and urban population raise the question of food security in India.

In this background, the study tries to find out the way of earning food and livelihood of marginalized people in Bankura district of West Bengal.

Literature survey: Agarwal and Narain (2000), Anna Hazare (1997), Anon (1998) represent the potential of generating wealth and well-being from rainwater harvesting and it takes short time to transform a poverty stricken destitute and ecologically devastated village to a rich and green village in Ralegan Siddhi, Tarun Bharth Sangha, Alwar and Madhya Pradesh case study. In all the cases resource base was created when people relating to the resource facing severe crisis.

In Sukhamajri village, villagers built a small tank to capture rain-water and agreed to protect their watershed in 1979 when they face severe drought. Subsequently, the economic and ecological changes have taken place. Village level Institution evolved out to manage the resource base, which is crucial for the entire exercise.

Krishna Bhaurao Hazare—A retired driver from the Indian army began work in the village Ralegan Siddhi in a drought prone area of Maharashtra, by constructing a storage pond, reservoirs and gully plugs in 1975. Every effort was made in the village to ensure people's participation including women and to ensure equitable access to the resources generated. Today not a single inhabitant of the village depends on drought relief.

In 1986, assisted by Tarun Bharat Sangha (a local voluntary agency) the villagers of Gopalpura (a poor and drought stricken village in Rajasthan) built three small earthen rainwater harvesting structures, locally called *johads* using traditional knowledge on their village grazing land to store monsoon rains. The storage water then used to irrigates their fields and increase percolation in the grounds to recharge wells. Today villagers has enough to eat and do not have to migrate any more. What is absolutely stunning today is to see the rebirth of several rivers in the region. The voluntary agency follows clear guidelines—villagers contribute land and labour while Tarun Bharat Sangha supplies external resources like cement for construction or diesel for tractors. Gram Sabha is the decision making body.

Watershed management programme of district Jhabua in Madhya Pradesh, has become outstanding example in which the government has been able to intervene in a way that promote public participation in environmental management.

These studies from India represent the transformation from a state of ecological poverty to a state sustainable economic wealth. These micro experiences are remarkable as they are testimony to the potential of generating wealth and well-being from rainwater harvesting and it takes short time to transform a poverty stricken destitute and ecologically devastated village to a rich and green village. These examples of community management of natural resources teach us that sustainable management will be succeeded when people are given the right to manage their natural resources base.

Objective of the Study

- To study the prospect of rain water harvesting in drought prone areas of Bankura District with community participation in making food and livelihood security of marginalized people.
- To highlight the development activity initiated by a tribal lady in raising the standard of living of tribal population in Chatmagara village of Bankura district.

Research Methodology

Scope of the Study

The study will help develop the strategy of successful community management to empowering and mobilizing labour resource towards the sustainable development of robust local economy based natural wealth and get out of their ecological poverty and lives with dignity.

Data collection: The primary data has been used for the purposes of the study. The primary data has been collected on the basis of sampling survey method.

Primary sources of data: The resource studied was a group of three water bodies (ponds) belonging to the tribal community in the village Chamtagara of Chhatna block in Bankura district, West Bengal, India. Primary data was collected from a voluntary organization of Chamtagara named Vivekananda Adibasi Kalyan Samity (VAKS). This voluntary organization evolved out from the committee constituted to construct and maintain water resources in 1961.

Sampling technique: Purposive sampling method is adopted to select the resource study and simple random sampling without replacement is used to select sample members belonging to the resources studied.

Sample size: A sample size of 16 was taken out of nearly 50 members. The necessary details about the sample are as under (Parenthesis indicate educational achievement of the respondent). Ist Chosen member is Anath Saren, 70 years old and class X passed, Husband of late Sundari Saren and secretary of Vivekananda Adibasi Kalyan Samity (VAKS), Chamtagara. Other chosen members consist of three women aged 60 years (just literate), 40 years (graduate), 20 years (class X passed); male members in descending ages are: 1. 67 years (just literate), 2. 66 years (class II passed), 3. 63 years (class I passed), 4. 59 years (class I passed), 5. 58 years (class I passed), 6. 45 years (class IV passed), 7. 40 years

(MBBS), 8. 37 years (class VII passed), 9. 36 years (VIII passed), 10. 30 years (class X passed), 11. 25 years (class X passed), and 12. 23 years (class XII passed).

Instrumentation technique: A structured questionnaire with multiple-choice questions followed by interview and group discussion has been used for the collection of data. Questionnaire was set in accordance with the objectives of the study. The survey was undertaken in December 2004 with interviews of Anath Saren, secretary of Vivekananda Adibasi Kalyan Samity (VAKS), Chamtagara to know about the history of the organization and its functioning. This was followed by interviews of 15 randomly Chosen members to identify their socio-economic characteristics and learn about their association with the committee to maintain Ponds. I held two group discussions with five members each randomly chosen (without replacement) consisting one female in first group and two females in second group. Finally, the audited financial records (financial year 2003-2004) of the VAKS was analyzed.

Tribal Sctting: The District of Bankura lies between 22°35 north latitude and 86°36 to 87°46 East longitudes. Administratively, it is located in the Burdwan Division in the Western Part of the state of West Bengal. It is known to be a backward district in terms of socio-economic development. Chamtagara village is situated in the drought prone Chhatna Block of Bankura District.

In the Chhatna Block, industry is non-existent. Agriculture is the major economic activity and characterized mostly by a mono-cropping system. Here soil is poor in nutrient contents and the rainfall is low and erratic. Irrigation facility in the Block is limited. As a result, agriculture production is very low. Low agricultural production may be the important cause of economic backwardness of the people which is severe particularly among the Schedule Caste (SC) and Schedule Tribe (ST) communities.

Above 50 percentage of the total population belongs to Scheduled Tribe (Santhals) in the Chamtagara village. They live in the West part of the village and in the East there live higher caste 'Tamboli' society.

Table 9.1: Distribution of tribal population in the Chamtagara village in 1962

0-1		*1-6*		*6-15*		*15-60*		*Above 60*		*Total*	
Male	*Female*	*Male*	*Female*	*Male*	*Female*	*Male*	*Female*	*Male*	*Female*	*Male*	*Female*
3	2	10	8	17	14	60	49	11	5	101	78

Source: VAKS.

Total tribal household = 33; Total tribal population = 179; Average size tribal household = 5.42; Total tribal working population = 109; Working population per tribal household = 3.3

Majority of tribal people in the village are agricultural labourers. As agricultural activity is seasonal, they do not get the scope of employment as daily labourer regularly throughout the year. To earn their livelihood they had to migrate three to four times in a year to the agriculturally developed Burdwan and Hooghly district and suffer a lot. Children and old parents of such migratory labourers stay in their home which in turn creates various problems. Economic backwardness among Scheduled Tribe population is manifested through high illiteracy rate, poor health status, ignorance, superstition and poor consciousness about sanitation, family planning etc.

Genesis and Evolution of Water Resources

In 1961 when new house wife Sundari entered her husband's village, Chamtagara visualized that they (Tribal Society) are dominated by higher community 'Tamboli' as in case of other villages in Bankura district. All the ponds are owned by Tamboli society. In summer ponds are dried up. The remaining little water in bottom is used for domestic needs, live-stock rearing etc. Due to ownership and dominant power, the member of Tambuli family, getting priority, but the tribal on the other hand had to wait till Tamboli's needs were met up.

Tribal, low caste, untouchable, Sundari had to return home without using water from nearby ponds after a long wait under scorching heat of mid-day of a summer like other days and other members of her society.

The fact struck her mind and she visualizes the problem of her entire society in her own eyes. She realizes that bathing; washing utensils and clothing and extinguish fire is must for normal living. There is no alternatives of water, alternatives of ponds. To get the required water for everyday use they needed ponds from where she, her family members, members for her society got water sufficiently, freely without any exclusion.

She came to know after discussion with her family members and members of her society that ponds gives more utility, it can reduce the damage of crop harvesting due to uncertainty of monsoon. To construct pond require land and labour. Most household in tribal society have fallow land and unemployed labour. To mobilize such valuable resources into productive purpose efficiently needed initiatives and devotion. Sundari Saren filed a project in PL-480 scheme with the help of a person of

Santiniketan involving village level Development project. The project was sanctioned. They bring their sanctioned food article from Calcutta port with the help from a rice mill owner of Jhantiphari, Bankura.

She faced another problem, the problem of selecting land for construction of ponds. They can use ponds for domestic needs and extinguish fire if ponds are within the hands distance; it fills by water if it is dug in the catchment of water flows, which also recharge ground water. It has to keep in mind how much lands are getting irrigated. Though main land area of projected pond belonging to the tribal community, the ponds cannot be constructed if the owners of few '*Kathas*' (1 *kathas* = 720 sq ft) of private property land are not agreed to give up.

Sundari, with her own initiatives, let them understand how a pond benefits society; solve their traditional problem of water, financial benefits of creating ponds to both those who gives land and labour. She involved the persons, even who will be landless after giving his small plot of land for ponds. She formed a committee for digging and maintenance of ponds involving her husband Anath Saren, other members of her family and her society. Three ponds were excavated one after another during the year of 1962-65. Average area of each pond is 12 *bigha* i.e. 1.61 hectare. They decided to dig 6 feet deep in each year. Land to build bank of the pond was separate. Now the tribal community of that village became the owner of these ponds. The entire member who gave either their land or labour got user rights of ponds. Heirs inherit membership. It was settled that the membership can also be transferred to persons nominated by the members. Any new individuals outside the community cannot be inducted into the committee.

They dig a cube of 20×20×20 cubic feet in the middle of the pond to connect with source of ground water.

Member of the committee discussed that the excavation of ponds, earthen canal and bunds (Johard Bandh) in the catchment which prevented to flow water beyond the village premises. Ground water will be recharged and the water levels in the earthen canal will rise. This will help the villagers to irrigate their land easily with local devise made of tin sheet, wood, pipe etc. without using diesel pump. To check the soil erosion and to conserve the run off rainwater, a number of jorbandh were constructed.

After solving water for domestic uses, irrigation etc., they think about problem of drinking water. The only well dug up with government sponsor in the entire village at higher caste belt. The tribal did not get drinking water before Tamboli's demand for water were met up, even in the case when they had to keep their child or sick family person at home alone.

They had forced to collect water from nearby small water bodies (doba). Disease like cholera and diarrhoea became part of their life. To solve it, they dig well in tribal belt of the village in the 1965. Separate committee was formed to maintain well. They also solve the problem of pollution by closing the open mouth of the well and put a hand pump in it. The waste water drained out to a nearby soak pit. In this way they dig 100 wells nearby and remote villages, one for each village with tribal concentration of Chhatna, Bankura-1 block of Bankura district.

At the time of survey some of the original members have grown older even some of them, including the dreamer Sundari Saren had died.

Analysis

(1) Water security:

(a) *Household needs:* As ponds were excavated, primary demand for water were met up. Tribals became free to use water from their own source for daily household activity. The age old dependency of tribal people upon higher caste Tamboli for their basic necessities of life were end up.

(b) *Sustainability*: The digging of a cube of 20 × 20 × 20 cubic feet in the middle of the pond made connection with sources of ground water. This indigenous technology provides water sufficiently for house-hold work in summer, when pond is dried up and even in time of drought.

(c) *Irrigation water*: The excavation of ponds, earthen canal and bunds (Johard Bandh) in the catchment which prevented to flow water beyond the village premises. Groundwater was recharged and the water levels in the earthen canals were rise up. These helped the villagers to irrigate their land easily with local devise made of tin sheet, wood, pipe etc. without using diesel pump.

(d) *Drinking water*: To solve the problem of drinking water, they dig well in tribal belt of the village in the year 1965. Separate committee was formed to maintain well. They also solved the problem of pollution by closing the open mouth of the well and put a hand pump in it. The waste water drained out to a nearby soak pit. In this way they dig 100 wells nearby and remote villages, one for each village with tribal concentration of Chhatna, Bankura-1 block of Bankura district.

(2) *Livelihood Security:* The age old traditional economic activity of the tribal people in that village was the forest related avocation namely collection and sale of Sal and Kendu leaves, seeds, wood, root etc. However, during the last few decades there has been large scale deforestation i.e. destruction of forest as a result of which the tribal population has been divested of their age old forest related economic activity.

During the time of digging pond, wells and watershed development, all the active people including both male and female of the age group 15 to 59 got jobs. On an average each household participated 23 days in a month. Generally, the works were done five to six month in the lien season, when agricultural activity is limited.

As a result each household with 3.3 working member on average gets 76 working days per month and 380 to 456 working days per year. In this way in each year 14 thousand man-days generated.

Initially workers got only food-grains as wage but when Sundari attracted government and non-government Aid, workers got food and money as wage.

Most impressive result is that the distress migration has reduced considerably.

(3) *Food Security*: When the work goes on every participant got 2 kgs of foodgrains daily. Male and female labourers got equal amount of foodgrains as wage. The foodgrains obtained in each household with 3.3 working members per family was sufficient to meet the daily requirement of whole family members with average family size of 5.4 including aged parents and children below 15 years. Side by side those workers had children below five years of age, they got extra allowance of barley, milk powder, baby food and soya bean etc.

Nutrition Security: The earthen bank of the newly created ponds was fertile and produced a huge amount of green vegetables like gourd, pumpkin, bitter pottel, green chili, banana etc. The harvested vegetable was distributed equally between all Santhal household. When large amount vegetable harvested, it was sold in the nearby market.

On the water of the ponds, fish was cultivated. They got fish three to four month in a year. Of these month fish was harvested once a week.

About 2 kg of fish was distributed to each household every week and extra harvested fish was sold in the market.

Tribal people also purchased green vegetables and fish in occasion and in festival at a subsidized rate.

As the ponds were dug in village premises, each of the tribal family kept 5 to 6 duck which produced egg and meat.

Production: Number of ponds, jorhbandh were constructed to conserve the run off rainwater and to check the soil erosion. Aforestation and land reclamation programme gained importance among the local people. These water conservation efforts resulted in increased availability of groundwater which in turn facilated development of community well.

Availability of water for irrigation raised the productivity of paddy. Between 1963 and 1969 rice production has been doubled from 1.5 quintal per *Bigha* to 3 quintal per *Bigha*, i.e. 1.05 ton per hectare to 2.10 ton per hectare. Mono-cropping farming now turns to multi-cropping farming including fruits and vegetables. Tribal people agreed to cultivate low water consuming crops in Rabi season.

Grass production has increased tremendously. Grass is best fodder. This led to increase in the number of livestock population. Each household started to keep 2 Bullock, two to three cow and 6 to 7 goat or ram. The composition of livestock also changes. The number of pig went down from 10 to 12 per family to nearly zero. The milk production has increased from zero to 0.75 litre per family. Increase in number of goat and ram led to meat production.

Availability of fodder of best quality at free of cost reduced the cost of maintaining Bullock, the most important input in traditional farming, which in turn reduces the cost of cultivation. Watershed protection has also resulted in increased tree density, which increased the production of wood and leaf both used as fire wood. Side by side wood was used for making Cart and Plough which again reduce the cost of cultivation.

In this way real income of the tribal people increase many fold. They found their way of sustainable livelihood. Most of the tribals who earlier to migrate with their men and women to work as labourers in cities are now returning to till their land which had been lying fallow for decades. People are still practising traditional farming but now they have enough to eat and do not have to migrate any more.

Heath Security

As soon as the tribal families use safe drinking water from protected well with closed mouth, hand pump, drainage to soak pit etc., the disease like cholera, Diarrhoea disorder were reduced immediately. This in turn reduces the infant mortality rate of the village.

Monetary Security

With money from selling of Fish, Vegetable… etc., they generate monetary fund. One of the members reminds that in the first year of creation of pond they generate a fund of Rs. 10,000 (Rs. 2000 from selling of vegetables and Rs. 8000 from selling of fish). As the development programme goes on the fund grow larger and larger.

This monetary fund protect the hard working poor tribal to mortgage their lands against loan in the hands of moneylender belonging to the higher caste community in case of illness or any other financial needs. This is another way to reduce the dependency of tribal people upon higher caste Tamboli. The result is that the age-old exploitative mechanism of moneylenders was end up.

Members of tribal society also get other benefits like educational Aid for their children, medical allowance for aged persons and children's.

Awareness Generation and Women Empowerment

It has been realized by Sundari Saren that one of the major causality of social and economic distortion among the indigenous people is the low spread of education both formal and informal particularly among the female. It has also been understood in course of time that education is not an isolated problem; it is rather associated with health, economic conditions and standard of living of the people concerned.

A number of problems like malnutrition, infection, lack of appropriate health awareness and lack of suitable housing and lack of adequate medical facilities continued to be accounted and even the most unwanted outcome, the death. Children and mothers are worst sufferers in this connection.

Sundari started health awareness and family planning programme involving worker of health sub-centre. Let them understand how frequent pregnancy effect badly in their physical health, productivity, income, nutrition and standard of living; about the evils of delivery at home instead of hospital.

It has also been observed that the family bondage among tribal people is not very strong. The wives are often looked upon not as a full time life partner, but as a working asset capable of undertaking both field and household work simultaneously. Whenever, the women become incapable of such hard work due to ill-health, pregnancy etc., they are driven out by their respective husbands and by their family members.

All male and female go to work to earn their livelihood. On the way of returning males spend their days earning in country liquor shop. Returning with drunked, they beat their wife for a negligible excuse. Due to ignorance of such tribal women's their social and legal rights, they become the victims of informal divorce. These women believe that it is the right of her husband.

Sundari after interaction with the Tribal community realized that most disadvantaged, neglected and oppressed a lot of the tribal population are the womenfolk who are often subject to various type of social subjugation on flimsy grounds.

Sharing the feelings with fellow women she realized that the problem is not exceptional but in general. She united all the tribal females including the victimized women and formed a committee. Unitedly, they faced the said drunked male partner and wanted to know the reason behind the disturbance in tribal belt. They said that your wife after doing the same work with you, collect fire-wood, making food, washing cloth but need no bear. Our children also learned the same as you done. If you do not go to liquor shop, you could save the money spend on liquor. By which you can purchase some nutritious food like egg or vegetables. Your children will be healthy. They will be less infected by disease. Their ability to doing job will rise. Income of your family will rise. Peace will return. You could send your children to school. The male member forced to keep the word that this fact (drunken) would not repeat in future. Being fear, others male member used to avoid liquor shop. Now except occasion no one drink alchohol.

When the problem of water, cultivation, livelihood, food, nutrition was solved, with Sundari Saren's awareness programme people think to raise their standard of living. They think they should send their children to school. In school they enrolled their children freely; tribal children got books, school uniform at free of cost and also got scholarship. So, to send their children in school is not burden. Gradually, all tribals started to send their children to school one after another. Tribal has reservation in government service. When one or two person get government job passed in class viii or class x, the interest to go to school increased many times. Now, a days most of the tribal children go to school. Occurrence of drop-out rate in secondary level is rare case.

Strategy of Successful Co-operation

In historical and socio-cultural context, the economic opportunities outside the domain of the resource were important variable affecting perceptions about cost and benefits. The labour market was extremely tight in the sense that unemployment and income is insecure. The uncertainty and risk of loss of livelihood created a complex situation where transaction costs in the form of search cost and insecurity of job reduces the efficacy of the labour market. Individuals can no longer be guided by market principles (in the form of seeking sectors with highest returns) in allocating labour.

Within geographical, historical, socio-cultural background, Santhals of Chamtagara village were locked in poverty trap. Sundari Saren's movement breaks the ignorance about the need of their (tribal people) pond. A small individual effort collectively produces a large productive asset which provides flow of benefits generation after generation and solves old age problems. Tribals people were motivated and unitedly promise to give up their land and labour to dig ponds. To start work they were needed food. Sundari was taking help from governments grant in terms of foodgrain. These initial investment acts as big push which breaks the poverty trap. As work were started forward and backward linkage were occur one after another and the beneficial stream became self perpetuating. Now, the poverty traps turns into cyclical self propagating forces which raise the standard of living. As the tribal people of the village use outside help in creating productive asset efficiently the self-perpetuating beneficial forces run sustainably even when the outside help stops.

Tribal society had their own culture, feeling of alienation from the mainstream culture, greater community sense, and a combative spirit. These shaped the perception and attitudes of the tribal and gave them a socio-cultural identity from that of higher caste Tamboli society of the village. They were able to communicate with each other easily, were willing to suffer great hardship, plan over a longer time period, discount individual sacrifices for group welfare, to a greater extent than the other caste of the villages. Thus, mutually consistent expectation what can be called a collective consciousness was created within the members, and gave them their collective identity. This created a sense of community amongst the members and served to reduce the transaction to cost of collective action. These makes Sundari Saren's task easy.

Louderadale *et al.* (1981) have shown in a game theoretic framework that the perception of a common threat may increase group solidarity. The creation of a group identity encourages co-operation because members of a social group tend to regard other members favourably and believe them trustworthy, honest and co-operative. Other members of the same group are expected, therefore, to reciprocate co-operative behaviour. In addition, inclusion with a social group reduces social distances between members so that they make less distinction between their own and other's welfare.

Hence, Sundari Saren's movement raises the consciousness about need of their own water resources and the threat of other community, dominancy; untouchables etc. and force the tribal society to co-operate. The small size and the homogeneity of the tribal community reduces the transaction cost of imposition of property rights.

Conclusion

Within geographical, historical, socio-cultural background, Santhals of Chamtagara village were locked in poverty trap. Sundari Saren's (A tribal lady) movement breaks the ignorance about the need of their (tribal people) pond. The threat of other community, dominancy; untouchables etc, lack of alternative livelihood opportunities force the tribal people to cooperate. Unitedly they promise to give up their land and labour to dig ponds. Government grants of food items acts as big push and breaks the poverty trap. Traditional cultivation became sustainable. Distress migration has been stopped. Awareness among female about education, health, family planning, sanitation and empowerment of women mainly inside the family raise the social and economic condition. Poverty traps turns into cyclical self-propagating forces which raise the standard of living.

Policy Prescription

Development of rural infrastructure like water harvesting structure through community participation with strong leadership using government development programme will lead to sustainable cultivation and hence food and livelihood security in drought prone areas of Bankura district where opportunity of alternative livelihood is limited.

References

Agarwal, A. and S. Narain, (2000): "Community and Household Water Management: The Key to Environmental Regeneration and Poverty Alleviation", in Dinesh K. Marothia (Ed.), *Institutionalizing Common Pool Resources*, Concept Publishing Co. Pvt. Ltd., New Delhi.

Banerjee Abhijit V. and Esther Duflo (2011): *Poor Economics: Rethinking Poverty and the Ways to End it*, Random House India.

Chopra, K., G.K. Kadekodi and M.N. Murty, (1989): "People's Participation and Common Property Resources", *EPW,* December 23-30.

Chopra, K., G.K. Kadekodi and M.N. Murty (1990): *Participatory Development: People and Common Property Resources*, Sage Publication, New Delhi.

Das, M. and A. Biswas (2005): "Food Security", *Kalodhvani*, Jan 2005, p. 15.

Census of India (1991): *District Census Hand Book, Bankura.*

Haldar, U. (2005): "Chamtagara Gram of Sundari Saren, ekti gram unnayan bhabnar etibritta", *Kalodhvani* 12(4).

Hunter, W.W. (1868, reprint 1996): *The Annals of Rural Bengal*, 10-17, 80-87.

Hussain, Z. and R.N. Bhattacharyya (2004): "Common Pool Resources and Contextual Factor: Evolution of Fishermen's Cooperative in Calcutta", *Ecological Economics* 50 (2004) 201-217.

Louderdale, P., P.P. Smith-Cunnier, J. Parker and J. Inveriarty (1981): "External Threat and the Definition of Deviation", *Journal of Personal and Social Psychology,* 46 (5), 1058-1068.

Singh, K. (1993): *Managing Common Pool Resources: Principles and Case Studies*, Oxford University Press, New Delhi.

10

Food Deprivation as a Choice Among Poor People in Backward Rural India During Liberalization

Jayanta Hajra and *Chandrasekhar Hajra*

I. Introduction

Planned development in India has been based on the notion of ensuring balanced regional development. Regional spread of heavy industrialization programmes, tax concessions for setting up industries in backward areas, easy and cheap lending facilities for small scale and cottage industries, priority sector lending programmes, investments in Social Overhead Capital (SOC) building projects in backward areas were designed to meet the said objective. The result was urban growth through industrial townships, development of linkage industries and increase in options in livelihood in many areas. All these government supportive measures helped to have some positive impacts on reducing regional imbalances. This accentuated the fiscal deficits of the government without any competitive edge of these industries in the global market. This unsustainable situation compelled government to adopt Liberalization, Privatization and Globalization (LPG) programme designed by Bretton Woods system (BWs). In this situation, we find that inequality between regions has grown farther.

Now, the problem of uneven development in the country has become a cause for concern. The worst suffering area is the rural part where most of the disadvantaged people live in a precarious condition. These people have very weak access to the opportunities of globalization, because it demands special skills to compete or even to sustain but unfortunately most of the rural people lack in this respect. Capability enhancing investments in these backward rural areas were mostly done by the government but in this age of liberalization, government is continuously withdrawing itself from such attempts. Private sector is not willing to invest in SOC in the rural backward areas. So, capability enhancement is not taking place causing the magnification of sufferings of rural people. Moreover, during globalization most adversely affected sector is agriculture which is the main source of livelihood of these people causing more and more deprivation in food, health, education and knowledge. The backward areas are becoming more backward for this reason.

People of backward regions are generally deprived in the basic human needs such as food, shelter, health and Knowledge. In this attempt we have tried to look into the food deprivation in backward areas. Hunger is the deprivation of the fundamental 'right to food' that human beings have sought to achieve ever since the origin of mankind. The means and ways of attaining food security has undergone vast changes since the days of hunting and gathering to expansionary food production and welfare measures of distribution as civilization has traversed through different epochs with varying modes of production. The persistence of a scourge like hunger even today among large sections of the world population in spite of astronomical distances covered by science and technology, especially over the last century, perhaps remains the greatest contradiction and challenge within the contemporary world system.

Global Hunger Index (GHI) has been one useful initiative in the recent years in tracking the comparative levels of hunger in different parts of the world and across individual nations. India, with a score of 23.3, figures among the countries with an alarming situation of hunger. The more worrisome fact, revealed upon comparison with last year's situation, is that India actually marginally slipped in its ranking from 94 among 118 nations in 2007 to 98 among 120 nations in 2008. The Indian case emphatically underscores the non-inclusive nature of the recent phase of high economic growth in the country, which has had little positive impact for her vast majority of poor population.

The dichotomy of high growth rates and persisting hunger among the Indian population has become an important area of study. The estimation of the Indian State Hunger Index (ISHI) comes as a new endeavour to throw light on the prevalence of hunger in our country at a more disaggregated level. The ISHI report published in 2008 constructs the hunger index for 17 major Indian states. While Punjab, Kerala, Andhra Pradesh and Assam have a 'serious' level of hunger; Madhya Pradesh fares worst in the 'extremely alarming' bracket of hunger with an index of 30.9. All the other remaining states record an 'alarming' level of hunger, which is also the general situation for the country. Bibek Debroy in his work entitled "District Level Deprivation in the New Millennium" showed the incidence of poverty and hunger in districts of different states of India and the result are shown in Table 10.1.

Table 10.1: No. of Poverty, Hunger Affected Districts (Lowest 25%) in Different States and UTs of India

Name of the State/ UT	*No. of Poverty affected Districts*	*No. of Hunger affected Districts*
Bihar	24	13
Uttar Pradesh	18	15
Orissa	23	23
Jharkhand	12	14
M.P.	22	09
Arunachal Pradesh	03	09
Karnataka	04	01
Chhattisgarh	08	08
Assam	13	14
Rajasthan	00	01
Nagaland	00	02
W.B.	06	14
A & N Islands	00	00
Andhra Pradesh	00	03
Chandigarh	00	00
D & N Haveli	00	00
Daman & Diu	00	00
Delhi	00	00
Goa	00	01
Gujarat	00	00
Haryana	00	03
Himachal Pradesh	00	00
J & K	00	00
Kerala	00	04
Lakshadweep	00	00
Maharashtra	11	05
Manipur	00	02
Meghalaya	00	00
Mizoram	00	00
Pondichery	00	01
Punjab	00	00
Sikkim	00	00
Tamil Nadu	02	00
Tripura	00	01
Uttarakhand	00	03
All India	146	146

Source: Distric Level Deprivation in the New Millennium by Bibek Debroy.

Independent and broader view of hunger can be based on the recommendations of the Report of The Task Force on Projections of Minimum needs and Effective consumption demand, 1979 of the Planning Commission. Taking into account that per capita per day calorie requirement is age, sex and occupation specific, the 1979 Task Force divided the population into 16 groups and estimated the average calorie requirement. This was 2435 kcal for rural areas and 2095 kcal for urban areas, which was rounded off to 2400 kcal and 2100 kcal respectively for convenience. Additionally, for the rural areas, a norm of 2200 kcal per capita per day, as this was the norm initially used to estimate poverty from the 1973-74 NSS data can also be used. Patnaik (2007) has made estimates of the proportion of the population with energy intake less than 2400 kcal and 2200 kcal per capita per day for rural India, which was used by Arindam Banerjee in the article named "Hunger and its Underlying Causes: A Broad Indian View, 2008". Here he constructed Hunger index as a simple average of three variables named Calorie Undernourishment, Proportion of Underweight among children below Five years and Under Five Mortility Rate per 100 (Table 10.2).

Based on these estimates, the Broad Hunger Index is a high 46.9 and 41.1 by the 2400 kcal and 2200 kcal norms respectively in rural India while in urban India the same is 34 implying an alarming prevalence of undernourishment and hunger.

Table 10.2: The Broad Hunger Index: Rural and Urban India

Norms	*Prevalence of Calorie Undernourishment*	*Proportion of Underweight among children <5 years*	*Under-five mortality rate reported as death per 100*	*Broad Hunger Index*
Rural				
2400 kcal	87	45.6	8.2	46.9
2200 kcal	69.5	45.6	8.2	41.1
Urban				
2100 kcal	64.0	32.7	5.2	34.0

Source: The rural figures of variable A are taken from Patnaik, 2007. The urban figure is estimated by the author using NSS data on Consumption Expenditure and Nutrition, 2004-05. Variables B and C are taken from the NFHS-III, 2005-06.

During the liberalization regime Indian agriculture has become more and more open to international market and the impact of that is not particularly helpful to the small and marginal producers. Percentage share of both agricultural export and import in the GDP from agriculture and allied product group has increased (Table 10.3) over time.

Table 10.3: Share of Agriculture in Export and Import of India

Year	*% share of agr. Ex. In GDP from agr. & allied product group*	*% share of agr. Im. In GDP from agr. & allied product group*
1991-92	4.22	0.80
2005-06	8.36	3.53

Source: R.S. Deshpande and S. Arora.

This increasing openness has adversely affected Indian agriculture due to change in world prices (Parikh, 1998). Table 10.4 shows change in world price due to India's trade in rice and wheat.

Table 10.4: Percentage Change in World Price due to India's Trade in Rice and Wheat

Qty. Traded (Million Tons)	*Rice*		*Wheat*	
	Import	*Export*	*Import*	*Export*
0.5	4.02	–3.69	0.57	–0.57
1.0	8.18	–7.11	1.56	–1.14
1.5	12.47	–10.26	2.27	–1.70
2.0	18.31	–11.87	2.98	–2.27
2.5	24.01	–12.94	3.55	–2.70
3.0	32.46	–14.42	4.26	–3.27
3.5	40.24	–16.16	2.97	–3.84
4.0	51.84	–17.64	5.68	–4.40
4.5	59.96	–19.05	6.53	–4.63
5.0	72.10	–20.52	7.24	–5.40

Source: Parikh, 1998.

With world prices affecting domestic prices under a trade-liberalized regime, the returns to agricultural production starts falling even within the domestic economies further compounding the problem for the large rural populace in these countries.

According to Arindam Banerjee, 2008, with non-increasing or declining returns in agricultural productions, the consumption levels of the rural population undergo deflation ovei time and hence the prevalence or aggravation of hunger incidence occurs. Falling returns in cultivation also leads to declining or non-increasing real wages of the large number of agricultural labourers in rural areas.

Along with this Michel Morisset and Pramod Kumar (2011) found in their studies that with falling expenditure on food the choice of people is also shifting towards high priced processed food basket causing smaller amount of purchase of the same. With falling income the inevitable result is low calorie consumption and spread of hunger.

In the analysis of the agriculturists we have not put enough emphasis on size of the holdings. The age of liberalization has entrapped small and marginal farmers in the market web. It has induced a range of new risks and uncertainties in the lives of small and marginal farmers. This type of holdings as a percentage of total holdings in India has increased from 74.47 per cent (1980-81) to 81.89 per cent (2000-01) (R.S. Deshpande and S. Arora, 2010). Notable risks can be traced as follows:

1. Size holding for marginal farmers has changed marginally from 0.39 hector in 1991 to 0.40 hector in 2001 and in the same time period size holding for small farmers has changed from 1.43 hector to 1.41 hector (R.S. Deshpande and S. Arora, 2010). In this size the scale effect of new technology is hard to achieve.
2. Till now Indian agriculture is seasonal by nature and dependent on monsoon. Irrigated cultivated area is only 40 per cent of the total in India (R.S. Deshpande and S. Arora, 2010). Non-irrigated areas cannot take advantages of new technology.
3. Investment in agriculture as per cent of GDP has decreased from 1.92 per cent to 1.37 per cent during 1990-91 to 1999-2000 (at 1993-94 prices). Further it has decreased from 2.2 per cent to 1.9 per cent during 1999-2000 to 2005-06 (at 1999-2000 prices) (Deshpande and Arora, 2010). This again goes against enjoying the benefits of modern agriculture for small and marginal farmers.
4. Local agricultural patterns and practices drew from a shared repository of knowledge much of which was transmitted and reproduced through the social and cultural structures of agricultural transactions and practices has changed after globalization. At present, commercialization of agriculture based on external inputs has increased the competitiveness among farmers regarding crop selection for getting the best market price. In this competition small and marginal farmers are in the disadvantageous position both in the input and output market due to their low bargaining power originated from their poor economic base.

The fact that calorie deprivation has increased in the rural India between 1993-94 and 2004-05 by whichever norm we follow (see Table 10.6) is largely explained by this shrinking of purchasing power of the rural population.

Apart from this few other problems are magnifying this acute problem of hunger and poverty namely, jobless growth in modern Indian Economy is pushing huge reserve of labour force to the uncertain world of unstable income through growth of informal sector and contractual employment regime. The result is expenditure in food itself has been one of the adjusting variable. And it has become more so due to inflation in general price level.

Table 10.5: Rural Calorie Deprivation by Various Norms: 1993-94 and 2004-05

Calorie Intake Norm (Kcal/person/day)	*Percentage of Population below Prescribed norm*	
	1993-94	*2004-05*
2400	74.5	87.0
2200	58.5	69.5
1800	20.0	25.0

Source: Estimates taken from Patnaik, 2007.

Also global spread of consumerism through powerful media has some impact through demonstration effect on the consumption basket of poor people. Lucrative offers on non-food luxury goods are siphoning off part of poor people's income from food items. Figures of Planning Commission 2008-09 supports this view. According to them during the period 1972-73 to 2004-05 food expenditure of rural people in India has decreased from 72.9 per cent to 55 per cent and the same figure for india has decreased from 64.5 per cent to 42.5 per cent. Reflection of it is also seen on NSSO figures of 2004-05. According to NSSO per capita calorie intake during the period 1983 to 2004-05 has decreased in rural India from 2221 kcal to 2047 kcal which is lower than the standard norm of 2400 kcal for rural areas and the same figure for the Urban India has decreased from 2089 kcal to 2020 kcal which is also lower than the standard norm of 2100 kcal for urban areas. This may in turn will affect the work efforts of these people causing more impoverishment of these people.

NSSO estimates only 5 per cent of Indian are owning 38 per cent of the resources of the country whereas 60 per cent people are owning 13 per cent of the resources. This means income generating investable capital is not owned by maximum people and after banking sector reforms banks are no longer interested in investing social priority sector. To fill the gap government are welcoming international capital on investor's favourable condition. Now, in India Government has already permitted FDI in retail trade. This in turn will deactivate rural activities of artisans petty traders and will make them dependent on production activities on the imposed terms of these FDIs. This will weaken the income earning capability and economic independence of the large section of common people. Again deprivation of food will become a natural corollary of this activity.

From the above discussion it is clear that the hunger and food deprivation is increasing but at the same time surprisingly poverty ratio is decreasing. The cause of this deprivation as envisaged by previous studies is fall in real income of farmers. But it is also true that government has propounded numerous poverty elevation programmes to enhance the economic situations of these poor people. This perhaps will be a judicious claim that due to these efforts poverty ratio has decreased over time during this period of globalization. So, perhaps only the fall in real income is not the sole cause of food deprivation. If some changes from nutritious food items to non-food consumer goods in consumption basket help the consumer to increase his immediate utility level then the loss in terms of calorie deprivation does not matter to the consumer in short run. Perhaps it is not realized by the consumers also. The new industrialization era based on the philosophy of spread of consumerism provokes poor people to shift his consumption basket in favour of more non-food items. In our attempt we shall try to reconcile the falling trend of poverty ratio with increasing spread of hunger in our following paragraphs.

In our analysis we shall try to explain the poor consumer's equilibrium by simple indifference curve approach. The basic assumptions of our model are as follows:

1. In this analysis we have assumed that food consumed by poor people are of two types—One, regular necessities as rice, wheat, and collected edible food items from common property resources. Two, nutritious foods such as pulses, seasonal vegetables, oil, fish, meat, sweets, milk, egg etc.
2. First type of food is gathered by individual efforts, family efforts, social help, government helps etc. to maintain sustainability level. Second types of food are purchased from the market.
3. In the non-food items we have considered, luxury items of poor people as sachet shampoo, soap, hair oil, tooth paste, cheap electronic equipments, small top up vouchers etc.

4. In our analysis we have considered the choice pattern is limited between second type of food items and non-food items and they are substitutable between each other.
5. Poor people's purchasing power is decreasing over time.
6. Second type of food price is increasing over time.
7. Unit level price of non-food items are decreasing at a faster rate compared to the fall in purchasing power of poor people.
8. Objective of the consumer is utility maximization.

II. The Model

The utility function: $U = U(Q_{f,} Q_{nf})$

$$Q_f = Q_{f1} + Q_{f2}$$

Q_{f1} – First type of food

Q_{f2} – Second type of food

Q_{nf} – Non-food items

Budget Constraint: $M = P_f Q_{f2} + P_{nf} Q_{nf}$

M – Money income of the poor consumer.

P_f – Second type of food price (composite price index)

P_{nf} – Non-food item's price (composite price index)

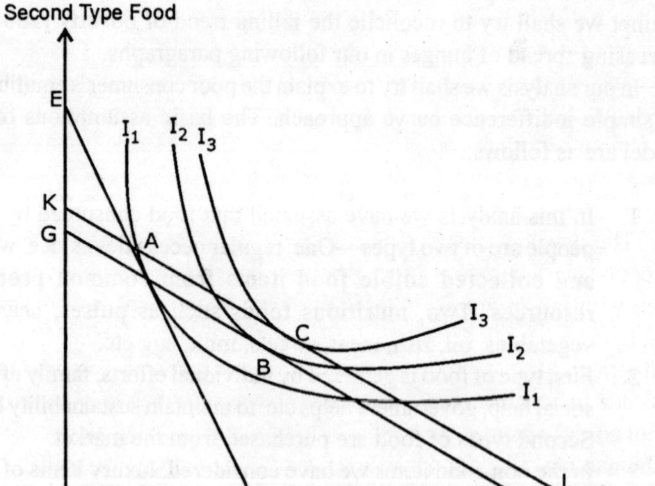

Fig. 10.1

Maximization study gives the first normal equilibrium at point A on the Budget line EF where his utility level is depicted by the indifference curve I_1I_1. Now when his purchasing power decreases point A no longer becomes attainable to him. His budget line will shift to GH due to increase in second type food price and decrease in unit level non-food price at a relatively higher rate in comparison with fall in purchasing power of the consumer. In this situation consumer will be in equilibrium at point B with higher level of utility depicted by indifference curve I_2I_2 compared to normal period equilibrium at point A. At point B, the consumer is substituting food items (Second type) for non-food items.

So, in this analysis we find with calorie deprivation the consumer is attaining higher utility level through substitution between second type of food and non-food items. This explains why the calorie deprivation is not realized at least in the short run by the consumer himself. With Govt. support programme to reduce poverty now suppose the consumer becomes enable to attain point A. This is shown by a parallel upward shift of the budget line from GH to KL. Even in this situation the consumer will be better off if a point like C showing even higher utility level I_3I_3 is chosen in spite of point A. Here also the consumer will substitute second type food items for non-food items. This explains how poverty reduction and increase in calorie deprivation takes place simultaneously.

In the long run due to calorie deprivation income earning capability of the consumer may decrease due to health ground leading to a downward shift in the budget line KL. But technological innovations reducing need for physical labour and high calorie requirement will partially offset this loss in earning capability of poor consumer. So, even in long run subsequent equilibriums may occur somewhere between A and C where he will be better off compared to point A. The possible results indicate that even with calorie deprivation in long run the consumer may attain higher level of utility.

The new age of industrialization is enabling firms to reduce their prices because in case of price elastic luxury products total revenue rises even with fall in prices. In this situation the price cut decision will be viable if cost escalation is controlled through technological innovation and remain lower than the rate of increase in revenue. The productivity loss due to negative health effects of calorie deprivation of poor people is not going to hamper the productivity of such non-food producing farms as human unskilled labour of poor people is replaced by skilled labour and machines and further through this they can control wage hike also. Thus both the demand and supply side factors will not be able to hinder this type of industrialization even though industry agriculture terms of trade moves against industry. Hence this is apparent that not only the decrease in purchasing power of poor people is responsible for calorie deprivation but modern industrialization based on consumerism philosophy is equally responsible for this type of problem.

The above analysis can also be supplemented by some other consumption behaviour of poor people as we all know part of their income is spent on some irrational items like lottery tickets, liquor, bidi etc. As this happens their effort to collect first type of food gets adversely affected and this also takes away a substantial part of their income which can otherwise be spent on normal consumption goods. It also causes the calorie deprivation more acute.

III. What Can Be Done

The problem of calorie deprivation is caused by two pronged problem as it is discussed above. One, the TOT is going against conventional Indian agricultural produce and second, affinity to purchase high priced processed food by common people. So, to ease out the situation either we have to withdraw ourselves from participation in conventional agricultural exports or we have to change our nature of export basket more in favour of agricultural processed food. This will help domestic consumers to have processed food at relatively cheaper prices whereas export potentiality of Indian farmers will increase without loss in TOT.

To achieve this focus of Indian agriculture needs to be readdressed. The role of Government, agricultural producers, processors and traders should be reassessed. A complementarity in all decision making nodes are required to achieve this broader objective. The availability and accessibility of investible fund and technology towards agricultural commercialization in the above mentioned direction become more important now. Privatization and market orientation of agriculture can solve the problem of fund scarcity, but in the terms and conditions of private investor only. But small, fragmented and marginal farming society with a very low resource base and technical know-how remain untouched due to inaccessibility of the modern structural and technical upgradation of the agricultural system. Government has the role to make the technical knowhow accessible to its small and marginal farming society in such a way that private commercialization takes place and at the same time interest of the small producers are served. To make it possible, one contradiction in this regard requires to be addressed properly by the

Government Corporate capital demands scale economy in its investment. But a small and scattered holding of Indian farmers hinders to have the scale economy. So, a clear policy in this respect should be designed to facilitate an investor friendly agriculture superstructure.

IV. Conclusion

Globalization has increased the Indian GDP growth rate to the second highest level of the world but at the same time backward rural areas have become more deprived in many respects. Agriculture dependent rural unskilled or semi-skilled artisans are losing grounds at a high pace due to lack of skill factor. Accession to the basic needs are becoming hard to achieve for these people due to low accession to the work opportunities, uncertainty in employment and income, low bargaining power with high inflation. If this situation goes on for a long time then demand for industrial goods or even consumer goods will decline defueling the engine of liberalization and the dream of modern industrial India will be faded out. The need of this hour is the capability enhancement of these rural folk by govt. attempts not just the social security programmes as advocated by present-day policy-makers. A more judicious way of tackling the problem of hunger within such economies will be to revisit and implement the goal of national food security that constituted the erstwhile 'Food-First' doctrine.

References

Bhandari, Laveesh and Amaresh Dubey (2001): Calorie Deficiency, Poverty and the Public Distribution System—A Household Level Analysis for 1993-94, *RGICS Working Paper No. 24,* Rajiv Gandhi Institute for Contemporary Studies, New Delhi.

Bhandari, Laveesh and Amaresh Dubey (2003): Incidence of Poverty and Hunger in Indian Districts, *RGICS Working Paper*, Rajiv Gandhi Institute for Contemporary Studies, New Delhi (forthcoming).

Deshpande, R.S. and Arora Saroj (2010): *Agrarian Crisis and Farmer Suicides,* Sage; New Delhi.

Government of India (2002): *Selected Educational Statistics 2000-2001,* Planning, Monitoring and Statistics Division, Department of Secondary and Higher Education, Ministry of Human Resource Development, New Delhi.

FAO (2003): *FAO Methodology for the Measurement of Food Deprivation,* FAO Statistics Division, October.

Guilmoto, Christophe Z. and S. Irudaya Rajan (2002): District Level Estimates of Fertility from India's 2001 Census, *Economic and Political Weekly,* February 16, 2002, pp. 665-672.

Gwatkin, Davidson R. and Garima Deveshwar-Bahl (2001): *Immunization Coverage Inequalities: An Overview of Socio-Economic and Gender Differentials in Developing Countries,* The World Bank, September 2001.

IIPS (2007): "National Family Health Survey 2005-06 (NFHS-3). National Report", *International Institute of Population Sciences,* Mumbai.

Menon, Purnima, Anil Deolalikar and Anjor Bhaskar (2008): *The India State Hunger Index: Comparisons of Hunger across States,* International Food Policy Research Institute, available at http://www.ifpri.org/pubs/cp/ishi08.asp.

Michel Morisset and Promod Kumar (2011): *Trends and Patterns of Consumption of Value-added Foods in India,* www.isid.ac.in/~pu/conference/dec_11_conf/./MichelMorisset.doc

National Commission on Population (NCP) (2001): *District-wise Social Economic Demographic Indicators,* Government of India, New Delhi.

Patnaik, Utsa (2007): "Neoliberalism and Rural Poverty in India", *Economic and Political Weekly,* Vol. 42(30): 3132-3150.

Planning Commission (1979): *Report of the Task Force on Projections of Minimum Needs and Effective Consumption Demand,* Government of India, New Delhi, mimeo, *(available at http://planningcommission.nic.in/aboutus/taskforce/tsk_mneff.pdf).*

Planning Commission (March 2002): *National Human Development Report 2001,* Government of India, Oxford University Press, New Delhi.

United Nations Development Programme (UNDP) (2001): *Human Development Report 2001,* Oxford University Press, New York.

United Nations Development Programme (UNDP) (2002): *Human Development Report 2002,* Oxford University Press, New Delhi.

Von Grebmer K., Fritschel H., Nestorova B., Olofinbiyi T., Pandya., Lorch R., and Yohannes Y. (2008): "Global Hunger Index Report 2008", *Welt hunger hilfe,* International Food Policy Research Institute, Concern.

http://www.aecf.org/kidscount/kc2001_static/sum_4.htm, 2001 KIDS COUNT ONLINE, The Annie E. Casey Foundation Website.

http://millenniumindicatoRsun.org/unsd/mi/mi_series_results.asp?rowID=562, United Nations Millenium Development Goals, Infant mortality rate (0-1 year) per 1,000 live births (UNICEF estimates)

http://www.medivisionindia.com/children/diseases.phtml?did=663&id=66&x=25&y=13, Dr. Nitin Shah in general discussion on immunization posted on the Medivision India's site

www.networkideas.org/featart/nov2008/Hunger.pdf, *Hunger and its Underlying Causes: A Broad Indian View* by *Arindam Banerjee.*

www.isid.ac.in/~pu/conference/dec_11_conf/./MichelMorisset.doc *Trends and Patterns of Consumption of Valueadded foods in India*

11

Focusing on the Factors Influencing the Rural Livelihoods in India

Poulomi Bhattacharya

"Not Life, but Good Life is to be chiefly valued".
—Socrates.

I. Introduction

Inclusive Growth, i.e. growth with development should be focused on. Growth takes into account the overall GDP or GNP level. However, for growth with development per capita levels is focused. Moreover, it takes into account the decline in rural-urban disparities in facilities provided and the inequality in any sphere between sectors and within sectors, so that the country moves towards development with growth. Here we will come across many such factors which not just affect rural livelihoods but also affect its growth.

India's rural people do not lead the same life as the urban people. In spite of being the suppliers of primary products, they are deprived of the comfort and the luxuries of life enjoyed by the urban people. Transformation in employment and income from agro-based rural economy to industry-based urban economy is associated with a vibrant rural non-farm sector.

Lack of convergence in the rural employment and poverty eradication programmes is the reason which holds the rural sector from developing to the extent it is targeted for.

II. Factors Influencing Rural Livelihoods

- *Behavioural:* Most rural male farmers have a tendency to use their money in buying assets, luxuries and liquor while women's income directly benefits family and cover expenses of food and basic needs. It is this realization that led to the development of income generating activities for women. However, the strategy did not fully succeed for these poverty-stricken women due to lack of skills, education, and access to technologies, tools and productive assets. **Women participation** is important.
- *Geographical:* About 55 per cent of our agriculture is rain-fed where delayed, deficient, low and erratic rainfall, lead to reduction in crop output or even total crop failure. They are the sufferers of the 'vagaries of monsoon'. Rain-fed regions are mainly hilly, undulating and mountainous with no opportunities for widespread irrigation. Moreover, soil depth, soil quality, land degradation, water availability can vary within a single village. Thus, **rural non-farm sector** should be given importance.
- *Technical*: Rural farmers often lack proper tools and draft power. Low productivity, lack of technical know-how, and frequent crop failure leave the rural farmers with no investible surplus and they become highly indebted. The green revolution framework focused only on "above the ground" issues and not on the "below the ground" issues such as soil-water-microbe dynamic remain neglected. **Education, both general and technical**, is important.
- *Financial*: Neglect and low investment in development resources give low returns. Moreover, the rural women face many financial obstacles when it comes to their involvement in economic activities. **Involvement of more NGOs and other government financial institutions which provide funds to these people and requirement to let the rural people know about these facilities.**

III. Strategies and their Flaws—Need for Convergence

- *Fragmented Programming:* There are now large budgets IWMP, RADP, NHM, MGNREGA, Minor Irrigation etc. for rural development. Although the activities promoted under these are highly relevant for the development of rain-fed areas, yet each of these is conceived and implemented in departmental silos and there is no unified mechanism for coordination and convergence. Thus, these programmes do not lead to "area development", potential synergies are lost, and investments, interventions remain sub-optimal.

- *For convergence*, a single steering mechanism should be created at the State and District levels for IWMP, MGNREGS, RADP, NHM etc. The policy making, programming, budgeting and implementing silos need to be dismantled. Mechanisms need to be created to ensure that policy making is focused on "development of rain-fed areas" as a single theme and schemes relevant for this theme converge in the field regardless of their origins in Central and State Ministries. In the present, at least MGNREGA, IWMP, Minor Irrigation, RKVY/RADP and NHM must be planned and implemented in a convergent manner.
- *There is a need to create mechanisms* to pool from various government and non-government agencies, the knowledge resources and to harness the grassroots capabilities of NGOs.
- For rural livelihood focus and sustainable management MGNREGS should include maintenance of watershed works. Although MGNREGS permits 40 per cent capital expenditure, one-fourth of it has to be borne by the states. Other Capital intensive projects such as roads take precedence in using up the 40 per cent. Moreover, being demand driven, MGNREGS cannot be converted into a watershed programme even though a watershed approach can and should be mandated for natural resource works under it.
- The 66th National Sample Survey Organization (NSSO) paints a grim picture of low job creations between 2004-05 to 2009-10, drop in labour participation rate (especially rural females) and slow growth of employment in non-agricultural sector. That this decline in rural employment took place in spite of the National Rural Employment Guarantee Act (NREGA) indicates a steep fall in rural work.

IV. A Comparitive Study of Past and Present Scenario and Rural-Urban Disparities

Table 11.1 shows although rural female literacy is increasing, it is less than the urban female literacy in India.

Table 11.1: Female Literacy in India

Year	*Rural (%)*	*Urban (%)*	*Overall (%)*
1961*	10.10	40.50	15.35
1971*	15.50	48.80	21.97
1981*	21.70	56.30	29.76
1991*	30.62	64.05	39.29
2001*	46.58	72.99	54.16
2011**	58.75	79.92	65.46

* Relates to population 5 yrs and above.

** Relates to population 7 yrs and above.

Source: GoI, www.censusindia.net, as on Jan 2012.

Table 11.2: Share of Employment in Various Industries in India in (%)

	Rural 2004-05	*Rural 2009-10*	*Urban 2004-05*	*Urban 2009-10*
Agriculture and allied activities	72.7	67.6	8.8	7.5
Mining	0.5	0.6	0.8	0.6
Manufacturing	8.1	7.2	24.6	23
Construction	4.9	9.4	8	10.2
Electricity, gas and water supply	0.2	0.2	0.7	0.6
Transport, storage and communication	2.5	2.9	8.6	8.7
Public administration and other services	4.5	4.8	18.7	18.5

Source: GoI.

Table 11.2 shows that over the years, farm activities have declined both in rural and urban areas. Rural people have switched to non-farm activities and urban people to construction and transport, storage and communication.

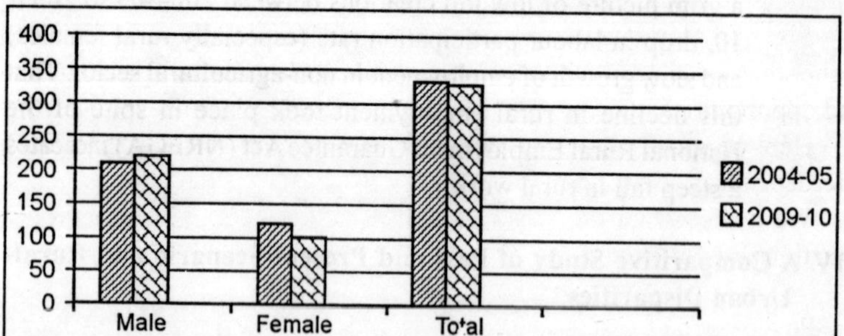

Fig. 11.1: Number of Rural persons in workforce (in million)

Source: Table Sl.1 in indicators of employment and unemployment in India 2009-10, NSSO Publications.

Tables 11.3 and 11.4 show some features of rural-urban disparities on calorie intake at different expenditure level and rural-urban poverty in India. Moreover rural sector's calorie intake is always low except for the expenditure class 255-300 and rural poverty is always higher than urban poverty.

Table 11.3: Calorie Intake at Different Expenditure Level (1999-2000)

Rural			*Urban*		
Expenditure class	*Calorie intake*	*% Expenditure on food*	*Expenditure class*	*Calorie intake*	*% Expenditure on food*
0-225	1383	67%	0-300	1398	64%
225-255	1609	67%	300-350	1654	64%
255-300	1733	66%	350-425	1729	62%
300-340	1868	65%	425-500	1912	60%
340-380	1957	65%	500-575	1968	58%
380-420	2054	64%	575-665	2091	56%
420-470	2173	63%	665-775	2187	54%
470-525	2289	62%	775-915	2297	52%
525-615	2403	60%	915-1120	2467	49%
615-775	2581	58%	1120-1500	2536	45%
775-950	2735	55%	1500-1925	2736	41%
950-more	3778	46%	1925-more	2938	32%

Source: Nutritional Intake in India NSS 55th round. Report No. 471.

The higher the expenditure group the higher the difference between food and non-food consumption as the poorer sections have no other option but to curtail (Table 11.5).

Fig. 11.2 shows that male participation in Rural non-farm sector is higher than the female participation. So, this creates inequality of rights and opportunities.

Here we use econometric tool to see how poverty and education are interdependent.

We demonstrate the structure of the model here. The structural equations are following...

$$\text{Poverty} = \alpha_0 + \alpha_1\text{*education} + \alpha_2\text{*employment level} + \alpha_5\text{*population} + \mu_1$$

$$\text{Education} = \beta_0 + \beta_1\text{*poverty} + \beta_2\text{*income} + \beta_3\text{*government expenditure on education} + \mu_2$$

Table 11.4: Poverty in India

States	*Rural*				*Urban*			
	Official Estimates		*Our Estimates*		*Official Estimates*		*Our Estimates*	
	Poverty line	*Poverty ratio*	*Poverty line*	*Poverty ratio*	*Poverty line*	*Poverty ratio*	*Poverty line*	*Poverty ratio*
A.P.	262.94	10.5	565	89.4	457.40	27.2	775	62.8
Assam	365.43	40.3	675	92.9	343.99	7.5	775	60.0
Bihar	333.07	44.0	470	79.8	379.78	33.5	535	60.2
Gujarat	318.94	12.4	775	86.5	474.41	14.8	775	53.6
Haryana	362.81	7.4	615	47.5	420.20	10.0	847	54.7
H.P.	367.45	7.5	560	44.75	420.20	4.6	575	11.3
Karnataka	309.59	16.8	681	84.6	511.44	24.6	838	58.5
Kerala	374.79	9.4	950	79.6	477.06	19.8	1014	68.6
M.P.	311.34	37.3	497	79.25	481.65	38.5	665	62.1
Maharashtra	318.63	23.2	950	94.9	593.71	26.7	915	62.2
Orissa	323.92	47.8	498	82.9	473.12	43.5	425	34.3
Punjab	362.68	6.0	775	66.6	388.15	5.5	717	46.2
Rajasthan	344.03	13.5	525	55.8	465.92	19.4	620	46.8
Tamil Nadu	307.64	20.0	950	94.5	475.60	22.5	840	58.8
U.P.	336.88	31.1	496	68.5	416.29	30.8	616	59.7
W.Bengal	350.17	31.7	615	85.6	409.22	14.7	621	45.3
Delhi					505.45	9.2	1120	53.6
All India	327.56	27.0	567	74.95	454.11	23.5	718	54.9

Sources: 1. Household Consumer Expenditure in India 1999-2000 Key Results NSS 55th Round, Report No. 454.

2. Nutritional Intake in India 1999-2000. NSS 55th Round, Report No. 471.

There are two endogenous variables i.e. *poverty* and *education*. The exogenous variables are **employment level, population, income, govt. expenditure on education.** Error terms of the equations are μ_1 and μ_2. Here have used the total number of persons below the poverty line as poverty level and total number of literates as education level here for the year 2010-2011.

Both the equations are found to be **over identified.** Since 3SLS is an improvement over OLS and 2SLS so we run 3SLS regression. Moreover, OLS gives inconsistent and biased estimates as this is a simultaneous equation system.

Table 11.5: Consumption Pattern in Rural India

Per capita Monthly Expenditure in Rs.

Item	*Expenditure Groups*	
	300-340	*525-615*
Cereals	99.25	117.77
Gram	0.35	0.79
Cereal substitutes	0.17	0.41
Pulses & their products	14.18	22.12
Milk & Milk products	16.29	57.68
Edible Oils	13.48	21.93
Meat, Fish and eggs	9.54	20.14
Vegetables	23.12	35.43
Fruits (Fresh)	2.75	8.32
Fruits (dry)	0.67	1.65
Sugar	7.33	14.52
Salt	0.93	1.19
Spices	9.86	15.28
Beverages, refreshment	10.02	24.55
All food	**207.94**	**341.79**
Pan	1.57	3.47
Tobacco	5.57	9.01
Intoxicant	2.65	4.23
Fuel & Light	26.23	43.65
Clothing	23.92	39.22
Footwear	2.97	6.3
Misc. Consumer Goods	15.71	30.03
Misc. Consumer Service	12.69	31.66
Rent	0.24	1.58
Taxes and Cesses	0.29	0.91
Education	3.69	10.74
Medical (Institutional)	1.65	7.35
Medical (Non-Instt.)	11.07	25.76
Durable Goods	4.61	10.83
All Non-Food	**112.85**	**224.74**

Source: Household Consumer Expenditure in India 1999-2000 Key Results. NSS 55th Round, Report No. 454.

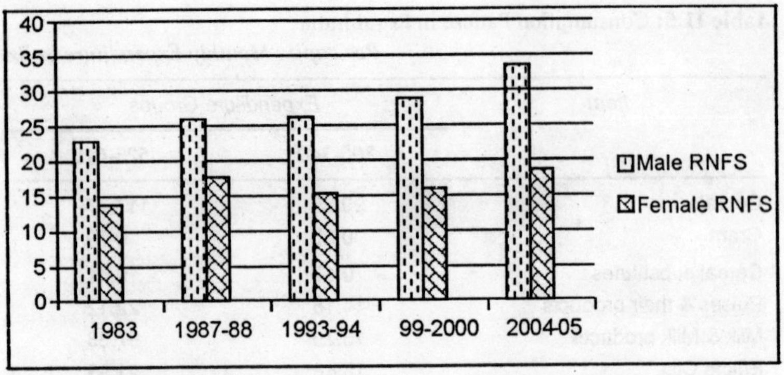

Fig. 11.2: Share of RNFS in Rural India

Stata Command: reg3 (poverty education employment level population) (education poverty income government exp on education).

From this regression table, we get that all variables are significant. They show good results and these are compliant with the theory. The null hypothesis is rejected for all variables and they explain the endogenous variables efficiently.

Three-stage least-squares regression

Equation	*Obs*	*Parms*	*RMSE*	*"R-sq"*	*chi2*	*P*
poverty	18	3	27.5961	0.8646	120.40	0.0000
education	18	3	.3368921	0.9609	450.78	0.0000

	Coef.	*Std. Err.*	*z*	*P>|z|*	*[95% Conf.*	*Interval]*
poverty						
education	-105.3355	28.51649	-3.69	0.000	-161.2268	-49.4442
employment level	-1.161378	.3704475	-3.14	0.002	-1.887442	-.4353142
population	1.418975	.254846	5.57	0.000	.919486	1.918464
_cons	-4.687036	13.31992	-0.35	0.725	-30.79359	21.41952
education						
poverty	.0109072	.0015283	7.14	0.000	.0079117	.0139027
income	.0038089	.0012365	3.08	0.002	.0013853	.0062325
govt exp on education	12.57386	6.357977	1.98	0.048	.1124493	25.03526
_cons	-.355651	.1949965	-1.82	0.068	-.7378371	.026535

Endogenous variables: poverty education
Exogenous variables: employment level population income govtexponeducation

Our analysis from the results have been satisfactory and consistent with the economic theory except for the fact that although education causes poverty but poverty does not cause education i.e. there is a one way causality, which is surprising. However, poverty plays a significant role in the determination of education. Moreover, the other factors namely government expenditure and income were also significant factors in the determination of education. After a thorough study of the results, we conclude that there is a policy implication. Although there should be a negative relationship between education and poverty in the education equation, we get a positive relationship which is attributed to the significant government expenditure on education in the backward areas.

Governments at the lowest levels—in townships and countries—**shouldered the bulk of the financial burden to provide education** for children and adults mostly in the more backward areas.

The factors namely employment level and population are significant factors in the determination of poverty which we get from poverty equation. Moreover, the education factor in the poverty equation has a significant role in determining poverty with a negative relationship with poverty, which is consistent with the economic theory.

We know the **cycle of poverty can be broken through education**. So, the Central and provincial governments should shoulder a bigger share of the financial burden needed to make education truly free, starting with the poorest 10 per cent of school-age kids.

Such a move will help bridge the "education gap", or inequities in education-giving equal access to all children and relieving the poor of the pinch of education cost.

V. Conclusion

Department for International Development (DFID) of United Kingdom has made a substantial contribution in improving the rural livelihoods in India.

According to the UN State of the World Population 2007 Report India's population would be 60 per cent rural in 2030. A 2010 report by McKinsey Global Institute, titled, 'India's Urban Awakening: Building Inclusive Cities, Sustainable Growth', presents a similar prognosis. Rural population would remain very large even when a majority begin to live in cities.

Thus, we can conclude that *"Its not enough, to know, one should also use; its not enough to want, one should also act."*

References

Leach, F. and Sitaram S. (2002). "Microfinance and Women's Empowerment: Lessons from India", *Development in Practice,* 12, 575-588.

Planning Commission *(2012-2017), Final Report of Minor Irrigation and Watershed Management for the Twelfth Five Year Plan,* Government of India, New Delhi.

www.rbi.org.in

www.indiastat.com

SECTION III
Case Studies

12

Rural Livelihoods in India Viewed from the Perspective of Women

Mriduchhanda Chattopadhyay

> "Some historians believe that it was woman who first domesticated crop plants and thereby initiated the art and science of farming. While men went out hunting in search of food, women started gathering seeds from the native flora and began cultivating those of interest from the point of view of food, feed, fodder, fibre and fuel."
>
> —*M.S. Swaminathan*
>
> "Give a man a fish, he'll eat for a day. Give a woman microcredit, she, her husband, her children and her extended family will eat for a lifetime."
>
> — *Bono*

I. Introduction

India forms the largest democracy in the world with population of more than 1.2 billion. Over the last few years, India has successfully been able to integrate herself with the global economy, emerging out as a global player with world's fourth largest economy in PPP terms. India showed an impressive growth rate of 5.4 per cent in the year 2012-13.

In spite of this impressive growth rate, a sharp inequality is observed between urban India and rural India or Bharat, as it is popularly called due to the gap in the standards of living. Agriculture is the main occupation of the people in rural India. Approximately 70 per cent of the households in rural India even today, depend on this sector for their livelihood. The agricultural sector has shown a growth rate of 2.9 per cent in 2012-13, contributing to 14.6 per cent of the country's GDP and 13 per cent of its exports.

Traditionally, women have always played an important role in agriculture. They have shown their expertise not only in crop cultivation but also in other areas like horticulture, livestock rearing and fisheries.

M.S. Swaminathan, the famous agricultural scientist commented, "Some historians believe that it was woman who first domesticated crop plants and thereby initiated the art and science of farming. While men went out hunting in search of food, women started gathering seeds from the native flora and began cultivating those of interest from the point of view of food, feed, fodder, fibre and fuel." In India, in over-all farm production, women's average contribution is 55-66 per cent in 2011-12. (*Data source: Dashora, Kavya: Women Farmers: From Seeds to Kitchen, Infochange News and Features, July 2010*)

Between the time periods, 1970-2012, the GDP share of agriculture has fallen from 43 per cent to 14.6 per cent while that of the service sector has increased by as large as 57.2 per cent. This is largely because of the rapid economic growth in services, industrial output and non-agricultural sectors in India between 2000-2010. With the declining agricultural sector, India had witnessed rapid migration of people (mainly men) from rural to urban India in search of jobs, higher wages and better opportunities in the service and industrial sector. According to 2001 census data, rural to urban migration had been 20.5 million. As a result of this, the proportion of women working in agricultural sector has increased to 78 per cent while that of men has fallen to 58 per cent over the years. (*Data source: Dashora, Kavya: Women Farmers: From Seeds to Kitchen, Infochange News and Features, July 2010*)

Moreover, in the present days, in many parts of rural India, women have been mobilized to form small self-help groups for savings and credit for improving the economic conditions of women and boosting their self-confidence.

With men moving to urban India for higher-paid jobs and better social security, the future of Bharat lies mainly in the hands of the women who have now started to take part in rural credit market to gain economic independence.

II. Feminization of Agriculture

Participation of women in Agriculture

According to Lastarria-Cornhiel's article "Feminization of Agriculture:

Trends and Driving Forces", feminisation of agriculture refers to women's increasing participation in the agricultural labour force (that might include their participation as independent producers, or as unpaid family workers, or as agricultural wage-earners). Feminisation of agriculture basically entails the following:

1. An increase in women's participation rates in the agricultural sector, either as self-employed or as agricultural wage workers; in other words, an increase in the percentage of women who are economically active in rural areas.
2. An increase in the percentage of women in the agricultural labour force relative to men, either because more women are working and/or because fewer men are working in agriculture.

Table 12.1 shows the increase in participation of women in agriculture and thus we can comment that India in the recent years have witnessed feminization of agriculture.

Table 12.1: Percentage Distribution of Workers (main + marginal) According Categories of worker by Sex in Rural Areas during 2001 for India

Categories	*Rural*		
	Female	*Male*	*Total*
Cultivators	36.46	42.19	40.14
Agricultural Labours	43.4	27.48	33.20
Industry and other Workers	14.70	27.49	22.90
Household Workers	5.44	2.83	3.77
All workers	100	100	100
Total workers (main+ marginal in millions)	111.46	199.20	310.66

Source: The National Commission for Women Report (2005): Impact of WTO Women in Agriculture.

Women have always been active participants in agriculture as farmers, co-farmers, family labourers, wage labourers and managers of farms in India. The selection, preservation and maintenance, the development and sharing of seeds-stocks have been under the female control for long.

In India, in agriculture sector, a man works for 1212 hours and a woman works for 3485 hours on an average in a year on a one hectare farm, a figure that illustrates women's significant contribution to agriculture (*Data source: Dashora, Kavya: Women Farmers: From Seeds to Kitchen, Infochange News and Features, July 2010*).

However, the agricultural sector data hides the actual picture of variation of male-female distribution in that sector. The female work participation rate varies across states, districts, villages and even across different groups and families. A variety of factors determine the women work participation rate in agriculture. Some of them being are the nature of crops grown (women participate more in food crop production), type of crops grown, availability of the scope of irrigation, technological equipments available in the farm, various socio-economic and political reasons like poverty, backwardness of the place, conservativeness of the family, social class, social and cultural norms.

Data of fifteen Indian states regarding female work participation rate has been calculated and the states are classified into two groups on the basis of the female work participation rate (WPR) and the incidence of female casual labour in agriculture. In group-1, the states included are Himachal Pradesh, Andhra Pradesh, Tamil Nadu, Karnataka, Maharashtra, Gujarat, Rajasthan and Madhya Pradesh. These states show a considerably high WPR over the years. Except, Himachal Pradesh and Rajasthan, these states show a high incidence of female casual labour. For Himachal Pradesh and Rajasthan, the rates are relatively lower (2% and 12% respectively). In group-2, the states included are West Bengal, Bihar, Uttar Pradesh, Kerala, Punjab, Haryana and Orissa. These states show a low female WPR. However, the bulk of women in agriculture in these states are quite high. The figures are the following: Haryana (91%), Punjab (90%), UP (87%), Bihar (86%). Except West Bengal and Kerala, the other states have a moderately high incidence of female casual labour. The incidence of female casual labour for WB and Kerala are 59 per cent and 57 per cent respectively. However, the north-eastern states like Arunachal Pradesh, Mizoram, and Manipur show a high WPR but low incidence of female casual labour (4-5%).

Hardships Faced

Despite their importance to agricultural production, women face severe hardships and problems in their daily life. They face meagre wage, long hours of strenuous and hazardous work and even sexual harassment. They do not get any medical help when ill and maternity leave or recuperation period after child birth. In fact, they are the largest group of landless labourers with little real security in case of break-up of the family owing to death or divorce; inheritance laws and customs usually gives verdict against them, land reform and settlement programmes usually give sole title and hence the security needed for obtaining production credits to the husband or the brothers. Agricultural development programmes are usually made by the men and for the men.

Gender-wise Wage Disparity in Agricultural Sector

There is also a discrimination of wages between a male and a female worker. Women are preferred as agricultural workers because the farmer is faced with the increasing costs of production required for modern agriculture which can be cut down by employing lower-paid women workers. Chart 12.1 gives a glimpse of the disparity of male-female daily wage rates.

It is quite clear from the chart with aggregate data from the 2001 census women gets much lower wage than men in India. In Mizoram a female agricultural worker gets Rs. 66.24 per day (the highest daily wage given to any female worker among the other states in India) while the daily wage rate of the male in the same state is Rs. 97.77. In India, the highest daily wage rate of a male worker is Rs. 100.78 in Kerala while in the same state, a female gets only Rs. 56.65. The difference in male-female wage rate is highest in Kerala. This picture is quite shocking in contrast to the picture of Kerala where the women show high literacy rate and the man-women ratio is high. The lowest daily wage given to a female agricultural worker in India is Rs. 23.34 (Orissa) while the lowest daily wage given to a male is Rs. 30.15 (Madhya Pradesh).

Gender-wise Decision Making Disparity in Agricultural Sector

Another important thing that is to be mentioned here is that rural women efficiently carry out their dual responsibilities within and outside the home. In rural India, the prosperity of the household depends on the prosperity of agriculture and allied occupation in any particular point of time *vis-à-vis* the role of women in innumerable activities connected to farming, dairying, sericulture etc. However, the women hands are invisible even to this day, so it is not surprising that the agricultural extension activities are still mainly a male oriented pursuit.

Though women take part in agricultural activities more than the men, the decision making power is still in the men's hand. This is mainly due to the mindset of the people. Generally, women have less access to

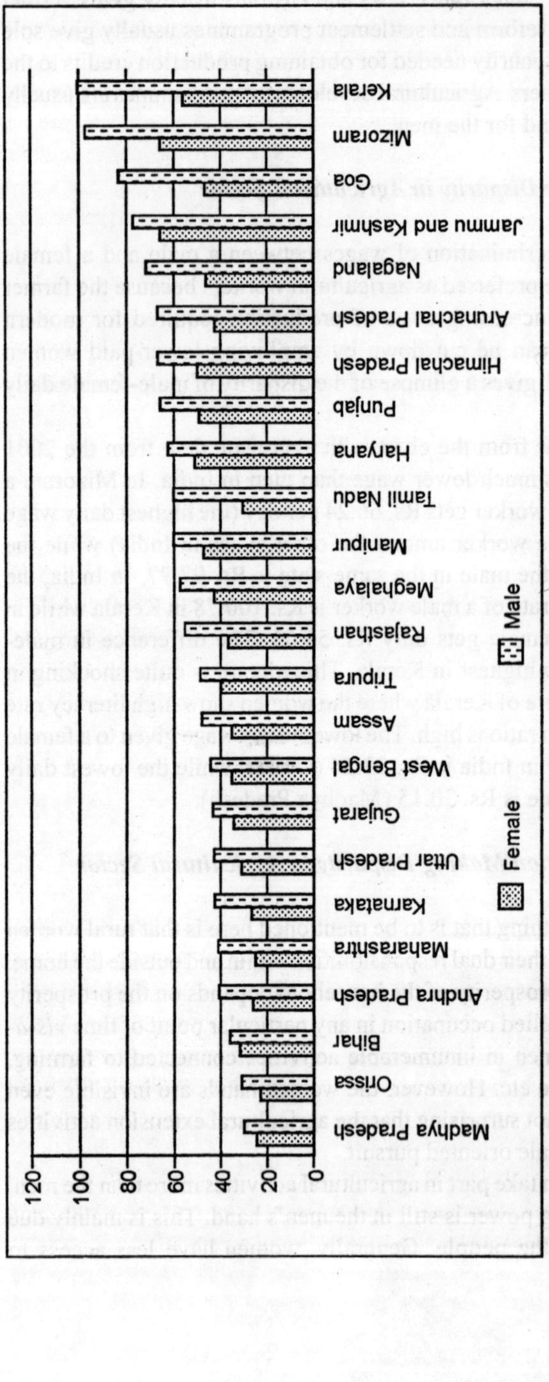

Chart 12.1: Wage Differentials between Male and Female workers in Indian States

Source: Vepa, S.S (2005): Feminisation of Agriculture and Marginalisation of their Economic Stake, *Economic Political Weekly* (June 18 2005).

information about technology as lack of proper education and relative isolation from public life. Thus, they feel a constant hesitation to come out, interact and express their decisions. Even, there are instances where the suggestions of knowledgeable rural women are ignored or are not taken seriously because men consider it disgraceful to accept the decision of women. This is because traditionally men have been the major lawmakers of the society. Many policies and decisions neglect women and undermine their abilities and roles.

Table 12.2 gives an idea of the domination of male in decision making in agricultural activities in rural India.

Table 12.2: Decision-Making in Agricultural Activities

	Male (%)	*Female (%)*	*Male + Female (%)*
Purchase of fertilisers	90.2	2.9	6.8
Purchase of animals	93.1	—	6.8
Purchase of agricultural equipments	92.1	1.9	5.8
Changing of crops	96.0	—	3.9
Selling of products	83.9	10.7	5.3

Source: The National Commission for Women Report (2005): Impact of WTO women in agriculture.

This table shows the clear picture of gender-wise disparity in decision-making in agricultural sector.

III. Feminization of Poverty

By, the late 1980s, international institutions like the World Bank had argued that women are more vulnerable to the extremes of poverty. However, empirical results from Africa and Latin America had proven this argument wrong. Women become the heads of households legally due to demise, dissertation or divorces of their husbands or the acting heads due to migration of men. According to 55th of National Sample Survey (NSSO, 2001), the proportion of female-headed households increased from 9.7 per cent in 1993-94 to 10.4 per cent in 1999-2000. 27.8 per cent households indicated that one male and one female member were usually employed. Of the female households 22.8 per cent reported that none of their family member was actually employed and 39.6 per cent mentioned that only one female member was actually working. (*Data source: The National Commission for Women Report* (2005): *Agriculture sector in India*). These households were found to be among the poorest.

So, measures to enable women's access to resources were recommended to be the surest way to eradicate poverty for women.

Several poverty eradication programmes were launched by the Government of India during the Fifth and Sixth Plan period (1974-78 and 1980-85) and are being launched even in the present days. These factored in women in various ways—some were designed with particular attention to women such as IRDP (1978), some with minimum quota such as TRYSEM (1979), Swarnajayanti Gram Swarojgar Yojana (1999) and some were targeted exclusively for women such as Rashtriya Mahila Kosh (1993). These schemes were designed to look after the empowerment of women and unlike other schemes, they treat women as active participants of economic activities and these schemes were designed in such a way that it keeps gender equality in mind in terms of wages and employment, at least theoretically. MGNREGS talks about equal wages to both male and female. However, when it comes for application of schemes in the practical sense, the curse of gender imbalance creeps in.

IV. Women's Participation in Micro-Finance

Women in rural India generally do not get access to formal education and hence do not get knowledge about the outer world. However, their livelihoods and empirical knowledge helps them to realise their deteriorating situation both economically and socially. They know that they are the victims of different social malpractices like dowry, child marriages which would lead to early motherhood. Their financial dependence and hesitance have made them the constant victim of male domination which they cannot fight back.

With the inspiration and knowledge from the different NGOs and other organisations, the women of rural India have realised that micro-finance could be a way out of their age-old problem of financial dependence and they form the self-help group to enjoy the collective benefit and support from the group in their everyday life. They have realised that this would give them a platform to realise their own selves and an opportunity to lead a better life, to use the locally available resources, to get economic independence and develop the habit of savings that would in turn help their households as well as to have a good relation with the neighbours and fellow group-members so that they can fight their challenges and problems together.

Micro-credit movement had started in India through the formation of self help groups (SHG hereafter) that work with the principles of self help and mutual help during 1990s. Prior to micro-finance and SHG were the Kisaan Credit Card schemes however, those were meant only for agricultural purposes. MF and SHGs show a much wide spectrum for credit in comparison to the KCC scheme. NABARD annual report of 2010 shows the fact that in 1998-99, 0.78 million of KCC were issued but the number of KCC issued had sharply decreased to 31.64 lakhs in 2009-10. This decline is mainly due to the strong emergence and establishment of micro-finance and micro-credit sector.

A SHG is a group of about 20 persons (generally women) who have volunteered to build up a common fund of resources (from where they can take loans when required) by contributing something and had come forward in their struggle to lead a better life. As they become accustomed in handling money, the Bank-credit linkage enables them to get credit from formal banking sectors (without any collateral and market rates of interest) and further scale up their common fund size. SHG had emerged out as way to provide credit on easy terms in rural India. Apart from finance, these SHGs provide a platform for the women to identify their potential and become self sufficient to face the challenges and hardships of life with confidence. It had given them the chance to live life on their own terms and have some social mobility. This has also given them the opportunity to fulfil their basic needs of consumption and production. According to a report giving the status of micro-finance in India, in 2009-10, there are 69.5 lakh savings linked SHGs and 48.5 lakh credit linked SHGs covering a household of about 9.7 crores had been observed. The increased number of SHG reflects the relevance of micro-finance as a tool of poverty alleviation, employment generation and women empowerment in rural India.

Now, credit is necessary for any economic activity. The participants of the SHG should have the awareness and proper knowledge about the availability of credit and proper utilisation. Different organisations (mostly NGOs e.g. Grama Vikas in Karnataka) have come forward to impart these knowledge to the rural women.

The group members make some common law and rules for the group which each member should follow. After the formation of group, the group members open an account in nearby banks where they can make regular contribution and build up a common fund. Group meetings generally take place at regular intervals. The group members generally are present regularly; however, if anybody fails to report, then the serious reasons are accepted for the absentee. The groups generally keep a systematic record of all the transactions of the groups, the contributions made to the common pool of resource and loans taken. Peer pressure ensures timely repayment of the loans. The financial discipline and the rules adopted by the members of the groups helps them to learn how to handle pools of fund that are much beyond their individual capacity.

Once the SHG members show mature financial behaviour by appreciating that resources are limited and have a cost associated with it, the formal banking sectors are willing to give them loans in certain multiples of their accumulated savings. Often, the formal banking sectors give them loans at the market rate of interest and without any collateral. Thus, these SHGs help the women to get rid of the malpractices of the informal money-lenders and the problems of not being able to access the formal banking sector due to lack of bank-acceptable assets.

NABARD in association with different government and non-government agencies are trying to upgrade the SHG-bank linkage programme to enable the rural poor to access the credit through formal agencies. This programme brings benefit to the bank as well. The banks will be able to provide credit to the poorest families of rural India but this programme will help them to reduce their transaction cost and risk cost in delivering small loans. Table 12.3 shows the number of SHG-bank linkage in the financial report 2010-11.

Table 12.3: An Overview of the SHG-bank Linkage in 2010-11

Sl. No.	Items	Physical amount (no. in lakhs)	Financial amount (Rupees, crores)
1.	Total SHG linked with banks	74.62	7016.30
2.	Total SHG linked with banks that are exclusively run by women	60.98	5298.64
3.	Total SHG credit linked with banks	11.96	14547.73
4.	Total SHG credit linked with banks that are exclusively run by women	10.17	12622.33

Source: *NABARD annual report (2011): Status of Micro-finance in India, 2010-11.*

These data clearly interprets how much the once "dominated" women of rural India are willing to form SHG and gain financial independence and stability.

V. Conclusion

Thus, in conclusion we can say that the women who are the age-old victim of male domination even if, they take part actively in agriculture and poverty alleviation, have been able to gain some financial independence via micro-finance. Micro-finance also has helped them to realise their hidden potential, break-free from the confined four walls of their dwellings and live their life in their own terms.

References

Dashora, K. (2010): "Women Farmers: From Seeds to Kitchen", *Infochange News and Features.*

Hemalatha, A.V. (2011): "Micro-finance for Poor Women: A Study of Self-Help Groups in Kerala", *Financial Inclusion and Inclusive Growth: Scope and Dimensions.*

Lastarria-Cornhiel, S. (2006): *Feminization of Agriculture: Trends and Driving Forces*, November 2006, Version-1.

NABARD (2011): "Status of Micro-finance in India", *Annual Report 2010-11.*

The National Commission for Women (2005): "Impact of WTO women in agriculture", *Annual Report.*

Vepa, S.S. (2005): "Feminisation of Agriculture and Marginalisation of Their Economic Stake", *Economic Political Weekly,* July 18, 2005.

www.wikipedia.com//:microfinance

www.wikipedia.com//:self-help groups

13

Dalits and Rural Livelihoods in India

Shilpi Majumder

"Indians today are governed by two different ideologies. Their political ideal set in the Preamble of the Constitution affirms a life of Liberty, Equality and Fraternity. Their social ideal embodied in their religion denies them." —*Dr. B.R. Ambedkar*

"I do not want to be reborn. But if I have to be reborn, I should be born an untouchable, so, that I may share their sorrows, sufferings and the affronts levelled at them, in order that I may endeavour to free myself and them from that miserable condition. I, therefore prayed that, if I should be born again, I should do so not as a Brahmin, Kshatriya, Vaishya or Shudra, but as an Atishudra". —*The Mind of Mahatma Gandhi*

"*Swaraj* is a meaningless term, if we desire to keep a fifth of India under perpetual subjection and deliberately deny to them the fruits of national culture. We are seeking the aid of god in this great purifying movement, but we deny to the most deserving among his creatures the rights of humanity. Inhuman ourselves we may not plead before the throne for deliverance from the inhumanity of others". —*The Mind of Mahatma Gandhi*

1. Introduction

1.1 The Historical Background

Sixty five years later, India still witnesses the similar contradictions of the socio-economic order. The first 14 years of the 21st century have passed but India is yet to resolve its contradictions. In spite of the constitutional commitment of the post-colonial state towards the goal of equality, liberty and justice the age old structure of inequality has not been dismantled. Social and economic inequality still is the centre of attraction and requires great concern. A vast section of the Indian population is deprived socially, economically, politically and educationally. The ideals of social democracy and distributive justice remain unidentifiable. The various social opportunities offered by the state are confined to the privileged sections of the society and the deprived and disadvantaged are still exposed to the vast and cumulative inequality.

Socio-economic inequality is not the only problem which the unprivileged sections of the Indian population face. They are also subjected to caste discrimination. The English word 'caste' has been derived from the Portuguese word 'Casta' means 'Race'. This word seems to have applied to India by the Portuguese in the middle of the 15th century. The first literary traces of caste system were found in *Rig Veda* and *Purushasukta* hymn. In *Bhagavad Gita*, caste system is sought to be justified on the basis of the idea of *Guna Karma* (deed) and *Dharma* (religion). In the age of *Smritis* and *Sutras* the society had been divided into various castes. They had framed strict rules regarding the occupation, food conduct and marriage which were mandatory. During that period these castes became so diversified that they could not come together in the due course of time. That also gave rise to the feeling of untouchability.

"Caste" is a term which is used to specify a group of people having a specific social rank. The Indian term for caste is *jati*, and it resembles a group that can vary in size from a handful to many thousands. Each *jati* has its own rules and customs and according to the tradition were arranged in a hierarchical order to fit into one of the four basic *varnas*[1]—

- Brahmans, commonly identified with priests and learned class.
- Kshatriyas, associated with rulers and warriors including property owners.
- Vaishyas, associated with commercial livelihoods (traders).
- Shudras, the menial labours.

Another category of people whose position are not clearly defined and are kept out of the Varna scheme are the "untouchables". Their jobs cause them to be considered as impure and thus untouchable. They were not permitted to enter the temples and other public places and were not allowed to attend any kind of public meetings. In 1950, legislation was passed to prevent any kind of discrimination towards the untouchables but the practice is still visible in considerable parts of the Indian society.

Initially caste system had formed the social and economic framework for the life of the people in India and now in its essential form, caste as the system of social and economic governance is based on certain rules:

- Division of people into social groups where rights assigned would be determined by birth and are fixed and hereditary.
- The basic rights assigned among various castes is unequal and hierarchical, with those at the top enjoying more rights coupled with less duties to perform and those at the bottom have to perform more duties with no rights to enjoy.
- The system is maintained through rigid enforcement of social ostracism[2] in case of any deviations.

The United Nations defines the above problem as the "Discrimination on the basis of work and descents". It is a traditional form of oppressed, hierarchical social organisation that arranged people according to their family of birth. Despite its legal abolition, this problem still persists in the Indian economy because of its religious sanction, the social and economic persecution of those who broke caste 'rules' and segregation between castes. Caste system continues in its both traditional rural forms of physical and occupational segregation and economic exploitation, in access to land and criminal justice, in modern Indian schools and universities, in marriage and dining and in access to new employment opportunities.

Dr. B.R. Ambedkar, who is accredited with framing the Indian constitution and also a great and enlightened founder of independent India, was himself an 'untouchable'. He also wrote extensively on 'caste' and gave in to Mahatma Gandhi's pleas that 'untouchables' should not break away from the rest of the Hindus but remain united in the freedom struggle. Because of Dr. Ambedkar's strong emphasis, Mahatma Gandhi's moral indignation against caste system and the modernizing zeal of the freedom fighters, discrimination on the basis of caste is illegal and is a punishable offence. The parliament and the various state legislative assemblies have reserved constituencies for their political representation and there are seats reserved in educational institutions and in government offices for members of these communities. According to Gandhi, "it is wrong to destroy caste because of the outcaste, as it would be to destroy a body because of an ugly growth in it or a crop because of weeds. The outcasteness, in the sense we understand it, has therefore to be destroyed altogether. It is the excess to be removed if the whole system is not to perish. Untouchability is the product therefore not of the caste system but of the distinction of high and low that has crept into Hinduism and is corroding it. The attack on untouchability is therefore an attack on the 'high-and-low'-ness. The moment untouchability goes caste system itself will be purified, that is to say, it will purify it to my dream of *varna-dharma*, the four divisions of the society each complementary of the other and none inferior or superior to any other each as necessary for the whole body of Hinduism as any other".

Caste discrimination however continues to be a social evil experienced everyday in several covert forms. The British listed the untouchables as the 'Scheduled Castes' and this nomenclature remains the official one till date. Mahatma Gandhi in order to remove the social stigma of untouchability coined the term '*Harijans*' which has now been rejected in favour of the term '*Dalits*'.

Poor people identified as *Dalits* are refused housing in communities dominated by upper castes, in urban areas. Also in rural areas they suffer the most. The status of *Dalits* has often been associated with occupations regarded as ritually impure. Engaging in those activities was considered to be polluting the individual and this pollution was considered contagious. *Dalits* were commonly segregated and banned from participating in Hindu social life and were expected to be submissive. Minimum wages established by law were rarely paid. Bonded labours and most of the out of school working children were more often *Dalits*. They have historically been poor, deprived of basic human rights and treated as social inferiors in India. They are subjected to economic, social, cultural and political discrimination in the name of caste. This hidden apartheid has perpetuated discrimination and denial of their human rights and as a result *Dalits* not only represent a disproportionate amount of poor in India but it also creates numerous obstacles that hinder their ability to change their situation.

1.2 Caste System and Dalits

The social structure of India is unique because of its caste structure. Several social scientists have put in lot of effort in studying the Indian social system. Many social reformers, political and social scientists have expressed their concern over the increasing influence of caste on politics and many other spheres of life. Despite their efforts, the social scientists are far from providing a definition to this Indian caste system. The *Varna* model provides a framework within which the innumerable variations of caste throughout India are found. Each caste is ranked higher or lower on the basis of ritual purity. Member of the higher castes on the whole tend to be more prosperous than member of the lower ranking castes. Tradionally castes were associated with an occupation such as high-ranking Brahmins, middle ranking farmers and artisan groups and low ranking *Dalits*. All these low ranking jobs were low paid and therefore many lower caste people living in conditions of poverty and social disadvantage.

One needs to understand the caste system, which controls and regulates the social, political, economical and religious life in India, in order to explain the Indian reality. Social and racial differences do exist in some forms or the other in different parts of the world but the kind of discrimination found in India, which is characterized by features like complexity, elaboration and rigidity is unique. The classification of the Indian population into groups is determined by birth. With the birth of an individual his status in society is determined by which caste he/she is born into. The reason that could be identified for the permanence of the caste system in India is the unity of social and religious rules. Initially, caste system was apparently an arrangement for the peaceful co-existence of several clans, tribes or other social groups. But as the time passed it developed rigidity and castes and communities multiplied themselves on the basis of occupation and other considerations. Another point that makes caste system significant is that it is linked with various aspects of an individual's life, that is, economical, political, religious, legal and moral.

Dalits were assigned the duties to serve three other *Varnas*, thus, they were deprived of higher training and social status. At the beginning, the caste system was merely based upon the division of labour for the purpose of fixing responsibility and duty, but with the passage of time it degenerated into pathogenic affairs where occupations changed into castes. It was believed that *Dalits* are part of the lowest of low Varnas. And thus for centuries *Dalits* were positioned at the bottom of the rigid Indian cast society.

People belonging to other castes who considered themselves to be superior, believed that *Dalits* were impure by birth and that their touch and presence could be polluting. For centuries *Dalits* were excluded from the mainstream society and were only allowed to perform menial occupations. They were discriminated in every sense. They did not have geographical isolation like the tribes, had to serve all classes of people around them and had to do all sorts of demeaning and stigmatized jobs and were also barred from entering the society in every sense. The road to knowledge for the *Dalits* was closed and so these castes remained socially, economically and politically backward. For years, *Dalits* suffered from social injustices and exploitations. They were denied entry into several occupations which were relatively cleaner. The *Dalits* suffered oppression at the hands of the upper castes for centuries, their economic condition remained poor, they were educationally backward and they lacked political skills to hold their own self against the upper caste leadership of the country. Charts 13.1 and 13.2 show the states with the highest percentage and highest number of Scheduled Caste people.

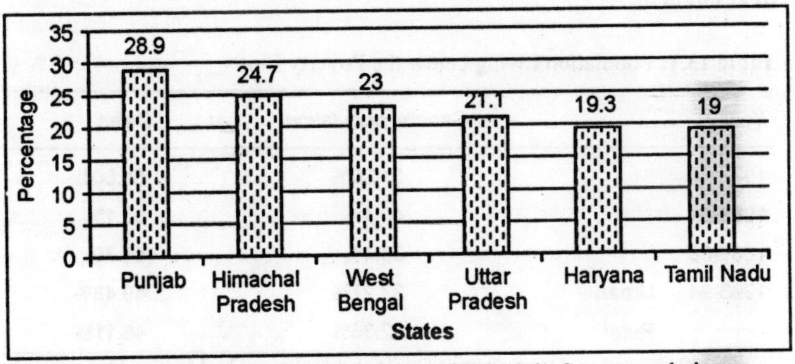

Chart 13.1: States with highest percentage of Schedule Caste population

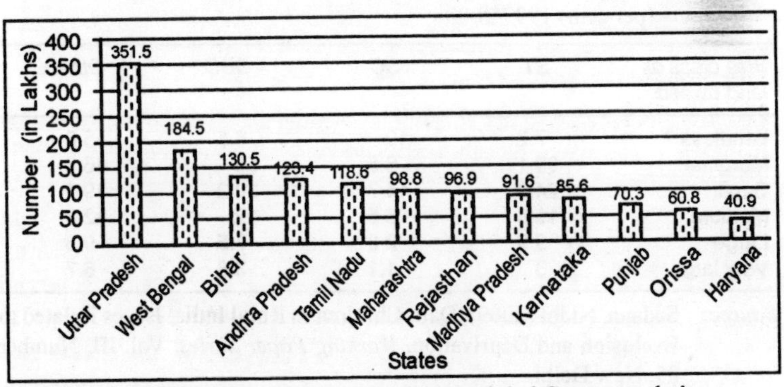

Chart 13.2: States with highest number of Scheduled Caste population.

We now move on to the next discussion which is the Millennium Dvelopment Goals and the *Dalits*.

2. The Millennium Development Goals and the Dalits

A significant observation regarding the implementation of the MDGs at the global level is that even in countries that have been most successful in the implementation of MDGs, specific sections of the population have been excluded or left behind. It is true for India more than any other country, especially related to the plight of the *Dalits*.

Ranging from the reports by the National SC/ST Commission and the Black Paper brought out by the National Campaign for Dalit Human Rights, there have been number of studies to prove that, in this country, Dalits have tended to be excluded and left behind other sections of population in literally every sense, that is, dimension of human and social development.

Table 13.1: Population Living below the Poverty Line

Year		*General population*	*Dalits*
1977-78		51.20%	64.60%
1983-84		40.4%	53.1%
1987-88		33.4%	44.7%
1993-94	Urban	37.27%	49.48%
	Rural	32.36%	48.11%

Source: "Millennium Development Goals and *Dalits*—The Missing Dimension".

Table 13.2: Land Owned by Size Class Across Social Groups in Rural India (per cent) 1999/2000

Size class of land owned	*ST*	*SC*	*OBC*	*Others*
Landless	7.2	10	6.5	5.8
Marginal	39.1	6.5	50	46.3
Small	24.3	14.7	20.2	19.1
Medium	16.5	6.5	12	12.8
Large	9.9	2.8	7.5	9.3
Very large	3	1.1	3.8	6.7

Source: Sadana, Nidhi (2009), Dalit Children in Rural India: Issues Related to Exclusion and Deprivation, *Working Paper Series,* Vol. III, Number 05, New Delhi.

- The percentage of Dalits below the poverty line in 1993-94

(49.48% in urban and 48.11% in rural areas) is an increase over that of 1987-88 (44.70%) is alarming.

- Above 50 per cent of Dalits in rural as well as urban areas live below the poverty line.
- In the year 1991, nearly 13.34 per cent of SC households were landless and 72.91 per cent were near landless. However, the year 2000 saw a decline and was 10 per cent. According to the Agricultural census of 1995-96 the bottom 61.6 per cent of operational holdings accounted for only 17.2 per cent of the total operated land area. On the other hand, the top 7.3 per cent of operational holdings accounted for 40.1 per cent of the total operated area.
- The high incidence of landlessness and near landlessness among SC candidates creates an enormously high proportion of wage labour households as was the case in 1987-88, when of the total of SC rural households, 63.14 per cent were wage labour households.
- In the year 2000, about 28 per cent of the SC households in rural areas had acquired access to fixed capital assets (agricultural land and non-land assets), this was half compared to the 56 per cent of the non SC/ST households who had some access to the fixed capital assets. In the urban areas this proportion was 27 per cent for the SCs and 35.5 per cent for others.

Table 13.3: Monthly Per Capita Consumption Expenditure (Rs.)

	Year	*Dalits*	*Non-dalits*
RURAL	1983-84	87	112
	1987-88	133	169
URBAN	1983-84	128	165
	1987-88	185	256

Source: "Millennium Development Goals and *Dalits*—The Missing Dimension".

- The difference between SCs and others in both rural and urban areas is very alarming and this difference increased from the year 1983-84 to 1987-88.
- 57.5 per cent of *Dalit* children whose age were 4 years or below were undernourished in the year 1992.
- In the year 2000 as against the national average of Rs. 4485, the per capita income of SCs was Rs. 3237. The average weekly

wage earning of an SC worker was Rs. 174.50 compared to Rs. 197.05 for other non-SC/ST workers.

Table 13.4(a): Health Status Indicator for Children in Rural Areas (1998-1999)

Health Status Indicator	*Dalits*	*Tribes*	*OBC*	*Others*	*All*
Infant Mortality Rate	88.1	86.9	82.2	69.3	73
Neo-Natal Mortality	56.2	55.1	54.7	45.1	—
Post Neo-Natal Mortality Rates	31.9	31.8	27.6	24.2	—
Child Mortality Rates	43	48.8	32.7	25.6	31
Under Five Mortality Rates	127.3	131.4	112.2	93.1	101

Source: Sadana, Nidhi (2009), Dalit Children in Rural India: Issues Related to Exclusion and Deprivation, *Working Paper Series*, Vol. III, Number 05, New Delhi.

Mortality is an important indicator of health status. Infant mortality rate for the *Dalit* children is as high as 88 per 1000 as compared to children from other social groups. In 1992-93, the Infant Mortality Rate among SCs was 91 per thousand live births. Infant Mortality Rate (IMR) for *Dalits* is higher than that of the STs and OBCs, while others have the least IMR. High infant/children mortality rate in *Dalit* population indicate low infant survival which is dependent on other factors related to care at birth some of which are place of delivery, type of assistance provided, major illnesses like pneumonia, fever, diarrhoea and the most important of all access to immunization. About 81 per cent of the births occurring to *Dalit* women and 86 per cent of the births occurring to the tribal women takes place at home while the corresponding for the 'other' social group is 70 per cent. Of the total deliveries of *Dalit* and tribal women that take place at home, about 47 per cent of them are attended by *dais*, traditional birth midwives attendants or while those attended by trained doctors and nurses are low. Also the percentage of *Dalits* and tribal women receiving vaccination was low.

Table 13.4(b): Death Rate

	Rural	*Urban*
Dalits	15.50%	12.90%
Non-Dalits	11.20%	8.40%

Source: "Millennium Development Goals and *Dalits*—The Missing Dimension".

Table 13.5(a): Literacy Rates and Level of Education by Social Groups (1999/2000)

Literacy level	*ST*		*SC*		*OBC*		*Others*	
	Male	*Female*	*Male*	*Female*	*Male*	*Female*	*Male*	*Female*
Illiterate	52.3	77.1	47.5	75.5	47.5	67.5	24	50.6
Literate up to Primary	23.9	13.3	25	13.5	27.1	16.9	26.1	22.4
Middle	12.9	5.4	14.8	6.8	18.1	9.2	21.2	13.8
Secondary	6	2.4	7.3	7.3	10.3	4.3	15.2	8.2
Higher Secondary	3.4	1.3	3.3	1	4.6	1.5	7.5	3.3
Graduate and Above	5.1	0.3	2	0.4	2.4	0.7	5.9	1.7

Source: Sadana, Nidhi (2009), *Dalit* Children in Rural India: Issues Related to Exclusion and Deprivation, *Working Paper Series*, Vol. III, Number 05, New Delhi.

Table 13.5(b): Literacy Gaps Between *Dalits* and Non-*Dalits*

Year	*Gaps (%)*
1961	17.59
1971	19.13
1981	19.84
1991	17.2

Source: "Millennium Development Goals and *Dalits*—The Missing Dimension".

- Only one-third of the SC candidates are literate.
- In the year 1993 enrolment at the primary level among SC candidates was 16.2 per cent while among non-SCs it was 83.8 per cent
- The national dropout rate among *Dalit* children is 49.35 per cent at primary and 67.77 per cent at middle and 77.65 per cent at secondary level.
- In the year 2001, the literacy rates among SC candidates was 54.7 per cent and among STs it was 47.1 per cent against 68.8 per cent for others. Among women it was 41.9 per cent for SCs, 34.8 per cent for STs against 58.2 per cent for others.

Table 13.6(a): Gender Inequality: sex ratio per 1000 males

Dalits	922
General population	944

Source: MDGs and *Dalits*—The Missing Dimensions.

Table 13.6(b): Female Literacy Gaps

Year	*All-India Total*	*All-India Female*	*Dalit Female*
1961	24.02	12.95	3.29
1971	29.46	18.72	6.44
1981	43.67	29.85	10.93
1991	52.21	39.29	23.76

Source: "Millennium Development Goals and *Dalits*—The Missing Dimension".

- According to the 1991 census, illiteracy rate of the SC women was 76.24 per cent and that of the general population was 47.79 per cent.
- The dropout rates of the SC females were always higher than that of either the SC boys or the general female population.
- The school attendance was 10 per cent less for SC boys than other boys and about 5 per cent less for SC girls than other girls.

Table 13.7: Sources of Drinking Water by Social Groups in Rural Areas (%)

Source of drinking water	*SC*	*ST*	*OBC*	*Other*	*All*
Piped water	7.8	8.45	11.08	16.85	12.18
Hand pump	50.47	29.61	41.78	41.19	41.38
Public tap	16.65	16.53	16.68	12.8	15.25
Well water	20.59	29.93	26.37	22.31	24.36
Surface water	4.49	15.48	4.1	6.85	6.83

Source: Sadana, Nidhi (2009), *Dalit* Children in Rural India: Issues Related to Exclusion and Deprivation, *Working Paper Series*, Vol. III, Number 05, New Delhi.

- The extent of SC population receiving the provision of drinking water has been the least (77.54%). Or in other words more than 20 per cent of the SC population does not have access to safe drinking water.
- Near about 70 per cent of *Dalits* households have no electricity and 90 per cent have no sanitation. Rural SC households are even more deprived of these basic amenities. Around 78 per cent of them have no electricity and more than 90 per cent have no sanitation facilities.

Over the period since the early 1990s, when the reforms regime overtook the Indian socio-economic scenario, the gaps between *Dalits* and Non-*Dalits* in all dimensions of social development have grown. One with regard to all the 8 goals, 18 targets and 48 indicators of the MDG's can say that *Dalits* have lagged behind and have been excluded. Almost every socio-economic indicator shows that the position of Scheduled Caste families is awful. Some of the socio-economic indicators for the year 2000 have been shown in Table 13.8.

Table 13.8: Socio-economic indicators for the year 2000

Socio- economic indicators	*Percentages*
Landless or near landless	75
Fixed capital assets	28
Agricultural labour	49.06
Child labour	40
Poverty	35.4
Unemployment	5
Reservation of government posts	15
Literacy rate	54.7
Sanitation	11
Electricity	28

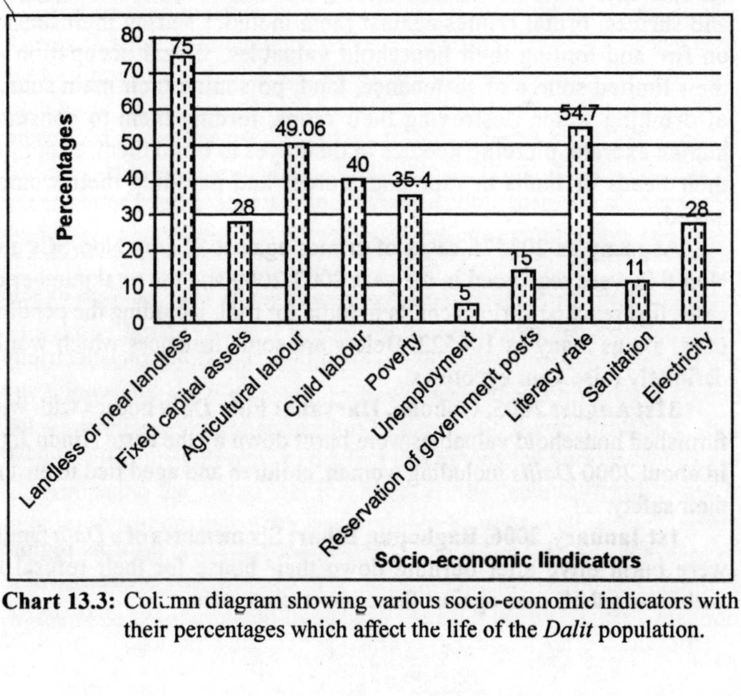

Chart 13.3: Column diagram showing various socio-economic indicators with their percentages which affect the life of the *Dalit* population.

We now move on to the next discussion which is on Crimes against *Dalits*.

3. Crimes Against Dalits

One of the important steps that independent India took was to implement special laws to protect the rights and dignity of *Dalits*. It has been more than sixty years of implementation of such laws and many developmental measures but the atrocities against *Dalits* remain as it is.

A recent study concludes that 'untouchability' is practiced in one form or the other in almost 80 per cent of the villages and it is most extensive in the private and religious spheres and least present in public and political spheres. Even today in one out of ten villages, *Dalits* are not allowed to wear new clothes or foot-wears or to ride bicycles. Besides untouchability, crimes against *Dalits* also continue and discouragingly the nature of such crimes has become more inhuman. It ranges from humiliating verbal abuses to brutal crimes. Apart from preventing them to fetch water from the common sources like pond, wells and community tube wells, drinking from common cups/glasses in the tea-stalls, using the common pathway, wearing foot-wears and clean and new clothes or from entering the religious places like temples and shrines, brutal crimes against them includes setting their houses on fire and looting their household valuables, illegal occupation of their limited source of sustenance, land, poisoning their main source of drinking water, destroying their crops, forcing them to consume human excreta, piercing needles in their eyes to blind them, chopping their heads or limbs or rape and murder and parading their women naked.

As many as 203576 cases of crimes against SCs by Non-SCs and Non-STs were registered in the year 2003-2009 and the total number of cases that reached various courts in India for trial, including the pending ones, are as many as 106522. Below are some instances which would definitely raise your eyebrows.

31st August 2005, Gohona, Haryana: Fifty *Dalit* houses with well furnished household valuables were burnt down by the caste Hindu Jats. In about 2000 *Dalits* including women, children and aged fled to ensure their safety.

1st January, 2006, Raghopur, Bihar: Six members of a *Dalit* family were burnt alive after burning down their house for their refusal to withdraw a theft case against three upper caste men.

27th September, 2006, Nagpur, Maharashtra: Four members of the same *Dalit* family were brutally murdered, but before committing the barbaric act of killing the women were tortured, paraded naked and gang-raped for asserting their right to protect their land, the only means of their livelihood.

21st April, 2010, Hisar, Haryana: Both father and daughter was burnt to death by the Jat mob which also looted 18 Balmiki houses.

Even in state like Tamil Nadu which progressed in several ways, there are some villages in which the *Dalits* live in terror. Many a time caste humiliation results in suicides. The SCs also depend on Hindus for livelihood and security. Most of the police officials in most of the police stations from local to state and also at national level were Hindus and thus the victims would not dare to register a complaint against the Hindu accused. So, it is undisputed fact that most of the crimes against the SCs go unregistered for obvious reasons of caste prejudice in society at large and among the police in particular.

The number of crimes committed against SCs was as many as 14318 in 1981, which increased to 17646 in 1991 and further to 33501 in 2001. Though the crime rate declined to 26252 in the year 2003 it again witnessed an increase in the year 2004 to 26887. It declined marginally to 26127 in the year 2005 and rose again to 27070 in 2006, 30031 in 2007 and 33615 in 2008. It declined again in 2009 to 33594. According to separate investigations by the National Campaign on *Dalit* Human Rights and Human Rights Watch, India discriminated against *Dalits* in distribution of aid in the wake of two major natural disasters in recent years: the Gujarat earthquake in January 2001 and the Indian Ocean Tsunami in December 2004. Following the Gujarat earthquake, the government allocated equal amounts of compensation and food supplies to all communities, the agencies did not ensure that the assistance went to *Dalit* communities. *Dalit* and Muslim population were not allowed to use the same shelter, electricity, running water and other supplies by the upper caste people. Following the Tsunami in 2004, it was found out that the *Dalits* were initially not guided on how to gain access to relief camps and were abused when they demanded of equal opportunities.

By taking a look at the state specific data we can say that the magnitude and trend of reported crimes against the SCs has in most cases changed over time across states. Some states have shown a decline, others have shown an increasing trend while some have remained more or less the same. The total number of registered rape cases against the SC women throughout India had increased during 2004 to 2008, with year 2009

Table 13.9: State-wise Incidence (I) and Percentage (P) Contribution of Crimes Committed against Scheduled Caste in India

State/UT's	*2003*		*2004*		*2005*		*2006*		*2007*		*2008*		*2009*	
	I	*P*	*I*	*P*	*I*	*P*	*I*	*P*	*I*	*P*	*I*	*P*	*I*	*P*
A.P.	3559	13.6	3255	12.1	3117	11.9	3891	14.4	3383	11.3	3998	11.9	4504	13.4
Bihar	1747	6.7	2646	9.8	1824	7.0	2043	7.5	2786	9.3	3617	10.8	3836	11.4
Chhattisgarh	709	2.7	698	2.6	454	1.7	444	1.6	511	1.7	600	1.8	466	1.4
Gujarat	1165	4.4	1309	4.9	1307	5.0	995	3.7	1040	3.5	1231	3.7	1182	3.5
Haryana	195	0.7	217	0.8	288	1.1	283	1.0	227	0.8	341	1.0	303	0.9
H.P.	107	0.4	89	0.3	55	0.2	92	0.3	91	0.3	71	0.2	88	0.3
Jharkhand	76	0.3	126	0.5	277	1.1	333	1.2	538	1.8	598	1.8	631	1.9
Karnataka	1844	7.0	1643	6.1	1780	6.8	1730	6.4	1844	6.1	2361	7.0	2174	6.5
Kerala	439	1.7	438	1.6	345	1.3	364	1.3	477	1.6	519	1.5	467	1.4
M.P.	5507	21.0	4699	17.5	4356	16.7	4214	15.6	4106	13.7	2965	8.8	3040	9.0
Maharashtra	697	2.7	715	2.7	865	3.3	1053	3.9	1166	3.9	1192	3.5	1096	3.3
Orissa	1157	4.4	1398	5.2	1439	5.5	1153	4.3	1355	4.5	1836	5.5	1709	5.1
Punjab	127	0.5	134	0.5	140	0.5	184	0.7	177	0.6	101	0.3	108	0.3
Rajasthan	4329	16.5	4360	16.2	3795	14.5	3910	14.4	4174	13.9	4302	12.8	4985	14.8
Tamil Nadu	1495	5.7	1156	4.3	1206	4.6	991	3.7	1743	5.8	1618	4.8	1312	3.9
U.P.	2821	10.7	3785	14.1	4397	16.8	4960	18.3	6144	20.5	8009	23.8	7522	22.4
Uttarakhand	129	0.5	137	0.5	99	0.4	68	0.3	71	0.2	42	0.1	58	0.2
Chandigarh	1	0	0	0	0	0	2	0	0	0	2	0	0	0
Delhi	3	0	4	0	21	0.1	21	0.1	24	0.1	34	0.1	33	0.1
Pondicherry	22	0.1	23	0.1	14	0.1	14	0.1	25	0.1	29	0.1	29	0.1

Source: Ramaiah, A. (2011), Growing Crimes against Dalits in India Despite Special Laws: Relevance of Ambedkar's demand for 'Seperate Settlement', *Journal of Law and Conflict Resolution*, Vol. 3(9), pp. 151-168, November.

witnessing a marginal decline. Madhya Pradesh had the highest share in the total number of rape cases in India for the entire stretch of 2003-2009 followed by Uttar Pradesh and Rajasthan. Kerala, the state with the highest literacy level and with a sizeable percentage of people egalitarian religion like Christianity and egalitarian ideology like Marxism, there is evidence of noticeable percentage of incidence of rape cases against SC women. However, in case of murder of the Scheduled Caste people Uttar Pradesh ranks first followed by Madhya Pradesh and Rajasthan.

3.1 Dalit Women in India—Victims of Caste Discrimination and Sexual Exploitation

Dalit women in India is highly patriarchal and caste based society bear the triple burden of class, caste and gender. Being positioned at the bottom of Indian society, SC women suffer from many forms of discrimination including lack of education, economic disadvantages, social disempowerment, domestic violence, political invisibility and sexual oppression. Despite having national laws and international human rights standard that prohibit any physical, sexual or psychological violence against women, varying forms of violent acts specifically targeting the SC women still take place in a large scale. Abuses are used to remind her of her caste and keep her oppressed. On the average 1000 cases of sexual exploitation and 1316 cases of rape was reported in the year 2001 alone. Social exclusion and untouchability faced by *Dalit* community takes shape of an institutionalized system in some places in context to *Dalit* women called "*Devadasis*".[3] The *Dalit* women also face humiliation and violence when they try to access rights and entitlements provided by the constitution and government. Apart from these they also face sexual and other kinds of physical violence. A significant proportion of *Dalit* women in India suffer multiple forms of systematic discrimination which includes verbal abuse, physical assault, sexual harassment and assault, domestic violence, naked parading, ingestion of human excreta, individual and gang rape. About 90 per cent crimes against *Dalit* women are not reported to the police for the fear of social ostracism and threat to personal safety and security. Also the legal proceedings are so complicated; time consuming, expensive and unfriendly to *Dalits* that they usually do not approach courts or other law enforcing agencies.

3.2 Dalit Children in India—Victims of Caste Discrimination

There are 260 million *Dalit* people around the world of which 166,635,700

Table 13.9: Number of Women Facing Various Forms of Violence

Form of violence	*Number of women who have faced the form of violence*	
	Number of women	*Per cent of total Dalit women (500)*
Physical Assault	274	54.8
Verbal Abuse	312	62.4
Sexual Harassment/Assault	234	46.8
Rape	116	23.2
Sexual Exploitation	44	8.8
Forced Prostitution	24	4.8
Kidnap/Abduction	24	4.8
Forced Incarceration	23	4.6
Medical Negligence	17	3.4
Female Infanticide	2	0.4
Child Sexual Abuse	23	4.6
Domestic Violence	215	43.0

Source: Ramaiah, A. (2011), Growing Crimes against *Dalits* in India Despite Special Laws: Relevance of Ambedkar's demand for 'Seperate Settlement', *Journal of Law and Conflict Resolution*, Vol. 3(9), pp. 151-168, November.

live in India. They are vulnerable to discrimination, exploitation and violence simply because of the caste they are born into. Caste discrimination dominates in housing, marriage, employment and education. According to unofficial estimates as many as 1.3 million Indian *Dalits* are employed as manual scavengers to clear human wastes. The children of manual scavengers are particularly vulnerable to discrimination in schools, where they are forced to perform cleaning and scavenging work, and where discrimination undermines all aspects of their education and often causes them to drop-out from schools. A survey conducted by the Indian Human Rights Organization reveals that teachers, community members routinely subject the children of manual scavengers to discrimination and forced labour as part of their daily experience of attending schools and living in their communities.

Discrimination against *Dalits* in the educational system is a widespread problem in caste affected countries. Social exclusion, alienation and physical abuse transcend all levels of education from primary to university. Illiteracy and drop-out rates among *Dalits* are significantly high due to a number of social and physical factors. The drop-out rate of *Dalit* children is generally high especially at the elementary level. According to the UNICEF, the drop-out rate among *Dalits* in India is 44.27 per cent in primary school. The difference in drop-out rates between *Dalit* children and other children has actually grown from 4.39 per cent in 1989 to 16.21 per cent in 2008. The various forms of structural discrimination, alienation and *Dalit* children face in schools are sometimes so disgraceful that they are forced to drop-out of schools. One of the main reasons is the discriminatory practice by the teachers in school. It includes harsh punishment, denial of access to school water supplies, segregation in classrooms and forcing *Dalit* children to perform manual scavenging on and around school premises.

Also *Dalit* children face discriminatory attitudes from fellow students and the community as a whole, in particular from upper caste members who perceive education for *Dalits* as a waste and a threat[4]. Along with this the extreme poverty in which most *Dalit* families live is another reason for the drop-out rates to be so high. Many families cannot afford to send their children to school and are dependent on their workforce to ensure the survival of the family. The distance to schools is also considered to be a huge barrier for Dalit children and it also explains the reason for low enrolment and high drop-out rates. As the upper caste people do not want to live with the *Dalits*, they often settle down in remote areas, away from the main villages and schools. First, the location of schools in the main village and the unwillingness of the upper caste people to mix with the *Dalit* children make it difficult for them to gain access to education and secondly, it is inconvenient for them to walk that far everyday resulting in high drop-out of the Dalit children.

Migratory labour is another reason that leads to high drop-out rates of Dalit children. Since most of them are landless they are forced to migrate as this is the only way to ensure the economical survival of their families. This continuous migration in search of jobs causes a disruption in their academic career and as a result they are unable to keep up with the other children. Finally, lack of proper facilities is a general problem in many schools. Injustice, harassment and prejudice towards *Dalit* children are not only found at the elementary school level but also institutions of higher education. Several incidents have occurred where discrimination is practiced by upper caste students, teachers, faculties and administrations.

We now move on to the fourth discussion which deals with the policy prescriptions prescribed for improving the socio-economic status of the *Dalits*.

4. Policy Prescriptions

Despite the passage of the Anti-Untouchability Act of 1955 and the Prevention of Atrocities Act of 1989, crimes against Dalits are still a major social problem and discrimination is widespread. Jawaharlal Nehru University professor and Director of the Indian Institute of *Dalit* Studies S.K. Thorat, recently said that approximately 18000 caste related discrimination cases filed annually with the Indian government are only a small fraction of the actual number. Vastly most cases go unreported, because Dalits in rural areas still live under feudal systems. The Constitution of India, adopted in 1950 was preceded by strong social, religious and political movements of the untouchables in the early part of the 20th century against caste and Brahmanism. The induction of these viewpoints was particularly facilitated by Dr. B.R. Ambedkar, who led much of the struggle against caste and untouchability as chairman of the Drafting committee of the Indian constitution. This philosophic ethos of the constitution proclaimed justice, equality, fraternity and liberty to all Indian citizens as against rights based on birth. Also the democratic form of government with elected representatives also provided an opportunity for members of different sections to participate in the decision making on the common platform. In addition to the general frame of justice and equality, the Constitution also recognised the need for distinct and special provisions related to the protection for *Dalit* community.

Constitutional Provisions for Protection and Development of Scheduled Castes

1. The Constitution emphasizes 'safe guards' for SCs under the 'Special Provisions Relating to Certain Classes' in Part XVI of the Constitution of India. The constitution also provides for protection and promotion of their social, economic, educational, cultural and political interests to bridge the gap between them and other sections of the society.
2. The constitutional provision include general measures found in-equality before law (Article 14), Prohibition of Discrimination (Art. 15), Protection of life and personal liberty (Art. 21). The provision and safeguards for Backward Classes especially SCs and STs have been incorporated in the Constitution. These are classified under the following broad categories:

   I. *Social Safeguards*: Article 17 relates to abolition of

untouchability being practiced in society. Article 23 prohibits traffic in human beings and 'beggar' and or other similar forms of forced labour and provides that any contravention of this provision shall be a punishable offence. Article 24 provides that no child below age 14 years shall be employed to work in any factory or mine or engaged in any hazardous employment. Article 25(2)(b) provides that Hindu religious institutions of a public character shall be opened to all classes and sections of Hindus.

II. *Economic Safeguard*: Article 23, 24 and 46 form the part of the economic safeguards for the SCs and STs. Article 46 states that "The State shall promote with special care the educational and economic interests of the weaker sections of the people, and in particular, of the SCs and the STs, and shall protect them from social injustice and all forms of exploitation."

III. *Educational and Cultural Safeguards*: Article 15(4) empowers the state to make special provisions for the advancement of any socially or educationally backward classes of citizens and for SCs. This has enabled the state to reserve seats for SCs in educational institutions, in general and professional courses, etc.

IV. *Political Safeguards*:

- *Article 243 D–Reservation of Seats*: Seats shall be reserved for SCs and STs in every Panchayat. Not less than one-third of the total number of seats reserved under clause (I) shall be reserved for women belonging to SC or, as the case may be to STs. Not less than one-third (including the seats belonging to SC and ST women) of the total number of seats to be filled by direct election in every Panchayat shall be reserved for women and such seats may be allocated by rotation to different constituencies in a Panchayat.
- *Article 243 T–Reservation of Seats*: Seats shall be reserved for SCs and STs in every Municipality. Not less than one-third of the total number of seats reserved under clause (I) shall be reserved for women belonging to SC or, as the case may be to STs. Not less than one-third (including the seats belonging to SC and ST women) of the total number of seats to be filled by

direct election in every Municipality shall be reserved for women and such seats may be allocated by rotation to different constituencies in a Municipality. The offices of the chair persons in the Municipalities shall be reserved for SCs and STs and women in such a manner as the Legislature of a State may, by law, provide. Nothing in the part shall prevent the Legislature of a state from making any provision of reservation of seats in municipality offices in favour of the backward class citizens.

- *Article 330–Reservation of seats for SCs and STs in House of People*: Seats shall be reserved for: (a) Scheduled Castes, (b) The Scheduled Tribes except the STs in the autonomous districts of Assam, (c) The Schedule Tribes in the autonomous districts of Assam.
- *Article 332–Reservation of Seats for SCs and STs in the Legislative Assemblies of the state*: Seats shall be reserved for the SCs and STs except the STs in the autonomous districts of Assam in the Legislative Assembly of every state. Seats shall also be reserved for the autonomous districts in Assam.
- *Article 334–Reservation of Seats and Special Representation to cease after 60 years*: (a) The reservation of seats for the SCs and the STs in the House of Pecple and in the Legislative Assemblies of the state and; (b) The representation of the Anglo-Indian community in the House of the People and in the Legislative Assemblies of the state by nomination shall cease to have effect on the expiration of a period of 60 years from the commencement of the Constitution.

V. *Service Safeguard:* They are contained in the Articles 16(4), 16(4A) and 335. In 2001, the Parliament through Constitution (85th Amendment) Act, 2001 amended the provisions contained in Article 16(4A). According to this amendment the SCs/STs promoted earlier than their counterpart in general category by virtue of reservation policy shall be senior to general category in the promoted scale/post.

3. *Important Legislations*:

(a) The Untouchability Offences Act later reformulated as the protection of Civil Rights Act (1955) and rules (1977).

(b) The SC/ST (Prevention of Atrocities) Act, 1989 and Rules 1995.

(c) Bonded Labour (System) Abolition Act, 1976.

(d) Employment of Manual Scavengers and Construction of Dry Latrines (Prohibition) Act, 1993.

(e) Devadasi System Abolition Act in the states of Andhra Pradesh, Maharashtra and Karnataka.

(f) Child Labour (Prohibition and Regulation) Act, 1986

(g) Minimum Wages Act, 1948

(h) Equal Remuneration Act, 1976

(i) Land Reforms Act in different states.

4. *The Need for International and European Union Action*: IDSN has produced a set of recommendations for a comprehensive EU policy to address caste discrimination:

- The EU should give recognition to caste discrimination as a priority human rights and development issue and lend its united support to the endorsement of the draft UN principles and guidelines for the Effective Elimination of Discrimination based on work and descent.
- The EU should ensure that caste discrimination is dealt with as a major, cross-cutting issue in human rights and policy dialogues with affected countries and is included in programming and discussions and country strategy papers.
- EU supported programmes, including in the educational sector, must include targeted measures for Dalit inclusion and benefits and take fully into account the needs and circumstances of Dalit women and the vulnerability of Dalit children.

References

Kethineni, Sesha and Gail Diane Humiston. (2010): *Dalits* the "Oppressed People" of India: How are their Social, Economic and Human Rights Addressed, *War Crimes, Genocide and Crimes against Humanity,* Vol. 4, 99-140.

Ramaiah, A. (2011): Growing Crimes against *Dalits* in India Despite Special Laws: Relevance of Ambedkar's demand for 'Seperate Settlement', *Journal of Law and Conflict Resolution,* Vol. 3(9), pp. 151-168, November.

Sadana, Nidhi (2009): Dalit Children in Rural India: Issues Related to Exclusion and Deprivation, *Working Paper Series,* Vol. III, Number 05, New Delhi.
Vijapur, Abdulrahim P. (1993): *Education of Ex-untouchables (Dalits): Plight of Human Rights Education in Indian schools.*
http://en.wikipedia.org/wiki/Dalit
www.cpim.org
http://indian-social-affairs.blogspot.in/2012/04/problems-of-dalits-in-india.html
http://en.wikipedia.org/wiki/History_of_the_Indian_caste_system
http://www.mtholyoke.edu/~epandit/page2.html
http://www.thehindu.com/news/the-india-cables/the-cables/article1568910.ece
http://www.hurights.or.jp/pub/hreas/10_02/15Education%20of%20Ex-Untouchables,%20Daiits.pdf
http://www.indianet.nl/pdf/CastAnEye.pdf
http://idsn.org/fileadmin/user_folder/pdf/New_files/India/Dalit_children_in_India_-_victims_of_caste_discrimination.pdf
http://idsn.org/fileadmin/user_folder/pdf/New_files/Key_Issues/Education/DALIT_EDUCATION_IDSNbriefingpaper.pdf
http://shodhganga.inflibnet.ac.in/bitstream/10603/3691/9/09_chapter%202.pdf
http://swtn.org/publications/MDGs_and_Dalits_Special_Component_Plan_2004_Single_Page_View.pdf
http://indiacurrentaffairs.org/problems-of-dalits-in-india/

Appendix 1

Case Study: Situation of Dalits in Nepal

The Nepal Legal Code of 1854, the Muluki Ain, formulated on the basis of Hindu orthodoxy included five hierarchical categories: (1) Tagadhari (wearers of holy thread); (2) Non-enslavable alcohol drinkers; (3) Enslavable alcohol drinkers; (4) Impure but Touchable; (5) Untouchable castes. It is accepted that the political ideology of Nepal as a Hindu state (which changed as of 2007—Nepal has now been declared as a secular state) has remained highly exclusionary. Despite the legal provisions caste based discrimination is still practiced. Moreover, discrimination is practiced among their own group, that is, between upper caste and *Dalits* and also within *Dalits*. Unlike in India, Nepal has no single defined schedule of castes. As the list fluctuates the numbers of *Dalit* population also vary according to different sources. The *Dalit* community in Nepal is also not homogenous. They can be divided into three broad groups—(1) *Dalits* in the hill areas, (2) *Dalits* in the Newari community, (3) *Dalits* in the Terai areas.

In Nepal, *Dalits* are poorer than most other social groups. The proportion of population below national poverty line is 31 per cent nationally, out of which 47 per cent of *Dalits* live below the national poverty line. 86 per cent of *Dalit* households have an income lower than national average. Multiple regression analysis of Nepal Living Standards Survey found that per capita consumption of *Dalit* households is about 46 per cent lower than the highest Hindu caste groups. Poor families have less to spend on their children's education. Child labour is prevalent among poor families although employment of children below 14 years is prohibited by the Child Act, 1991. Many *Dalit* families work in the informal sector through daily wage labour, often involving seasonal migration, to earn their living.

In Nepal the social and economic status of women is much lower than that of men. This is manifested in the lower health and nutritional status of *Dalit* women, as well as in the political representation of *Dalit* women, which is negligible. 44 per cent of Dalit men are literate against 24 per cent of *Dalit* women. Poverty affects schooling of girls more than boys. In Nepal, *Dalits* lag behind other social groups in terms of educational attainment. At least, 8,00,000 children of primary school going age are estimated to be out of school. Students, teachers and parents all acknowledge that beating and humiliating children in the name of discipline is very common in schools. The more 'disadvantaged' students tend to suffer more. Also *Dalits* have been excluded from savings and credit in programmes which hinders *Dalit* families from engaging in decision making process.

Discriminatory practices against *Dalits* and their exclusion from educational opportunities continue in both India and Nepal despite the legal provisions in the Constitution, various government Acts, policies and plans.

Appendix 2

Case Study: Dalits in West Bengal

West Bengal was continually ruled by the Left Front government since 1977 with its redistributive ideology of social goods. Therefore to contextualize the study of social mobility of *Dalits* including their existing reality requires elaboration.

In West Bengal *Dalits* constituted 23 per cent of the total population and shared second largest *Dalit* population in India. As per census 2001, total *Dalit* population in West Bengal was 18,452,555 out of which

9,469,659 (51.32%) were men and 8,982,896 (48.68%) were women. The state registered 14.8 per cent decadal growth of *Dalit* population in 1991-2001 compared to 17.77 per cent of total population of the state. The sex ratio of *Dalit* population is 949 which are substantially higher than total population of West Bengal. About 18.85 per cent of *Dalit* population live in urban areas which is lower than the average rate of urbanization of the state (27.97%). So, it seems that the *Dalit* population is essentially rural. The literacy rate of total population in West Bengal is 68.6 per cent and that of the total rural population is 63.4 per cent. The literacy among *Dalit* is only 59.04 per cent which reduces to 48.91 per cent among rural *Dalits*.

A total of 63.3 per cent of *Dalit* in age group 5-14 years has been attending any educational institutions. However majority of *Dalit* students drop out at below primary to primary level. Only 15 per cent *Dalit* students reach middle or elementary level and a negligible 2.56 per cent reaches graduation and above graduation level. Around 11.6 per cent of total *Dalit* in West Bengal are having education above Matriculation. The percentage of *Dalit* workers to total population (WPR) is 38.8 per cent which is lower than the aggregated figure for *Dalit* at the national level (40.4%), but slightly higher than total population in the state (36.77%). The female WPR is 22.31 per cent against 54.37 per cent of males.

With the agrarian structure of West Bengal characterized with high incidence of landlessness and equal distribution of land with those possessing, 52.1 per cent of *Dalit* main worker is found to be dependent on agriculture. Only 19.61 per cent of arable land in West Bengal is owned by *Dalits*. Also only 12.42 per cent *Dalit* households use electricity as source of lighting, 1.14 per cent of *Dalit* households have access to clean source of fuel and around 96.24 per cent of *Dalit* households do not have proper sanitation facilities. In respect of levels of living measured in terms of monthly income, *Dalits* are significantly below than rest of the population. In 2000 as against the national average of Rs. 4485, the per capita income of *Dalit* was Rs. 3237. According to census 2001, only 32.91 per cent of *Dalits* live in good houses and 11.08 per cent residing in dilapidated houses. In reducing the incidence of poverty, the Left's effort through land reforms and in revitalizing panchayat seem to have positive impact, when compared with the states of Eastern India, but lags behind when compared with All-India level. The NSS data revealed that the proportion of rural population below poverty line declined from 60.51 per cent in 1973 to 26 per cent in 1998.

Notes

1. Early Indian texts like *Manusmriti* and the *Puranas* speak of '*Varna*' which means order, category, type or colour and groups the society into four main categories—the Brahmins, the kshatriyas, the vaishyas and the shudras. The *Varna* system was mainly based on occupations. The first three *Varna* is called "twice born". It implies that they have come of age and are eligible to study Sanskrit and the Vedas and perform Vedic rituals. The thread ceremony marks the second birth among the Indian males and the thread tied around the hands of the girls during their marriage marks the second birth among the girls.
2. A system of social and economic penalties. Ostracism means being excluded from society—it might mean that people would not speak, work or allow someone to take part in such things as group activities.
3. Under *Devadasi* system, a Scheduled Caste family dedicates/marry its young daughter to the village goddess, and when the girl reaches puberty she becomes an available sexual partner of the priest and all upper caste men in the village.
4. This is linked to a perception among some upper caste people that if *Dalits* receive education, the educated *Dalits* might pose a threat to village hierarchies and power relations.

14
Rural Livelihoods in India
Issues, Measurement and Policies

Piyali Chatterjee

1. Introduction

Whenever I come across the words 'rural' and 'livelihood', clubbed together in the context of India, immediately it gives me two kinds of images, one is of lush green fields spread across thousands of acres and another of rural people toiling under the sun for their daily livelihood. Rural livelihood as defined by FAO (Food and Agriculture Organization) is "the capabilities, assets and activities that rural people require for a means of living". Livelihood in the rural sector is the means of earning for sustaining life. The principal means of earning in the rural area is agriculture which represents basically the rural farm sector (RFS). Besides this, there is the rural non-farm sector (RNFS). Rural livelihood also includes allied activities apart from agriculture like fishery, animal husbandry, forestry, etc. which falls under the broad dimension of RNFS.

The era of globalization beginning from 1991 also affected the rural livelihood of India through influencing agriculture, allied activities and non-farm economic activities in the rural area. The opening up of the economy led to many changes in the exports and imports statistics of the agriculture and allied activities. The agricultural sector, since decades, has been playing a key role in the composition of Indian exports. The share of agricultural exports, for instance, declined from 18.2 per cent in 1998-99 to 13.5 per cent in 2000-01 and further reduced to 11.7 per cent in 2002-03. It implies India's share of exports in tea, tobacco, sugar and molasses has been slowly declining in the global market. Also besides this, in spite of several hurdles, production of some produces like coffee, rice, fish, etc. have been entering the global market by raising their shares. There were also changes in policies on the import front. For instance, the average tariffs on agricultural imports were reduced from 100 per cent in 1990 to 30 per cent in 1997. However, the growth of farm business income started declining in the 1990s. There had also been widening of disparities between agricultural and non-agricultural income which did also put the farmers in distress in this period.

The rural lives and livelihood also witnessed days of radical banking reforms in the 1960s in the form of social control and later by nationalization of banks, which lead to a rapid expansion of banking in the rural areas. However since economic reforms in the year 1991, the number of rural bank branches reduced from more than 34,000 to 32,000 during the period 1990-2003. This posed a serious constraint on the flow of bank credit in the rural sector specifically to agriculture, and as such led to disastrous consequences. Such a situation was juxtaposed with the policy of regional rural banks functioning on commercial principles of increasing the interest rates charged. In scheduled commercial banks, the number of agricultural loan accounts declined from 27.7 million in 1992 to 20.3 million in 2002. The small farmers' share in bank credit declined steeply from 21.9 per cent in 1992 to 7 per cent in 2001. As such, the small farmers were compelled to look forward to non-institutional sources like village money-lenders for credit. The decade of economic reforms therefore lead to rise in farmer indebtedness and along with this saw a rise in farmer suicides due to high debt; the suicide mortality rate had gone up to 10.4 per cent in 2003 from 9.3 per cent in 1991. The state of Maharashtra was the first state where farmer suicides were reported in the 1990s. The total number of farmer suicides in Maharashtra in the period 1995-2011 was 53,818.

In spite of all these disruptions, rural poverty at all-India level reduced in the post-liberalisation period from 37.27 per cent in 1993-94 to 28.3 per cent in 2004-05. The reason behind such a decline can be attributed to the implementation of rural poverty alleviation programmes for employment generation through non-farm activities. Some of the rural development programmes are National Rural Employment Guarantee Act (NREGA), Integrated Rural Development Programme (IRDP), Swarnjayanti Gram Swarozgar Yojana (SGSY), Sampoorna Grameen Rozgar Yojana (SGRY), etc.

2. Rural India: A Glimpse of the Past

If we gently turnover the pages of history, a vivid picture of rural India comes in front of us. The rural sector of India has undergone incredible changes since pre-Independence through post-independence and of late through the globalisation era. The arrival of the East India Company in India proved to be havoc for the resources of the country. There was a two-way depletion of resources since the British would buy raw materials from India at cheaper rates and the finished goods were sold at higher than normal price in Indian markets. The pre-independence period was a phase of near economic stagnation for the country. There was acute poverty all across the country. Even at the time of independence, the economy got stuck into a vicious circle of poverty. Low income levels lead to low savings level, which in turn lead to low capital formation leading to low productivity and as such low income levels. Therefore, it can be easily concluded that the standard of rural and urban India was absolutely quite unsatisfactory.

At the time of Independence, the economy was predominantly an agricultural economy reflecting its overwhelming rural character with nearly 85 per cent of the population living in villages and deriving their livelihood primarily from agriculture and other related pursuits, using traditional and low productivity-generating techniques. Around 70 per cent of Indian working population were engaged in agriculture. In spite of such intense involvement in agriculture, there were serious dearth of food and raw materials for industry, which was manifested in deficiency in average food availability for the masses. The relative importance of

Table 14.1: Sector-wise percentage contributed to national income and workforce engaged

Sector	*National Income (%) (1948-49)*	*Workforce (%) (1950-51)*
1. Agriculture, Animal Husbandry, Forestry, Fisheries	49.1	72.3
2. Mines, Manufacturing Industries, Small Enterprises	17.1	10.7
3. Trade, Transport and Communications	18.5	7.7
4. Other Services, Professions, Administration, Domestic Services	15.7	9.3
Total	100	100

Source: Uma Kapila (2008-09).

various industrial activities in terms of percentage contributed to *national income* and *workforce* engaged in these activities is given in Table 14.1.

Table 14.1 clearly highlights a few mind-boggling facts of the then Indian economy. The dominant sector, as mentioned before, was the agriculture and allied activities, both in terms of contribution to national income and workforce participation. This not only explains the existence of the large rural sector in sharp contrast to the urban sector, but also the predominant contribution of rural farm and rural non-farm sector in the growth of the economy as a whole. It is also important to mention here, that the high percentage of workforce participation in rural sector during the beginning of the five year planning is invariably the reason for such a large contribution of the rural economy to the national income, the percentage being around 72 of the total workforce. Hence, the importance of gearing up for high growth of rural sector and paving a way for future sustainable development was felt necessary since the post-independence era.

The First Five Year Plan (1951-56) was all focussed on developing agriculture and as such through various steps taken by the government was at last able to achieve its objectives. The decades that followed, however, witnessed a sharp fall in the share of agriculture and other allied activities like forestry and fishing, in the national income. The Share of Agriculture in the National Income from 1950-51 to 1997-98 is given in Table 14.2.

Table 14.2: Share of Agricultural Sector in Total Gross Domestic Product (GDP) at Factor Cost (at 1980-81 Prices) Rs. Crore

Year	*Agriculture*	*GDP at Factor Cost*	*% of Agricultural Contribution*
1950-51	23,741	42,871	55.4
1960-61	31,995	62,904	52.5
1970-71	40,214	90,426	44.5
1980-81	46,649	1,22,427	38.1
1990-91	65,653	2,12,253	30.9
1997-98*	2,77,418	10,49,191	26.4

Note: Here Agriculture includes agriculture, forestry and fishing.
*At 1993-94 prices.

Source: Central Statistical Organisation (CSO).

Table 14.2 clearly shows that between 1950-51 to 1997-98, the share of agriculture in GDP sharply declined from approx. 55 per cent to approx. 26 per cent. The decrease in the share of agriculture implies the increase in the shares of manufacturing and service sectors. During the Ninth Five Year Plan (1997-2002) agriculture industry growth rate was 2.1 per cent. In the Tenth Five Year Plan (2002-2007), GDP originating from agriculture and allied activities was 2.3 per cent compared to 8 per cent in the industrial sector and 9.5 per cent in the services sector. During this plan period the growth in the agriculture and allied activities averaged 2.3 per cent which is lower than that of 3.2 per cent during the 1990s and 4.4 per cent during the 1980s. During the Eleventh Five Year Plan (2007-2012), the growth rate of agriculture, forestry and fishing was estimated to be around 3.2 per cent. The share of agriculture and allied sectors to GDP was 14.5 per cent in 2010-11, which further declined to 13.9 per cent in 2011-12, according to the Economic Survey 2011-12. The current period which is the Twelfth Five Year Plan (2012-17) targets an agricultural growth rate of 4 per cent.

Factors influencing Rural Livelihoods in India

1. Employment

Agriculture and Allied Sectors: Rural livelihood in India is greatly influenced by agriculture and its allied sectors. Agriculture and allied sectors are undoubtedly considered to be indispensable for sustainable living in the rural areas. They are not only an important source of raw material but also a very important market for the huge industrial sector of the modern economy. The linkage between agriculture and industrial sector undeniably is a strong truth behind the development and flourishing of the large rural economy. Agriculture and allied sector apart from comprising the crop production, is further divided into several correlated segments, namely, horticulture and its allied sectors (like flowers, fruits and vegetables, plantation crops, spices, aromatic and medicinal plants), the fisheries, the animal husbandry and livestock, and the sericulture. Livelihood is persistently affected by the level of employment in agriculture and allied sector. Table 14.3 shows the rural employment data for the period 1983-2010.

In Table 14.4, the production of crops is utilising the highest percentage of labourers than in allied sectors. The employment share in forestry and fishery is absolutely negligible in comparison to the crop production. The dependence on crop production continuously increased during the period 1983 to 2009-10. However, the animal husbandry sector

Table 14.3: Rural Employment as Distributed in Agricultural Sector (%)

Period	*Crops*	*Animal Husbandry*	*Forestry*	*Fishery*
1983	88.8	10.4	0.4	0.4
1993-94	92.2	6.8	0.4	0.6
2004-05	90.3	8.7	0.5	0.5
2009-10	93.2	6.1	0.2	0.5

Source: Anjani Kumar *et al.* (2011)

witnessed a sharp fall in employment share to 6.1 per cent in 2009-10 from 10.4 per cent in 1983.

As far as *sericulture* is concerned, sericulture is promoted as an agro-based, labour-intensive rural oriented cottage industry in India. It provides gainful employment primarily to the weaker and marginalised sections of the Indian society. In the year 2010-11, employment in sericulture sector was 72.5 lakh persons of which 52.20 lakh were farmers, 3.70 lakh were reelers and 16.60 lakh were weavers, as compared to 68.17 lakh in the year 2009-10. Around, 55-60 per cent of sericulture activities are undertaken by rural women.

Apart from these, the pattern of employment within the crop sub-sector is equally significant for studying the employment in agriculture. The pattern of employment diversification within crop sub-sector is given in Table 14.4.

Table 14.4: The pattern of employment diversification within crop sub-sector

(%)

Period	*Cereals & Pulses*	*Cash Crops*	*Horticulture*	*Agricultural Services*
1983	93.7	4.3	1.9	0.1
1993-94	92.2	5.1	1.9	0.8
2004-05	84.3	11.1	4.1	0.5
2009-10	86.2	9.8	3.5	0.5

Source: Anjani Kumar *et al.* (2011).

In Table 14.4, it is pretty clear that the employment share in the cereals and pulses category is highest as compared to the cash crops and horticulture. However, the employment share declined over the years from 1983 to 2009-10 from 93.7 per cent to 86.2 per cent. Within this period, the trend of decline was reversed after 2004-05 from 84.3 per cent to 86.2 per cent. The cash crops showed variations in employment share.

The percentage rose to 11.1 per cent in 2004-05 from 4.3 per cent in 1983, and then again declined to 9.8 per cent in 2009-10. Besides these, the horticulture sub-sector throughout the given period eventually emerged as a *catalyst* to the growth of agricultural sector. The share of horticulture in total crop sector employment did not rise as compared to its increase in share in agricultural income. The share of horticulture in crop sub-sector employment increased throughout the period 1983 to 2004-05, from 1.9 per cent to 4.1 per cent and declined slightly in the subsequent period of 2004-05 to 2009-10 to 3.5 per cent.

Apart from this, the RNFS is also growing in its importance with the passing time. This is not only manifested in the increase in number of establishments in RNFS but also in the increase in employment in it. For male it has increased from 16.2 per cent in 1972-73 to 33.2 per cent in 2004-05 and for female it has increased from 10.1 per cent in 1972-73 to 18.2 per cent in 2004-05.

Non-farm Sector

The rural non-agricultural establishments and employment in rural India in 1998 and 2005 is given in Table 14.5.

Table 14.5: The rural non-agricultural establishments and employment in rural India in 1998 and 2005

Own account Establishments				Establishments with hired workers				
No. of establishments	Employment			No. of establishments	Employment			
	Total	Female	Child		Total	Hired	Female	Child
Economic Census of 1998								
107145	158121	30112	6002	37923	179557	156085	38522	4707
Economic Census of 2005								
13262173	17302128	3216655	326967	6564894	24592025	21122316	5981652	700709

Source: Mukhopadhyay, Gangopadhyay and Nayak (2008).

It can be easily concluded from Table 14.5 that there had been an increase in the number of non-agricultural establishments from 1998 to 2005 in the rural sector. It as such clearly reflects the growing importance of non-agricultural economic activities. The employment data is also showing a rise in the number of employed. This implies the heavy dependence of the rural people on non-agricultural activities for earning their livelihood.

2. Wages

The wages prevailing in the rural area in India, undoubtedly affects the rural livelihood. Wages determines the pattern of employment in the rural sector which is manifested in the employment diversification in the rural sector. As per available statistics, during the period 2000-01 to 2006-07, there had been a fluctuation of real farm wages between 117 per day in 2001-02 and 111 per day in 2006-07, both wage rates measured at 2011-12 constant prices. However, since 2007-08, the period of 11th Five Year Plan (2007-11), the real farm wages have been consistently rising, and increased from a low of 111 per day in 2006-07 to a high of 154 per day in 2011-12, with an average annual growth rate of 6.8 per cent per annum in real terms. The reasons could be around 8 per cent per annum growth of the economy especially in the construction sector leading to drawing labour from agriculture, high growth in agriculture GDP coupled with rising farm prices, global food inflation followed by significant increases in MSPs (minimum support prices) of major crops and government intervention in rural labour market through MGNREGA (Mahatma Gandhi National Rural Employment Guarantee Act) that eventually empowered rural labour to negotiate higher wages for farm work (Gulati and Jena, 2012).

Table 14.6: Agricultural and Non-agricultural Employment Growth Rates

	1993-94 to 1999-2000	*1999-2000 to 2004-05*	*1993-94 to 2004-05*
Agricultural Self-Employment	–0.53	2.89	1.01
Agricultural Wage Employment	1.06	–3.18	–0.89
Total Agricultural Employment	0.03	0.85	0.40
Real Agricultural Wage Rate (CPIAL deflated)	**2.74**	**1.46**	**2.15**
Rural non-agricultural Employment	2.26	5.27	3.52
Average Real Non-agricultural Wage Rate (deflated by NAS consumption deflator)	**5.03**	**0.13**	**2.77**

Source: Planning Commission, Government of India, 10th April, 2012.

Table 14.6 clearly shows the growth rates in rural agricultural employment and rural non-agricultural employment. During the periods 1993-94 to 1999-2000 and 1999-2000 to 2004-05, the growth rates in employment in rural agricultural sector is less than that in rural non-agricultural sector, given significant change in the growth rates of real wages, of both agricultural and non-agricultural, wages. However, the overall growth rate of real wages during the period 1993-94 to 2004-05, is greater in the rural non-agricultural sector which is 2.77, than in the rural agricultural sector which is 2.15. This can fairly justify the growth rate in the rural non-agricultural employment which is 3.52 which is much greater than that in rural agricultural sector which is 0.40, during the same period.

Table 14.7 shows the change in real wages in the rural sector with a detailed classification of growth in non-farm wages.

Table 14.7: Change in Real Wages in the Rural Sector

Annual Average Growth in Real Wage				
Growth in Mean Wage (% per year)				
	83-93	*93-99*	*99-04*	*93-04*
Agricultural Wage	3.2	2.8	1.7	2.3
Non-farm Regular	2.9	4.9	–0.5	2.4
Non-farm Casual	3.5	4.1	1.3	2.8
Growth in Median Wage (% per year)				
Agricultural Wage	4.1	1.0	2.9	1.9
Non-farm Regular	2.9	2.8	–5.4	–1.0
Non-farm Casual	4.4	3.8	1.9	2.9

Source: Himanshu, Lanjouw, Mukhopadhyay, Murgai (2010).

Comparing the decades of 80s and 90s, it is seen that there has been a slowdown in regular non-farm wage growth, much faster as shown by the growth in median wage than the growth in mean wage. The slowdown in wage growth is clear in the 1999-2004 period and this extends to the non-farm casual sector as well. The fall in the median regular wage over the period 1999-2004 by more than 5 per cent, undeniably reflects the large public service pay increases associated with the Fifth Pay Commission, which was followed by the freeze in public sector hiring and also the rapid growth in low paid regular jobs.

In 2004-05, a negligible 6 per cent of self-employed workers were running enterprises that employed more than 5 workers. During the same period, around 41 per cent of self-employed workers worked out of their own dwellings, 12 per cent had no fixed location and an additional 10 per cent worked on the street. Also only one-fourth received a regular monthly or weekly payment, with the vast majority relying on irregular daily or piece rate modes of payment (Lanjouw, 2010). Some benefits like social security or paid leave were apparently non-existent. In some industries, earnings of self-employed workers are better than what salaried workers earn (Glinskaya and Jalan, 2005). Such enterprises and multiple occupations within households would explain the presence of self-employed workers at the top end of the income distribution.

3. Rural Credit

The effect of rural credit on rural livelihood is undeniably significant in a growing economy like India, where a major part of the economy is still *rural* in nature. The growth of the rural economy is absolutely important in the growth of the Indian economy. The change in rural income causes variations in the demand for products of the industrial as well as services sector. A study revealed that in 1993-94, one unit rise in agricultural output was likely to increase the demand for industrial products by 0.297 unit (i.e., more than three times as compared to 1968-69), while demand for services sector increased by around 0.149 unit in 1993-94 as against 0.035 unit in 1968-69 (Chakrabarty, 2003). But, the commercialization of agriculture, apart from increasing productivity and food security, also lead to the emergence of middlemen who weakened the agriculture channels by delivering the produce at inflated prices to the consumers and negligible margins to the producers as part of their exploitation.

The Reserve Bank of India (RBI) has already given prime importance to the agricultural credit delivery. The Reserve Bank of India Act, 1934 envisaged a significant developmental role for the Reserve Bank in the sphere of agricultural credit, specifically, with respect to financing seasonal operations and the marketing of crops. In July 1969, 14 major commercial banks were nationalised and as such, encouraged the commercial banks to be oriented towards meeting the requirements of the priority sectors of the economy with special attention to financing the needs of the small farmers. The National Bank for Agriculture and Rural Development (NABARD) came into existence in July 1982. Therefore, all major activities related to rural credit from the RBI were transferred to the NABARD.

The amount of credit flow in the rural sector in the decades of 1970s, 1980s and 1990s is clubbed in Table 14.8. It is clear from Table 14.8 that the Institutional credit for agriculture and allied activities increased by several times, during the three decades. The institutional credit were Rs. 2,235 crore approximately at the end of the year 1971-72 and increased to approximately Rs. 8,252 crore at the end of the year 1979-80. The institutional credit to the rural sector during this period increased by approximately Rs. 4, 580 crore on an annual basis (Chakrabarty, 2003).

Table 14.8: Institutional Credit for Agriculture and Allied Activities (Rounded Figures)

Year	*Loans Outstanding (Rs.crore)*
1971-72	2,235
1974-75	3,539
1979-80	8,252
1980-81	10,123
1984-85	19,035
1989-90	35,353
1990-91	37,408
1994-95	66,346
1999-2000	1,09,816

Note: Institutions cover co-operatives, scheduled commercial banks, Regional Rural Banks and Rural Electrification Corporation Ltd. Loans outstanding cover short-term and long-term credit direct as well as indirect.

Source: Reserve Bank of India Occasional Papers (2003).

Similarly, the level of outstanding loans increased between the period 1980-81 and 1989-90 from around Rs. 10,123 crore to around Rs. 35,353 crore, the figures achieved at the end of both the years. However on an annual average loans outstanding increased by Rs. 21,156 crore during this period and by Rs. 69,777 crore during the period 1990-91 to 1999-2000 and on an annual average basis by 15 times over the entire period 1971-72 to 1999-2000 (Chakrabarty, 2003).

It is worth noting here that the rural nominal income along with the flow of credit during this period increased significantly during the decades of 1970s, 1980s and 1990s. The yield per hectare of foodgrains increased from 872 kg/hectare in 1970-71 to 1704 kg/hectare in 1999-2000, nearly twice the growth, given the fact that the area under cultivation of foodgrains also increased from 124.32 million hectare in 1970-71 to 131.16 million hectare in 1983-84; with some variations in between over the years, the area was around 123.10 million hectare in 1999-2000 (Chakrabarty, 2003).

4. Prices

Price is essentially an important factor in influencing the rural livelihood. The price factor encircles both the agricultural commodities and the non-agricultural commodities. The rural labourer undeniably expects to earn a fair some of money, in exchange for the products sold, be it agricultural products or non-agricultural products. To ensure a minimum price in the case of agricultural products, the Government of India, introduced the Minimum Support Price (MSP) of various agricultural crops, on the recommendations of the Commission for Agricultural Costs and Prices (CACP). The MSP strategy indeed has been a cornerstone of the agricultural policy since 1965. Of course, it is important to mention here that the views of the concerned State Governments and Central Ministries/ Departments as well as other factors are considered relevant for fixing MSP. The objective was however, to ensure remunerative prices to the growers of agricultural produce with the motive of encouraging higher investment and production and, of course, evolving a balanced and integrated price structure in the context of the overall needs of the economy and also protecting the interests of the consumers by making available adequate supplies at reasonable prices. MSP is intended to offer a minimum guaranteed price for the farmers by the Government for their produce in case the market prices fall below that level. If the market offers higher price than MSP, the farmers are free to sell at that price. The MSPs of some of the major crops in, 2010-11, 2011-12 and 2012-13 are given in Table 14.9.

The MSP played a significant role in contributing towards sustained increase in agricultural production. There has been an increase of 5 per cent in area under Wheat, between 2006-07 and 2010-11 which culminated in an increase in production by 13 per cent. Also the area under cotton increased by about 22 per cent and its production by about 48 per cent.

The issue of *Price* in the rural areas of India stretches beyond the agricultural sector to the non-farm sector. The Price Factor affects the RNFS vastly through the changing level of prices of non-farm commodities which are sold in and out of the rural areas. The rural sector of India is a producer and consumer of innumerable non-agricultural commodities. Rural products of India can be said to be unique, innovative and have good utility and values. A major part of these products, namely, handicrafts items, food products, embroidery, clothes and other products, etc. supports and sustains a significant section of the population in rural areas. Though out of several attributes of these products, the *ethnic origin* and *indigenous design and appearance* attributes attract the most, these products are not marketed horizontally. Hence, they often first travel down to market through a long chain of intermediaries and then up to more difficult locations in the rural areas. In the process, the people in rural

Table 14.9: Minimum Support Prices of some of the Major Crops for 2010-11, 2011-12 and 2012-13

Commodity	*Variety*	*2010-11*	*2011-12*	*(#) increase in MSP 2011-12 over 2010-11*	*2012-13*	*(#) increase in MSP 2011-12 over 2010-11*
Paddy	Common	1000	1080	80 (8.0)	1250	170 (15.7)
	Grade 'A'	1030	1110	80 (7.8)	1280	170 (15.3)
Cotton	Medium Staple	2500	2800	300 (12.0)	3600	800 (28.6)
	Long Staple	3000	3300	300 (10.0)	3900	600 (18.2)
Wheat		1120@	1285	165 (14.7)	1350	65 (5.05)
Jute		1575	1675	100 (6.3)	2200	525 (31.3)
Sugarcane		139.12*	145.00*	5.88 (4.2)	170.00*	25 (17.2)

Source: Department of Agriculture and Cooperation, Ministry of Agriculture, Government of India.

@ An additional incentive bonus of Rs.50 per quintal is payable over the MSP.

* Fair and Remunerative Price.

Figures in brackets indicate percentage increase.

areas suffer from both low prices as producers and high prices as consumers. Thus, the rural entrepreneurs face acute loss and rural markets become stagnant.

Branding and Marketing of Rural Products: The era of Marketing in India, undeniably affected the urban manufactured goods sector as well as the rural manufactured goods sector. The rural sector, witnessed the growth of the agricultural sector and also the growth of the non-agricultural sector. The tool of marketing to promote agro-products in the national and domestic market has been highly effective. The retail outlets in the urban areas are seen flooded with packaged farm products like rice, wheat, oats, etc. and other food grains including vegetables. The effective use of marketing mix i.e., the 7Ps of marketing, Product, Price, Place, Promotion, People, Process and Physical Evidence, have undoubtedly affected the branding and marketing of rural products, specifically agricultural products. This in turn, has affected the price, at which these products are sold in the market. Some leading Indian brands selling agricultural products are ITC (Indian Tobacco Company), MPS, Kohinoor, HUL (Hindustan Unilever Limited), etc.

Agricultural marketing can be defined as commercial functions involved in transferring agricultural products consisting of farm, horticultural and other allied products from producer to consumer. In this, the retail giants who are the major buyers goes for purchase in bulk quantity and they constantly look for differentiated, graded, standardized, processed and packaged products rather than undifferentiated ones. They also look for qualitative and quantitative supply of agricultural stocks continuously to beat the competition in the retail sector. The farmers on the other hand, are also benefited through effective agricultural marketing. The purchase of agricultural produce in bulk by the marketing organizations directly from the farmers, have not only reduced (or eliminated) the presence of intermediaries in between, but has also resulted in payment of fairly acceptable prices to the farmers. For example, ITC in its agri-business has established strong backward linkages with its farmers. This has led to the building of a highly cost-effective procurement system. To web-enable the Indian farmer, it has created a networking system known as 'e-Choupal' where internet kiosks are provided to farmers to access on-line information related to the weather, crop conditions, prevalent efficient farming practices, current prices at the international level, etc. which is so very relevant for the farmers. As such, this system has not only led to enhanced supply chain management but also better farm productivity. The farmers on the other hand, are also benefited through effective agricultural marketing. From the above observation, it is clear that major Corporates (like ITC), are using internationally acclaimed pricing strategies namely, **farm gate pricing**. While implementing, *farm gate pricing* we observe that the company in mention and the farmer are in a win-win situation; this situation, comes because the company gets good raw materials which will cater to the apparently insatiable end-consumer. By adhering to the quality requirements as per the customer levels, the company gets more revenue (in terms of turnover/ market share) which in turn creates demand for the products and fosters well-being among the farmers.

Even in the case of non-farm products, there have been significant effects of branding and marketing. For example, the cooperative named Anand Milk Union Limited (AMUL) based at Anand in the state of Gujarat, spurred India's ***White revolution***, which led the country on its way to becoming the world's largest producer of not only milk but milk products, eventually making Amul one of the largest food brand in India and encouraging to venture into overseas market. This cooperative was formed to prevent the exploitation of milk producers, who were mainly marginal farmers in the hands of traders or agents of the then only existing dairy, the *Polson (brand)* dairy, in the small town of Anand (in Kaira District of Gujarat). This has not only led to marketing of milk and milk products produced by the Milk Unions under Amul, but also establishing a distribution network for marketing of milk and milk products along with, deciding on the prices of milk and milk products to be paid to Milk Unions.

Another example that can be cited with respect to marketing of non-farm products is of the Khadi Gramodyog Sangh, which aims at attaining the objective of disentangling the rural people from their acute poverty through stepping up steadily the Khadi and Village Industries sales and providing employment to the rural masses. The Khadi Gramodyog Bhavan under the Khadi Gramodyog Sangh in Chennai, introduced modern marketing techniques after scrutinizing customer's preference and fashion trends and to cater to the needs of the customers, pursued measures like introducing Khadi made garments, apart from selling a wide range of village industries products like honey, edible oils, soaps, pulses, etc. Also, in order to keep alive the varied forms of village arts and crafts, Khadi Bhavan also arranges a number of exhibitions like of dolls, sandalwood and rosewood products, *pooja* articles, jewellery, leather goods, teak wood furniture, etc.

5. Government Employment Schemes

The Government of India, since Independence, undertook the policy of providing employment through introducing wage programmes and as such reducing the then rampant poverty. One such successful programme had been 'The Jawahar Rozgar Yojana' (JRY) introduced in 1989 and got continued till 2006. Later, JRY lead to the formation of NREGA (National Rural Employment Guarantee Act) in the year 2006, later renamed as MGNREGA (Mahatma Gandhi National Rural Employment Guarantee Act) on 2009. The MGNREGA is apparently the largest wage employment scheme in the world. As such, it has provided employment to around 25 per cent of rural households in India, 50 per cent of which contributes to the SC/ST categories and around 48 per cent of unskilled labours fall under woman category (Joshi, 2013).

However, NREGA came after almost 56 years of experience of other rural employment programmes which includes both the Centrally Sponsored Schemes and those launched by State Governments. These consist of National Rural Employment Programme (NREP) 1980-89, Rural Landless Employment Guarantee Programme (RLEGP) 1983-89, Jawahar Rozgar Yojana (JRY) 1989-99, Employment Assurance Scheme (EAS) 1993-99, Jawahar Gram Samridhi Yojana (JGSY) 1999-2002, Sampoorna Grameen Rozgar Yojana (SGRY) from 2000, National Food for Work Programme (NFFWP) from 2004 were national rural employment schemes. The SGRY and NFFWP have been merged with NREGS in 2005. The Maharashtra Employment Guarantee Scheme (MEGS), launched in 1972-73 (the Act was passed in 1977), is an important state programme. These programmes generated the required wage employment for the targeted rural unemployed and poor people (ISWSD NREGA Final Report, 2006). All these schemes had their positive contribution, towards creating rural employment.

Table 14.10 shows the allocation in Union Budget on Rural Employment Schemes as per cent of Gross State Domestic Product (GSDP).

The fluctuations in allocation of the Union budget in rural employment generation schemes as percentage of GSDP are clearly noticeable. Since the late 90s post-liberalization, the allocation dipped considerably and then rose in the early year of the previous decade, falling again in the later years. However, there had been several *drawbacks* in the implementation of the employment generation schemes like, low level of funds allocation and lower utilization, minimum wages not being paid due to high productivity norms, enormous delays in wage payment,

Table 14.10: Allocation in Union Budget on Rural Employment Schemes as per cent of GSDP

Allocation in Union Budget on Employment Schemes as % of GSDP	
Year	*Rural Employment*
1998-99	0.21
1999-2000	0.19
2000-01	0.13
2001-02	0.20
2002-03	0.40
2003-04	0.37
2004-05	0.23
2005-06	0.33
2006-07	0.33

Source: ISWSD NREGA Final Report.

worksites devoid of any facilities, meager level of women participation, low number of person-days of wage employment provided per family, etc. (ISWSD NREGA Final Report). Hence, it can be concluded that, though the employment generation schemes in the rural areas benefitted the masses, it nonetheless carries its own loopholes.

6. Globalization and the Way Ahead

The effect of Globalization or the opening up of the Indian economy to the world economy is believed to have both positive and negative effects on the rural livelihood. At one end, if globalization led to growth in export potential, it has also its apparently negative effects in the form of Special Economic Zones (SEZ). Globalization can be defined as the integration of the economies of the world leading to interchange of goods, services, ideas as well as culture. As a result, the local markets blends with the larger global market. Globalization in India has a unique face of its own and inevitably along with time, has turned out to be a major topic of discussion and debate among the policy-makers and the other concerned groups of the country. Going back to the decade of 1990s when the policy of LPG (Liberalization, Globalization and Privatization) was adopted, it had been observed that the agricultural growth has been relatively sluggish in the 1990s compared with the 1980s, or even with the 1970s, except for non-food crops. There has also been a decline in rural income as a share of total income due to fall in the share of agriculture in the total income. On the other hand, the income earning opportunities from rural non-agricultural activity narrowed down in the 1990s. However, agricultural exports accounted for about 13 per cent to 18 per cent of total annual export of the country. In 2000-01, agricultural products valued at more than US $ 6 million were exported from the country.

The most persistent effect of globalization of late has been of SEZ (a geographical region that has economic laws that are more liberal than a country's typical economic laws), which are created across India to promote industries and exports. As such, a certain degree of vulnerability of the rural economy can be perceived with respect to the existence of SEZ. In 2007, the total amount of land to be acquired across India was estimated to be around 1,50,000 hectares, which were predominantly agricultural and typically multi-cropped and was capable of producing near to 1m tones of foodgrains (Hiremath, 2007). Hence, such kind of structural changes in the economy can be easily said to endanger the food security of the country. Nonetheless, we can argue that creation of SEZ develops the particular area, by not only adding on to the existing employment opportunities but also leads to urbanization of the economy.

Conclusion

In spite of the mind-boggling issue of globalization and its impact on rural livelihood of India, it is important to remember that the Indian rural sector is indispensable to the overall growth and development of the economy. The rural sector is undoubtedly carrying its own linkage effects (forward and backward), with the ever-expanding industrial sector. As such, both the sectors are supporting each other, given their own structural volatility and constraints, and have undoubtedly ended up in being both the cause and the effect behind the existence of each other. We should neither flaunt our well-performing industries by over-shadowing our 'green' rural sector nor stick to the stereotype way of running the pre-dominantly agrarian economy. Hence, a balanced growth of the economy with equal importance on both rural sector and urban sector is all desirable on the part of the policy-makers in specific and the nation builders as a whole, to do justice to both the urban, and the equally important rural masses.

References

Chakrabarty, Tapas Kumar (2003): "Rural Income: Some Evidence of Effect of Rural Credit During Last Three Decades", *Reserve Bank of India Occasional Papers*, Vol. 24, No. 3, Winter 2003.

FAO (2003): *Corporate Document Repository: Produced by Agriculture and Consumer Protection* (Committee on Agriculture 17th Session, Rome 31 March–4 April, 2003).

Glinskaya, E. and J. Jalan. (2005): "Quality of Informal Jobs in India", Background paper prepared for *Draft World Bank Report*, India's Employment Challenge: Creating Jobs, Helping Workers. New Delhi: World Bank.

Government of India (2010): *Wage Rates in Rural India (2008-09)*, Ministry of Labour and Employment, Labour, Shimla/Chandigarh, 2010.

Gulati Ashok and Jena Anjan. K. (2012): "Rural Prosperity No Mirage", *The Economic Times*, October 4, 2012.

Hiremath B.N. (2007): "The Changing Faces of Rural Livelihoods in India", *Theme Paper*, National Civil Society Conference, December 4-6, 2007.

Indian School of Women's Studies Development (2006): *e-Monitoring and evaluation of National Rural Employment Guarantee Scheme with Special Focus on Gender Issues*, October 2006, ISWSD NREGA Final Report.

Joshi, Avinash (2013): "Mahatma Gandhi National Rural Employment Guarantee Act – A Prevailing Instrument for Inclusive Growth of Rural India", *Tenth AIMS International Conference on Management*, January 6-9, 2013.

Kapila, Uma (Ed.), (2009): *Indian Economy Since Independence*, 19th Edition 2008-09, Academic Foundation Publication.

Kumar Anjani, Kumar Sant, Singh Dhiraj K. and Shivjee (2011): "Rural Employment Diversification in India: Trends, Determinants and Implications on Poverty", *Agricultural Economics Research Review*, Vol. 24 (Conference Number) 2011 pp. 361-372.

Landes Maurice and Burfisher Mary E. (2009): *Growth and Equity Effects of Agricultural Marketing Efficiency Gains in India*, Economic Research Report No. (ERR 89) 43 p., December 2009, United States Department of Agriculture (USDA).

Lanjouw Peter, Himanshu, Mukhopadhyay Abhiroop and Murgai Rinku (2010): "Non-farm Diversification and Rural Poverty Decline: A Perspective from Indian Sample Survey and Village Study Data", Draft September, 2010.

Mukhopadhyay A.K., Gangopadhyay D. and Nayak Saswati (2008): "Non-farm Occupation in Rural India: S&T for Rural India and Inclusive Growth: India", *Science and Technology*: 2008.

Paul Sharma, Vijay (2011): "India's Agricultural Development under the New Economic Regime: Policy Perspective and Strategy for the 12th Five Year Plan", *W.P. No. 2011-11-01*, November 2011, Indian Institute of Management, Ahmedabad, India.

Satyasai K.J.S. (2012): "Access to Rural Credit and Input Use: An Empirical Study", *Agricultural Economics Research Review*, Vol. 25 (Conference Number) 2012, pp. 461-471.

Singha, Komol (Ed.), (2010): *Rural Development in India: Retrospect and Prospects*, Concept Publishing Company Pvt. Ltd., New Delhi.

15

Disaster—A Menace to Rural Livelihood *via* Environmental Hazards

Anasuya Kar

> **"....We will not make genuine progress in mitigating climate change until we learn to speak of the atmosphere from the inside, understanding it as the breath of life.... What is needed is a reverential ecology...a way of seeing that reminds us that Earth doesn't belong to us but, rather, that we belong to Earth!"**
>
> —*Christopher Uhl*

I. Introduction

Disasters throw challenges to life and livelihood along with displacement on a mass scale and disrupts the social and economic living via severe environmental damage. A large section of rural people dependent on primary sector (e.g. agriculture, fishing, etc.) has to run into loss of livelihood. Besides its short-run effects, the multi-dimensional effects of disaster in the long-run, directly vis-à-vis indirectly jeopardize the security and pattern of family management which may ultimately lead to flotsam and jetsam.

The World Disaster Report (2010) published by the International Federation of Red Cross and Red Crescent Societies (IFRC) reveals that during 2000-2009, as many as 85 per cent of disaster-affected people belonged to the Asia-Pacific region. India and Bangladesh, with large number of population and high population density among disaster-pronc countries in South Asia, are highly vulnerable to floods and cyclones. In India as many as 200 million people are exposed to recurring floods every year. Besides, millions of people here live in vulnerable areas prone to geological, hydro-meteorological, man-made and technological disasters. The Vulnerability Atlas prepared by Building Materials Technology Promotion Council (BMTPC) highlights that of the geographical area in India 58 per cent lies within seismic zones with moderate to very high intensity, 12 per cent faces recurring floods, changing course of rivers and river erosion. Along the 7516 k.m. coastline, about 5700 k.m. are vulnerable to storm serge, cyclones and tsunami. More than 68 per cent area is vulnerable to drought. Landslide and snow avalanches in unstable slopes and high altitude terrains also occur frequently. Pressures of the fast pace of urbanization, modernization and industrialization bearing threats to man-made and technological disasters have also increased substantially. Needless to say, all these disasters have immense effects on livelihood—especially on the rural one.

According to the World Bank, during 1996-2000, India lost approximately 2.25 per cent of her GDP and 12.2 per cent of revenue annually due to disasters. It is evident that the damages and economic losses by disasters are far exceeding the acceptable levels (of financial allocation) and are wiping out the had-earned gains of development from the affected areas and the government exchequer as well. Further, the deployment of scarce resources for post-disaster relief, construction and recovery are making a substantial dent on resources for other sectors like health, education, social welfare, etc.

The colossal direct and indirect effects of disasters, a moving process with cumulative nature, on livelihood, the basic necessity for living, among others have made it imperative to incorporate disaster management into total development perspective for successful achievement of 'inclusive growth'.

II. Environment, Ecology, Climate Change and Disaster

Environment, a term derived from the French word 'Environner' means 'to surround'. As per the Environment (Protection) Act, 1986, environment includes all the physical and biological surroundings of an organism along with their interactions. Thus, environment may be defined as "the sum total of water, air and land and the interrelationships that exist among them and with the human beings, other living organisms and materials".

Environment often changes after some time. Although many organisms have ability to adopt to these changes—the tolerance level varies.

The world ecology is derived from the Greek word 'aikos' meaning 'household' and 'logos' meaning 'study'. Thus, the study of the environmental house includes all the organisms in it and all the functional processes that make the house habitable. Ecology then literally is the study of 'life at home' with emphasis on "the totality or pattern of relations between organisms and their environment".

The quality of human life is directly related to the quality of Environment—a system of physical, chemical and biological factors in dynamic equilibrium. Although a healthy environment is essential for human survival, man dominates the world and exploits all the available resources and, of course, becomes its prime victim. Ecological overshoot is a vastly underestimated threat to human well-being and the health of the planet and one that is not adequately addressed. Human activity via ecological footprint among others is a major cause of environmental change. Environmental degradation has an impact not only on human beings but also on all species and most natural symptoms.

Climate change is a long-term change in the statistical distribution of weather patterns over periods of time—ranging from decades to millions of years. It is caused by the factors that include oceanic processes, biotic processes, variations in solar radiation received by Earth, plate tectonics and volcanic eruptions and human-induced alterations of the natural world. "Taken as a whole" the IPCC (International Panel of Climate Change) says "the range of published evidence indicates that the net damage costs of climate change are likely to be significant and to increase over time."

A volatile mix of erratic weather, natural and man-made disasters and enormous pressures on the availability of clean air, water and energy together with the problems of poverty and hunger continues to be of great concern for policymakers, particularly in the developing countries like India. The impact of climate variability is redefining the hazard profile of many States in India—livelihood being the ultimate victim.

Disaster is defined as "Catastrophic situation where the normal pattern of life or ecosystem are required to preserve lives and/or the environment" (Ministry of Home Affairs, 2011). The Disaster Management Act (2005) has included man-made disasters to define disaster as "a catastrophe, mishap, calamity or grave occurrence in any area, arising from natural or man-made causes or by accident or negligence which result in substantial loss of life or human sufferings or damage to, and destruction of, property or damage to, or degradation of environment and is of such a nature or magnitude as to be beyond the coping capacity of the community of an affected area".

Disasters may be natural or man-made. High Powered Committee (HPC) on Disaster Management (1999) has identified thirty-one disasters categorized into five sub-groups.

Nuclear, Chemical and Biological threats are apparent in the present scenario. Moreover, deliberate national and international terrorism or accidental secondary fall out can be fatal.

III. Disaster and Livelihood

Hazard, be it natural or man-made, is an incident that hampers the normal life of the affected area temporarily with loss and damage to some extent. Hazard turns into disaster when it crosses the normal limit—which again depends on some factors, like magnitude of the event, vulnerability of the location, population density or desolation, etc. Actually the size and scale of disasters are determined by us.

Disasters cause loss of life, injury or other health impacts, property damage, loss of livelihood and services, social and economic disruptions and severe environmental damage. Although the vulnerability or the extent of exposure differs the marginalized sections, by virtue of their poverty, are much more affected by the vagaries of nature's fury than the normal populace. In fact, they are the worst sufferers of any kind of disaster via joblessness (livelihood) and displacement.

Livelihood is defined as a set of activities, involving means of securing the basic necessities of life (food, fodder, water, medicine, shelter, and clothing) and the capacity to acquire these necessities working either individually or as a group by using endowments (both human and material) to meet the requirements of self and the household on a sustainable basis with dignity. The activities are carried out repeatedly. A farmer's livelihood, for instance, depends on availability and accessibility of fish.

The concept of sustainable livelihood puts an attempt to go beyond the conventional definitions and approaches to poverty eradication. It is now recognized that more attention must be paid to various factors and processes (e.g. vulnerability and social exclusion) which either constrain or enhance ability of the poor to make a hiring in an economically, ecologically and socially sustainable manner.

According to Robert Chambers and Gordon Comray (1992), "A livelihood comprises the capabilities, assets (stores, resources, claims and access) and activities required for means of living. A livelihood is sustainable which can cope with and recover from shocks, maintain or enhance its capabilities and assets and provide sustainable livelihood opportunities for the next generation......"

Disaster, whether it strikes rural or urban area, inevitably takes its toll on livelihood or source of earning. Rural economy as it is basically vulnerable and dependent on primary sector, rural livelihood is heavily damaged by disasters. Different impacts of disasters there include—colossal damage, loss of life, loss of cattle, loss of assets, total and partial dislocation of transport and communication, collapse and damage of dwellings, loss of agriculture and allied jobs, loss of crop and vegetation, pollution of different types etc.

IV. Account of Disasters and Vulnerability in the Indian Context

The main natural disasters in India include floods, earthquakes, droughts and cyclones while landslides, avalanches, hail storms, cloud bursts, forest fire are the minor ones. Among the 35 total States/Union Territories in India 25 are disaster-prone and most of the states experience more than one type of disaster. On an average about 50 million people are affected by one or the other disaster annually besides loss of property worth several millions.

According to UNISDR (United Nations International Strategy for Disaster Reduction), India ranked second in the world for natural disasters after China in 2010. India's hazard profile is mainly determined by the geo-climatic settings and topographic features and the underlying vulnerabilities result in annual disasters of varying degrees (See Table 15.1).

It is needless to say mention that the poor and the vulnerable section is worst affected by disasters, losing their everything—even their livelihood. River erosion (leading to displacement) presents a special case in this context. Erosion-affected people at Malda bordering Jharkhand are, in particular, a case where deprivation has reached the level of statelessness for the local people residing in West Bengal. A similar situation exists in Murshidabad (West Bengal). And adding salt to their injury, river erosion is not yet regarded as a disaster.

In addition to large-scale displacement and loss of life disasters result in loss of property, infrastructure and agricultural crops worth millions of dollars annually—resulting in a substantial loss of hard won development gains (economic, physical, social and environmental).

Table 15.1: People affected, lives lost and economic damage due to Disasters in India during 1980 and 2010

Year	Type of Disasters	People affected	Life lost	Economic damage (USD x 1,000)
1980	Flood	30,000,023		
1982	Drought	100,000,000		
	Flood	33,500,000		
1984	Epidemic		3290	
1987	Drought	300,000,000		
1988	Epidemic		3000	
1990	Storm			2,200,000
1993	Flood	128,000,000		7,000,000
	Earthquake		9,748	
1994	Flood		2001	
1995	Flood	32,704,000		
1996	Storm			1,500,300
1998	Storm		2871	
	Extreme Temp.		2541	
	Flood		1811	
1999	Storm		9,843	2,500,000
2000	Drought	50,000,000		
2001	Earthquake		20,005	2,263,000
2002	Drought	300,000,000		
	Flood	42,000,000		
2004	Flood	33,000,000		2,500,000
	Earthquake		16,389	
2005	Flood			3,330,000
	Flood			2,300,000
2006	Flood			3,390,000
2009	Flood			2,150,000

Source: "EM-DAT: The OFDA/CRED International Disaster Database.

The direct losses from natural disasters have been estimated up to 20 per cent of India's GDP and 12 per cent of Central Government revenue (World Bank, 2002). Disaster losses include not only the shocking direct effect that meet our eyes *via* media, but also indirect effects such as foregone and interrupted production and services. Post-disaster reconstruction activities strain public finances and divert funds from economic development which further escalates the losses.

Direct damages (stock) induce indirect damage (flow). If the long-term recovery goes unaddressed, the loss from flow gets added everyday ultimately creating a huge pressure on the economy. To assess the extent of damage and loss of different States due to disasters, BMTPC prepared a Vulnerability ATLAS based on the available information in 1997. Table 15.2 shows revised version (2006).

Table 15.2: Losses during 2005-06 to 2009-2010

Sl. No.	*Human Lives*		*Cattle*		*Houses*		*Crop Areas*	
	Top 10 states	*No.*	*Top 10 states*	*No.*	*Top 10 states*	*No.*	*Top 10 states*	*Lakh Ha.*
1.	Himachal Pradesh	379	Assam	11659	Gujarat	221664	Orissa	12.36
2.	Uttarakhand	488	Himachal Pradesh	13551	Rajasthan	269252	Gujarat	12.85
3.	Maharashtra	749	Gujarat	19365	Orissa	475618	Rajasthan	17.36
4.	Kerala	763	Bihar	20474	Assam	493228	Bihar	21.37
5.	Andhra Pradesh	770	Karnataka	23020	Uttar Pradesh	517918	Maharashtra	21.52
6.	West Bengal	921	Arunachal Pradesh	28409	Maharashtra	723325	Uttar Pradesh	22.87
7.	Karnataka	990	Maharashtra	46586	Andhra Pradesh	857027	Tamil Nadu	23.34
8.	Gujarat	1199	West Bengal	47526	Bihar	1089676	Andhra Pradesh	29.21
9.	Bihar	1684	Rajasthan	50894	Karnataka	1134080	West Bengal	31.38
10.	Uttar Pradesh	2763	Andhra Pradesh	481960	West Bengal	2096665	Karnataka	34.43
	Others	2340	Others	42668	Others	921314	Others	34.43
	Total	13046	Total	786112	Total	8799047	Total	259.15

The economic cost of disaster not only erodes all developmental gains, but also cuts across the political boundaries created by man. Disaster incident of one country may have serious impact on the other geographical regions of the world. The same disaster may affect many countries at the same time, e.g. the concurrent disaster Tsunami (2004) affected many countries. In the era of globalization, disaster happening in one country leads to huge loss in other countries *via* spill-over and snow-ball effects—thereby rendering the livelihood more vulnerable. It is evident that all types of damage and loss are ultimately manifested in utter vulneralbility of livelihood worsening the condition of the poor (specially in rural and underdeveloped areas) at the receiving end. Table 15.3 shows some of the major natural disasters that repeatedly and increasingly affectted India.

Table 15.3: Year-wise damage caused due to floods, cyclonic storms, landslides, etc. during last ten years in India

Year	*Live Lost [Human] (in No.)*	*Cattle Lost*	*Houses damaged (in No.)*	*Cropped areas affected (in Lakh hectares)*
2001-02	834	21,269	3,46,878	18.72
2002-03	898	3,729	4,62,700	21.00
2003-04	1,992	25,393	6,82,209	31.98
2004-05	1,995	12,389	16,03,300	32.53
2005-06	2,698	1,10,997	21,20,012	35.52
2006-07	2,402	4,55,619	19,34,680	70.87
2007-08	3,764	1,19,218	35,27,041	85.13
2008-09	3,405	53,833	16,46,905	35.56
2009-10	1,677	1,28,452	13,59,726	47.13
2010-11	2,310	48,778	13,38,619	46.25

Source: Ministry of Home Affairs (MHA).

It is quite difficult to assess, count or scale the precise cost of disasters in terms of loss of lives, property, livelihood, loss of development opportunities, etc. Cost of disasters is obviously inequitable—falling heavily on the poor. Disasters result not only in loss of shelter but also create hardship, non-availability of victual, temporary (sometimes permanent) loss of livelihood and disrupt socio-economic activities—situation being more aggravated in rural areas. While the contribution of agriculture to reduction in hunger and poverty is well recognized, the impact of disaster and bad weather on agriculture, on the income (livelihood) and food security of small and marginal farmers and marginal labourers has not been adequately addressed in any programme related to agriculture. Disasters rob them of their belongings, e.g., shelter, standing crops, livelihood, cattle, they become indebted, and are pushed back into the vicious circle of poverty. Disaster Risk Reduction measures incorporated in Rural Poverty Alleviation Programme can affectively help in reducing poverty in rural India through provisions for security of livelihood. It stands to reason that loss of livelihood security in the rural areas (which is already under stress due to high population density and growth, rapid urbanization, high rate of environmental degradation and frequent occurrence of natural disasters) make millions of people who directly or indirectly depend on primary sector vulnerable.

V. Need for Disaster Management

The need for preparedness to combat disaster is hardly understood until it happens. In short, disaster management is the process of preparedness to brave the disaster. Although India is highly vulnerable and disaster-prone, the four colossal disasters of last two decades—Earthquake in Maharashtra (1993), Super Cyclone in Orissa and Andhra Pradesh (1999), Earthquake in Gujarat (Kutch, 2001) and Tsunami in Andaman and Tamil Nadu (2004) worked as a milestone in initiating awareness for disaster management.

Disaster Management is a multi-disciplinary area where a wide variety of issues range from forecasting, warning, search and rescue, relief to reconstruction and rehabilitation. Also, it is multi-sectoral involving administrators, scientists, planners, volunteers and communities. Their roles and activities span the pre-disaster, during disaster and post-disaster plans and all these activities are complementary and supplementary to each other.

Disaster Management occupies an important place in the policy framework as it is the poor and the underprivileged who are worst affected losing even their livelihood on account of calamities and disasters. In 2004, Department for International Development (DFID, UK) made explicit links among disasters, development and poverty and concluded that "...sustainable poverty reduction is proving to be an elusive goal and this is particularly because disasters are not being factored into development."

In a changed viewpoint, now poverty (linked with insufficient or lack of livelihood) is measured in terms of human poverty indicators such as lack of access to resources necessary to sustain the basic human capabilities and Disaster Management is expressed in terms of hazard assessment, vulnerability analysis and disaster risk reduction. Thus, a paradigm shift in both the concepts—poverty alleviation and disaster management, is introduced.

The full-fledged National Disaster Management Framework has attempted to combine poverty eradication, capacity building and community empowerment with the disaster management related matters. Accordingly, the National Disaster Management Act (2005) shows a paradigm shift from relief-centric approaches to a pro-active regime that lays greater emphasis on preparedness, prevention and mitigation.

VI. Conclusion

Livelihood, in a nutshell, means earning—empowerment to living. Disasters among all other damages, impair livelihood the moot—especially in rural areas. For this reason, restoration and creation of livelihood along with relief and reconstruction demand equal attention, if not more. Taking the advantages of wretched condition created by disasters (e.g. displacement, lack of food, shelter, medical help, etc.) rackets of middle-men, cheats and human-traffickers become hyper-active. Lack and loss of livelihood, force thousands of people into their trap in search of livelihood. Mainly women, baited by jobs elsewhere are trafficked on a mass scale—and flesh-trading become a livelihood for some persons. This is a common picture of the rural areas. As the poor with poverty is prevalent in rural India disasters loom large on rural livelihood. The recovery process of disaster-damages is a short-run vis-à-vis long-run effort. Rural livelihood is mainly based on agriculture. But to make damaged arable land re-cultivable is a time-consuming process (e.g. after-Ayila Sundarbans). So it is very urgent to build substitute livelihood along with restoration of agricultural ones in the rural areas. Damages and losses are there but hunger knows no law. It may be concluded by quoting Sukanta Bhattacharyya, the poet—

> "Nothing else matter, in the World of Hunger,
> Even the full moon hangs like a singed bread."

References

Bhukta, Anindya (2012): 'ABCD of Disaster Management', *Dhanadhanye*.
Padmanathan, G. (2012): 'Hazard Profile of India', *Yojana*, March 2012, Vol. 56.

Menon, N. Vinod Chandra: Challenges in Disaster Management, *Yojana*, March 2012.

Kumar T. Nanda: Managing Disasters in India, *Yojana*, March 2012.

Kumar, K.J. Ananda and Ajinder Walia: *India Disaster Report*, NIDM.

Murthy, D.B.N. (2007): *Disaster Management: Text and Case Studies*, Deep and Deep Publications, New Delhi.

16

Livelihoods of Rural Van-Rickshaw Pullers are at a Stake

A Case Study in a Selected Village of Nadia District

Suhas Roy and *Swapan Kumar Roy*

I. Introduction

Rickshaws are Japanese in origin. The original word in Japanese is *Jinricksha. 'Jin'* means 'man'; *'riki'* means 'strength'; and *'sha'* means 'vehicle'. Rickshaws refer to man pulling vehicles. In 1900, Chinese immigrants brought these vehicles in Indian subcontinent and they remained in India as the most popular local means of transport. This type of tri-cycle is now found all-over India. With time they grew in numbers. They are pollution-free vehicles. According to *Concise Oxford Dictionary*, the word 'van' means "a covered motor vehicle used for transporting goods or people". But van-rickshaws found in rural West Bengal are not covered. Van-rickshaws are also tricycles. They are also pollution-free. The number of van-rickshaws grew with time. The structure of rickshaw is made to accommodate two passengers. There is a foldable shade above the heads of the passengers to protect them from sunlight and rain. Van-rickshaws do not have such shades. They can accommodate four to six passengers. Previously, van-rickshaws were used to carry goods only. Later it was found that they are more cost-effective in carrying passengers in relation to rickshaws as its capacity to carry more passengers. In 2000, a devastating flood was there in West Bengal. A large area of rural West

Bengal was waterlogged. Van-rickshaws were found to be most effective and affordable means of rural transport in rescue, relief and communication. It was found that the number of van-rickshaws crossed ordinary rickshaws plying in rural areas. Van-rickshaws became the most popular both in passengers as well as in goods carrying. They were found in playing the role of ambulance in rural areas. It is not a rare scene to see that patients are being sent to hospitals by van-rickshaws and saline bottle is held by someone. Even the corpses are being transported by van-rickshaws. Such a popular means of transport is facing viability threats from different corners by the end of the year 2012. The present paper intends to investigate the factors behind this viability challenge which raises the question of livelihood of the van-rickshaw pullers.

II. Coverage and Methodology of the Study

The study covers fifty van-rickshaw pullers operating in the two contiguous Gram panchayat areas, namely, Bethuadahari-I and Bethuadahari-II under Nakashipara Development Block in the district of Nadia. The samples were drawn at random from the van-rickshaw stands near Bethuadahari Railway Station, Bethuadahari Bus Stand and Birpur More. The study started in the last week of December 2012 and ended in the last week of January 2013. A set of questions were scheduled to ask the sample van-rickshaw pullers. The authors and three other associates took personal interviews on the basis of the schedule prepared.

III. Livelihood of Rural Van-Rickshaw Pullers

India is a labour-abundant country and its unemployment problem is acute. Rural youths having no specialized training, abilities and skills compel to rely upon their physical strength for their livelihoods. They involved themselves in unskilled jobs. A few rich people own quite a large number (ranges from ten to twenty) of van-rickshaws. They rent their van-rickshaws to pedallers per day basis. Since last two years it is Rupees twenty only, before that it was only Rupees ten per day. It is a good option to rural youths. They can earn more if they put more labour and time. The passenger carrying van-rickshaws stand near bus stoppages, railway station, hospitals, offices, market etc. the goods carrying van-rickshaws assemble near godowns, markets, shops and farmhouses. They can pay the rental charge by a single trip of journey. The rest trips amount to his income. As a result, many van-rickshaw pullers bought van-rickshaws on their own and became self-employed. Thus there are two types of van-rickshaw pullers – owner-puller and tenant-puller. Owner-pullers need not pay anything to others out of their earnings. But the tenant-pullers have to pay a certain amount of their earnings daily to the owners of their van-rickshaws.

Sometimes the urban intelligentsias argue that van-rickshaw pulling is an act of violation of human rights. Four human beings are pulled by a human by his physical labour is completely an inhuman activity. Rural youths do not bother with this human right. They want a handful of money after a day-long work. Van-rickshaw pulling gives them this opportunity. This apart, they can help fellow villagers by providing his service as and when needed. They are given importance by the villagers. They rely on the van pullers in sending their children to and bringing them from schools. They depend upon them in visiting doctor's place, hospitals. They rely upon them in sending marketed goods home and marketable goods to the right destinations. In short, the van-rickshaw pullers have personal relationships with their customers.

A van-rickshaw puller whether he pulls passengers or luggage makes ten trips (to and fro) on an average in a day. The number of trips varies within the range beginning from five to twenty in a day. Out of these twenty (ten up and ten down) trips, a passenger carrying van-rickshaw makes five to six trips to carry goods and luggage. Similarly, goods carrying van-rickshaw makes five to six trips to carry passengers out of their twenty trips.

Daily income of a owner-van-rickshaw puller on an average is Rupees two hundred only. The tenant pullers' income is on an average is Rupees One hundred eighty only. In twenty full trips, a owner-puller can earn Rupees four hundred only, but they earn only Rupees two hundred because in each trip they do not get four passengers. The passengers do not want to wait for more than five minutes to collect more commuters of the same route. The van-pullers have to start their trip keeping seats vacant. They are often found to carry two or three passengers at a time. The van-fare is fixed at Rupees five per commuter. This is minimum as well as maximum fare because the van does not go beyond a certain destination unless it is booked as reserved. In that case, the rate is fixed through negotiation. If the passengers drop in the midway of the route they have to pay the minimum fare. They do not get any concession for not travelling the full course. The rate of Rupees five per passengers is at least five years old. The van-pullers do not take the risk of increasing the fare anticipating losing their demands.

A van-rickshaw puller usually works from early morning. They take the passengers to the railway station (Bethuadahari) to avail the first local train towards Sealdah. They reach the station as early as 4-30 A.M. They try to attend all the Up and Down trains. They bring the passengers to the station and take them to the different part of the village. They have their meals in suitable gaps. At 9-00 P.M. they make their final trip, taking passengers of Bhagirathi Express. They again come to the station to receive the passengers in the midnight (Up Lalgola passenger train) if they are requested by any known villager. They try to respond positively round the clock, if any patient is seriously ill and needs to be brought to local primary health centre. Thus, they do not have any fixed time of work. In spite of this, the availability of van-rickshaws is less in the late noon (1-30 P.M. to 2-30 P.M.) and in the evening. The old, feeble, poor eye-sighted and alcoholic pedallers retire with the sunset.

IV. Factors Affecting their Livelihoods

There is no doubt that van-rickshaw pulling is a very laborious job. Unless nutritionally compensated physique of the puller does not endure this exercise for many days. They need adequate food, rest and sound sleep. Their income falls to zero if they become ill. Their health and physical fitness is the main factor that affects their livelihoods.

Many of them become alcoholic. It is dangerous for their profession. Firstly, it reduces physical strength. Secondly, it reduces the power of contribution to his family. Thirdly, it raises probability of road accidents. Finally, it reduces credibility of the pullers to the passengers and the latter avoid him consciously.

Recently, a close competitor of van-rickshaw has emerged in rural road transport system. The name of this competitor is lachhiman. They are also known as city van service, pick-up vans and bhatbhati vans. Lachhimans are motor run van-rickshaws. They are structured more strongly and bigger in sizes. They accommodate fifteen persons at a time. They run by diesel. They are designed and fabricated locally. Local smiths make the structure and mechanics install the machineries. The motor of the irrigation pump is used in the lachhimans. The fare of lachhiman is also Rupees five for the same distance. Moreover, it takes lesser time. It covers larger distance in a trip. From the point of view of the passengers, lachhimans are far better than van-rickshaws. Thus, recent phenomenon is that passengers are preferring lachhimans to van-rickshaws. When they are not getting lachhimans they are availing van-rickshaws. Thus, the market share of van-rickshaws is diminishing quickly in rural road transport due to introduction of lachhimans. But the lachhimans suffer from several serious limitations. Firstly, the design made by the indigenous smiths and mechanics are not proved to be adequately safe by any competent authority. Secondly, they carry beyond limits. Thirdly, they are accident prone. Fourthly, the vehicle is not pollution-free. They emit considerable black smoke in the air. Finally, they do not have legal support to be road worthy. The drivers do not need driving license! They do not need clear emission certificates from smoke checking centres! It is completely a local arrangement using local expertise and contrary to rules and regulations applicable to automobiles.

Once upon a time van-rickshaws enjoy almost monopoly in rural road transport system. Rickshaws were there but could not compete with van-rickshaws. Van rickshaws can carry more people at a time; they can be used to carry people as well as goods. They used to go anywhere in the interior villages. They do not require dry, smooth and all-weather roads. Unlike the rickshaws, the passengers of van-rickshaws share the cost of a trip. The fare is charged on per capita basis. The villagers found it more affordable than rickshaws. The fare of rickshaw is not shared. For this reason, the number of rickshaws dropped gradually in the interior village. But with the introduction of lachhimans, van-rickshaws are facing livelihood threats. The product life-cycle of van-rickshaws is now out of date. New technology has provided a better option and occupied the place of van-rickshaws.

The Prime Minister's Gram Sadak Yojana (PMGSY), NABARD's RIDF schemes built a well-knit rural road network. In addition to these, MGNREG Scheme has constructed many kuccha roads in the villages. This road network attracted different kind of vehicles in the rural areas. In the bus routes, the frequency of buses has increased. Lachhimans have been introduced. A number of reputed automobile companies like Tata (Magic) and Mahindra (Gio) have launched small cars (like auto-rickshaws but four wheelers) in carrying rural passengers in rural roads. These vehicles have already taken place as shared cabs in rural transport system. Gradually, their popularity is also on rise. All these are due to improvement of rural road and implementation of need based technology.

The improvement of economic condition of the rural people and the growing needs of quicker communication with distant places have encouraged villagers to own scooters, mopeds and motorcycles. The use of bicycle is being rapidly replaced by these bi-wheeler automobiles. These also have a negative effect on the demand for van-rickshaw pullers.

V. Findings of the Survey

The findings of the survey can be summarized in the following manner. In Table 16.1, the questions which can be answered by yes or no have been placed. The number of yes or no gives the general idea about the asked information.

Table 16.1: Survey Information in Yes-No Format

Sl. No.	*Question asked*	*Yes*	*No*
1.	Do you have your own van-rickshaw?	16	34
2.	Do you know that many van-rickshaw pullers are alcoholic?	45	05
3.	Do you earn more than rupees two hundred or more a day?	12	38
4.	Do you get four passengers in every trip?	00	50
5.	Do you have any cultivable land?	13	37
6.	Do you have Bank accounts?	32	18
7.	Have you any health insurance policy?	00	50
8.	Do you have any life insurance policy?	07	43
9.	Are you literate?	45	05
9(a).	Do you have passed Matriculation?	17	33
9(b).	Do you have passed H.S. Exam?	06	44
9(c).	Are you a graduate?	00	50
10.	Do you have any plan to switch over to another profession?	22	28
11.	Do you think lachhimans are posing threats to your livelihood?	41	09
12.	Do you think that Tata magic/Mahindra gio are your rivals?	35	15
13.	Do you think improvement of roads in the rural areas have attracted your rival means of transport to operate in your area?	30	20
14.	Do you think personal two-wheelers of the villagers have reduced your demands significantly?	15	35
15.	Do your children go to school?	40	10
16.	Do you want your children to continue in the same profession as you?	48	02

Source: Field Survey.

In Table 16.2, such questions are placed which have a specific answer other than yes or no.

Gallagher (1992) pointed out that rickshaw pullers have to work nearly as hard as Olympic athletes. They cannot continue it for long.

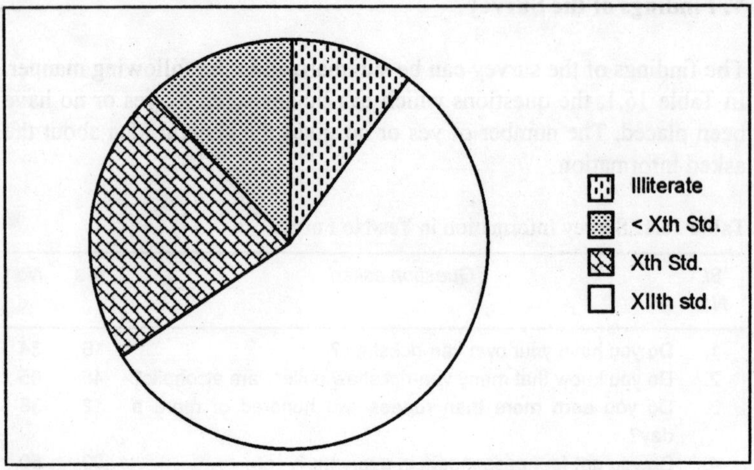

Fig. 16.1: Level of Education of the Respondent Van Rickshaw Pullers
Source: Field Survey.

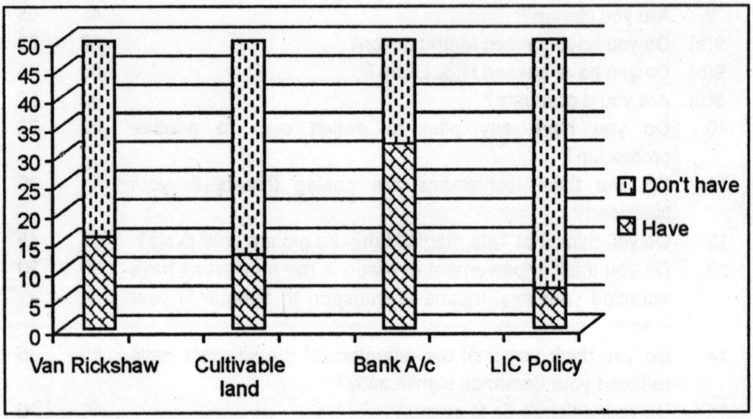

Fig. 16.2: Financial Position of Respondent Van-Rickshaw Pullers
Source: Field Survey.

When they enter into this profession their physical strength remains normal. But with time due to excessive physical pressure of job their condition of physical health deteriorates. They often suffer from cold, fever, gastro-enteric problems including acidity and ulcers. Their irregular food habits and long gap between the meals account for this type of illness. They also suffer from body ache, headache and physical weakness.

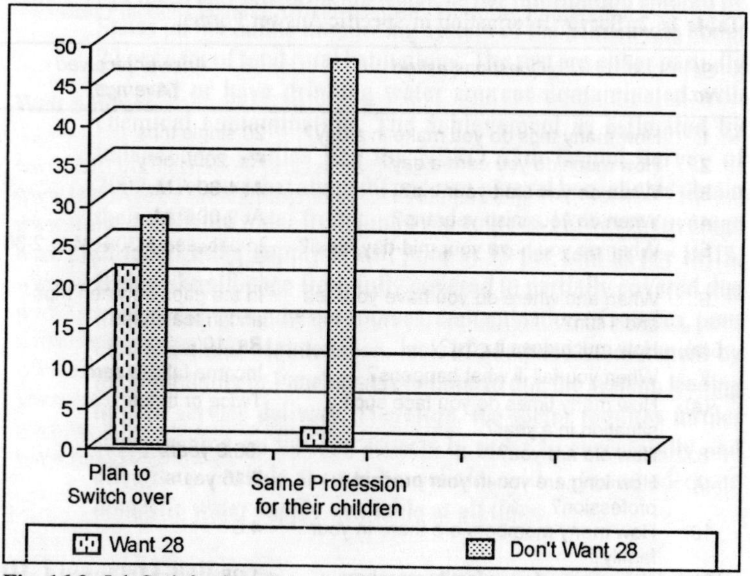

Fig. 16.3: Job Satisfaction of the Respondent Van-Rickshaw Pullers
Source: Field Survey.

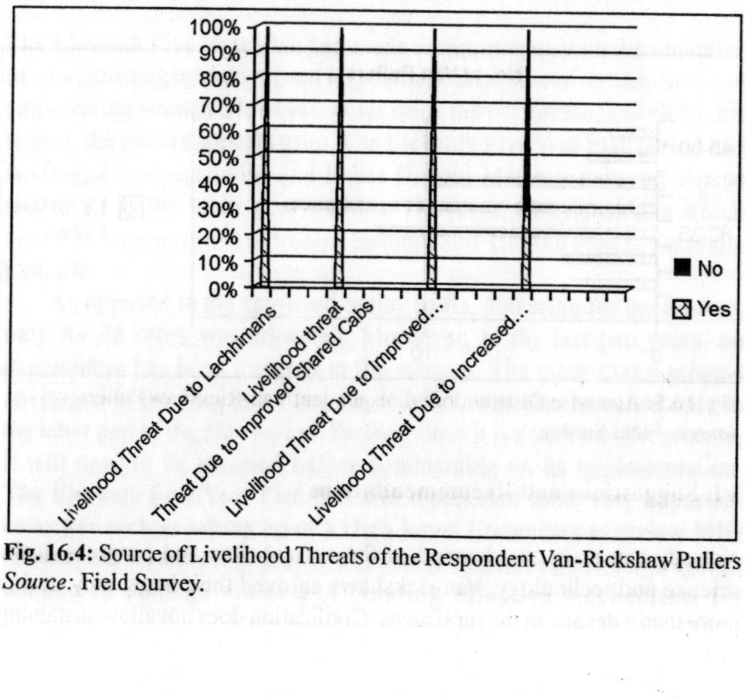

Fig. 16.4: Source of Livelihood Threats of the Respondent Van-Rickshaw Pullers
Source: Field Survey.

Table 16.2: Survey Information in Specific Answer Format

Sl. No.	*Questions asked*	*Answer received (Average)*
1.	How many trips do you make in a day?	20 single trips
2.	How much do you earn a day?	Rs. 200/- only
3.	When do you start your trip?	At 4-30 A.M.
4.	When do you finish your trip?	At 9-00 P.M.
5.	When do you have your mid-day meal?	In between 1-30 P.M to 2-30 P.M.
6.	When and where do you have your tea and Tiffin?	In the gaps between trips and in tea shops.
6(a).	How much does it cost?	Rs. 10/-
7.	When you fall ill what happens?	Income falls to zero.
7(a).	How many times do you face such a situation in a year?	Twice or thrice
8.	How old are you?	36.8 years
9.	How long are you in your present profession?	7.16 years
10.	How many members are there in your family?	4.6
10(a).	How many of your family members contribute to family income?	1.28

Source: Field Survey.

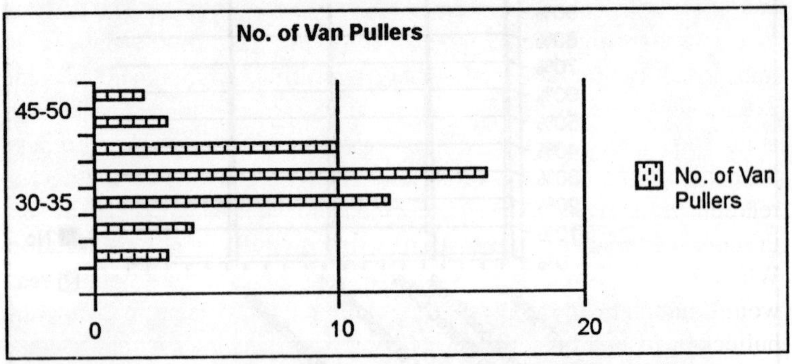

Fig. 16.5: Age-wise Distribution of respondent Van-Rickshaw Pullers
Source: Field Survey.

VI. Suggestions and Recommendations

Nobody can resist the demand of the current time and progress of the science and technology. Van-rickshaws enjoyed their hegemony during more than a decade in the rural areas. Civilization does not allow sustaining

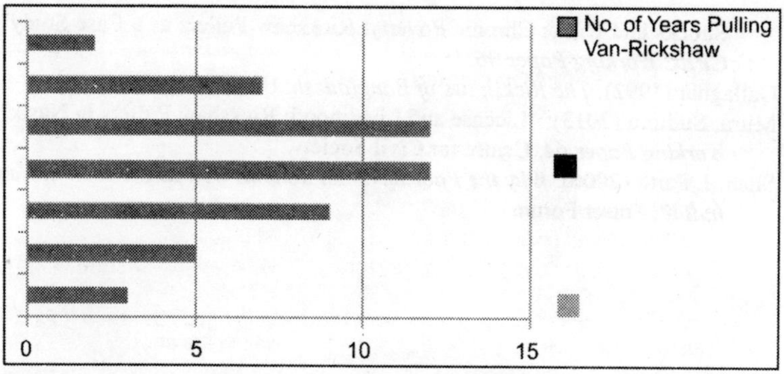

Fig. 16.6: Number of Years in Van-rickshaw Pulling
Source: Field Survey.

this hegemony forever. It is true that the way demand for van-rickshaws are declining it would become soon lose its economic viability. If a young person fails to earn his livelihood even after a day-long hard work, then it is not possible for him to continue the same work for indefinite period. These people are to be engaged in different occupations. They are to be trained to drive auto-rickshaws, mini cabs and matadors. They can also be given training to repair automobiles and replacement of spare parts of them. The running of lachhimans can be restricted for the time-being but the other rival mode of vehicles would fill in the gap soon. The existing van-rickshaw pullers can be given loans to purchase improved means of transport. As a pollution free vehicle, van-rickshaws should not become extinct altogether. Technological upgradation of existing van-rickshaws is not impossible. Geared pedals would increase the speed and reduce the hardship of the pullers. These models are needed to be competitive in relation with its rivals. The existing model of van-rickshaws is to be sent in more interior parts of the villages where roads are not yet metallic. Where there is all-weather roads are available improved means of transport would automatically come into operation. Like palanquins, caravan, bullocks cart and horse-driven chariots van-rickshaws would become extinct from the map of rural road transport. This paper is an attempt of rehabilitation of van-rickshaw pullers in alternative occupations and extension of lives of van-rickshaws in rural areas as a means of livelihood.

References

Begum, Sharifa and Sen, Binayak (2004): "Unsustainable Livelihoods, Health

Shocks and Urban Chronic Poverty: Rickshaw Pullers as a Case Study", *CPRC Working Paper 46*.

Gallaghar (1992): *The Rickshaws of Bangladesh*, UPL, Dhaka.

Mitra, Sudipto (2013): "License and Livelihood: Rickshaw Pullers in Nasik", *Working Paper 64,* Centre for Civil Society.

Shah, J. Parth (2006): *Why the Poor have not done as well as the Rich in New India?*, Fraser Forum.

17

Impact of Microfinance through SHG on the Livelihoods of the Rural Poor

A Case Study of a Village in Nadia District of West Bengal

Bhajan Chandra Barman

I. Introducton

The basic problem of our country is the problem of poverty and underutilization of the nationally cheap labour resource. India's effort to eradicate poverty has a long history. As we have seen, since the inception of our planning exercise, that various antipoverty programmes were being undertaken for the poverty-stricken population to reduce their number who lie below the poverty line. Still, even after six decades of planning, we have rather failed to reduce the number of rural poor in real term.

As a result, we have had another important problem that also crop up side by side in our rural society is the minimal use of the working potentiality of the employable female adults. This is equally true, more or less, for the men but for women it is in point of serious concern. From a recent village study it has been seen that more than 91 per cent employed female adults are failed to make use even 40 per cent of their labour power (Kar, 2009). Therefore, we have failed to expand the good opportunity of livelihood before the rural employable adults.

Needless to mention that India is an agro-based country where around 70 per cent of the population depends upon agriculture for their livelihood.

The rural poor farmers cannot get satisfactory services by the formal and informal financial sectors in our country. Most of the time, the poorest of the poor is deprived of credit due to absence of adequate and suitable collaterals. Besides, the poor need credit in small doses frequently and that should be made available when it is needed the most. Therefore, the access to credit by the rural poor is very much limited.

Under the above circumstances, we can think about the concept of microfinance which is a powerful tool and a new generation of anti-poverty programme. With the help of the formation of SHGs microfinance expand the scope of employment opportunities particularly among the rural poor adults.

II. Concept and Feature of Microfinance and SHG

Microfinance, a new anti-poverty programme, is a global phenomenon introduced by Dr. Muhammad Yunus of Bangladesh in the 1970s. Before Yunus, it was assumed that poor people were unbankable since they were only capable of taking out small loans, and had no collateral. But Dr. Yunus with the help of Grameen Bank in Bangladesh proved that poor are indeed responsible enough to manage credit and repay loans. Since then microfinance institutions have sprung up all-over the world and reached millions of poor people in the grass-root rural areas.

Researchers have explained the term 'microfinance' as the "provision of financial services and loans to the poor in which sum of money loaned out is repaid in small installments over a certain period of time" (Morduch, 2000).

Microfinance can be defined as "giving access to financing means, to a maximum of poor people, by allowing them to use their capacities in favour of a durable development" (Yunus, 2003).

Microfinance is a form of financial development that has primarily focused on alleviating poverty through providing financial services to the poor. Most people think of microfinance, if at all, as being about micro-credit, i.e. lending small amounts of money to the poor. Microfinance is not only this, but it also has a broader perspective which also includes insurance, transactional services, and importantly, savings (Barr, 2005).

The Canadian International Development Agency (CIDA) defines microfinance as, "the provision of a broad range of financial services to poor, low income households and micro-enterprises usually lacking access to formal financial institutions" (CIDA & Microfinance, 2002).

Microfinance gives access to financial and non-financial services to low-income people, who wish to access money for starting or developing an income generation activity. Microfinance as a discipline has created financial products and services that together have enabled low-income people to become clients of a banking intermediary (Murray & Boros, 2002).

The main features of the microfinance institution which differentiate it from other commercial institutions are:

> (i) a substitute for informal credit; (ii) generally requires no collateral; (iii) have simple procedures and less documentation; (iv) mostly group lending; (v) easy and flexible repayment schemes; (vi) financial assistance of members of group in case of emergency; (vii) the most deprived segments of population are efficiently targeted; and (x) groups interaction with each others.

The SHGs became a regular component of the Indian financial system since 1996. A brief note on SHG is given in this section. The Self-Help Group [SHG] is considered to be a voluntary association of poor people. They are mostly having some socio-economic background. They are involved in solving their common problems through self-help and mutual help. SHG creates small saving among the members and the amount is kept with any bank. The SHGs have a membership of 15 to 20 members. SHGs are either registered or unregistered groups of people who are economically homogenous; and the members are basically small and marginal farmers, landless agricultural labourers, rural artisans, petty rural traders, who voluntarily coming together to save small amounts regularly, to mutual help basis (Swain and Nayak, 2008).

According to Reserve Bank of India, SHGs may be registered or unregistered group of people, mostly micro-entrepreneurs having homogeneity in their socio-economic background, who join hands together to contribute regular savings to a common fund and meet their emergency needs on mutual help basis. The peer pressure and collective wisdom ensures the credit use and timely repayments. The peer pressure and collective wisdom substitute the collateral for loans.

It is also defined as a group of rural poor generally comprising of small/marginal farmers, landless agricultural labourers, rural artisans, women folk and other micro entrepreneurs who organize themselves to, achieve socio-economic development by raising resource at their level initially and linking with the bank subsequently with the help of NGOs [www.aidindia.org].

The self-help group has been defined by NABARD as a group of about 20 people from a homogeneous class who come together for addressing their common problems. They are encouraged to make voluntary thrift on a regular basis. They use their pooled resource to make small interest bearing loans to their members. The process helps them imbibe the prioritization of needs, setting terms and conditions and accounts keeping. This gradually builds financial discipline in all of them. They also learn to handle resources of a size that is much beyond individual capacities of any of them. The SHG in certain multiples of the accumulate savings of the SHG. The bank loans are given without any collateral and at market interest rates. The groups continue to decide the terms of loans to their own members. Since the groups own accumulated savings are part and parcel of the aggregate loans made by the groups to their members, peer pressure ensures timely repayments (NABARD 2001-02).

The SHGs are small, informal and homogenous groups. These groups have proved as cyclic agents of development in both the rural and urban areas. The SHGs after being formed start collecting a fixed amount of thrift from each member regularly. After accumulating a reasonable amount of resource, the group starts lending to its members for petty consumption needs. If the bank is satisfied with the group in terms of (i) genuineness of demand for credit; (ii) credit handling capacity of the members; (iii) repayment behaviour within the groups; and (iv) the accounting system and maintenance of the records, it extends a term loan of smaller amount to the group. Thus, financing through SHGs effects quite a few benefits like: (i) savings mobilized by the poor; (ii) access to the required amount of appropriate credit by the poor; (iii) meeting the demand and supply of credit structure and opening of new market for financing institutions; (iv) reduction in transaction cost for both lenders and borrowers; (v) tremendous improvement in recovery; (vi) heralding a new realization of subsidiless and corruptionless credit; and (vii) remarkable empowerment of poor women.

III: Objective and Methodology

Objectives

The main objectives of this write up are:

1. to measure the impact of microfinance through SHGs on the livelihood of the rural poor; and
2. to show the support of microfinance to rural livelihood programmes has transformed the quality of life and reduced poverty.

Methodology

It is found that there are two types of SHGs formed in the study district. They are: (1) SHGs formed under SGSY, and (2) SHGs formed by NABARD. We deal mainly with SHGs which are formed under SGSY scheme. We have collected primary data from 10 SHGs with 130 members under SGSY scheme. Accordingly, 10 SHGs with 130 women members who are involved in economic activities with microfinance will be the sample units for the present study. The survey was conducted in one village namely Khamarpara of Santipur Block. The logic behind choosing the village is that the SHGs in this village are functioning for a long time. We use some secondary data also. Various developmental officials, agencies and NGOs will be our secondary source of data.

IV. Profile of the Study Area

Khamarpara includes small and marginal farmers, agricultural labourers, artisans like weavers, mason, carpenter, tailors etc. and small traders such as petty businessman, shopkeepers, readymade garments seller, processing of *muri*, *chira*, and *khai*. Most of the households weave handloom and spinning. Some household cultivate paddy either on owned or leased lands. Agricultural labour is the other occupation. All members of a family (including children) work as labourers during the agricultural season.

Beedi rolling is another activity in Khamarpara village. It is a home-based activity and provides a primary source of income, which is available throughout the year and collect the production. It is an important stream of income for households, taking care of day-to-day needs such as expenses for schooling, vegetables, small festivals. Retailing is a popular enterprise option for women. The families that could combine this activity with some other means of income generation were relatively comfortable.

Some small shops were found to generate a surplus of around Rs. 9,000. This would be inadequate to meet the entire requirements of a family, but was a useful buffer when agriculture was not giving adequate returns. To set up a shop women generally borrow between Rs. 10-20,000.

Table 17.1: Gradation of SHGs

Grading	*No. of SHGs*	*Percentage*
Not any grading	1	6.67
1st grading	9	60.00
2nd grading	5	33.33
Total Group	15	100.00

Source: Field Survey.

Most of the SHGs are graded by bank officials for accessing credit. About 50 per cent SHGs are graded second time by bank officials and 30 per cent SHGs do not get any grade (Table 17.1).

Table 17.2: Distribution of SHG Members by Caste

Sl. No.	*Number of member*	*Percentage of total*
SC	83	63.85
ST	20	15.38
GEN	27	20.77
Total	130	100.00

Source: Field Survey.

Among the total sample members, most of the members (63.85%) belong to Scheduled Caste community (Table 17.2). The Scheduled Tribes and general caste members are 15.38 per cent and 20.77 per cent respectively.

Table 17.3: Distribution of SHG Members by Age

Age Group	*Number of member*	*Percentage of total*
Below-30	24	18.46
30-40	80	61.54
40-50	20	15.38
50 & above	6	4.62
Total	130	100.00

Source: Field Survey.

From Table 17.3 it is seen that a large number of SHG members are in the age group of 30 to 40 years. It shows that the younger generations have been actually involved in the thrift, credit and economic activities of SHGs in the study area.

Table 17.4: Distribution of SHG Members by Education

Education	*Number of member*	*Percentage*
Illiterate	34	26.15
Can just sign	23	17.69
Primary (class I-IV)	24	18.46
High School (class V- XII)	44	33.85
College & above	5	3.85
Total	130	100.00

Source: Field Survey.

Table 17.4 illustrates the educational status of the SHG members in the study area. The educational status revealed that 26.15 per cent members are illiterate, 17.69 per cent members can just sign, and 18.46 per cent members have completed primary education, i.e. up to class I to IV, 33.85 per cent members have completed High School, and 3.85 per cent members have completed college and above. Therefore, we see that there is no need for education for formation of SHGs. Illiterate as well as highly educated members are found in SHGs. Such variations found in these groups help the groups functioning properly.

Table 17.5: Distribution of SHG Members by Marital Status

Marital Status	*Number of member*	*Percentage of total*
Married	117	90.00
Unmarried	3	2.31
Widow	10	7.69
Total	130	100.00

Source: Field Survey.

From the Table 17.5 we see that maximum number of SHG members is married (90%). About 2.31 per cent unmarried and 7.69 per cent widows are found in the study area.

From Table 17.6 we see that most of the members join the SHG to get loan (61.54%). Moreover, they want to save too. Again we found 12 members who opined for joining SHG to start business and 8 members who join the SHG to get self-confidence and some sort of dignity from the society.

Table 17.6: Reason for joining SHG

Reasons	*No. of members*	*Percentage of total*
To get loan	80	61.54
To get loan and save	30	23.08
To get help to start business	12	9.23
To get self-confidence and dignity	8	6.15
Total	130	100.00

Source: Field Survey.

Table 17.7: Sources of Savings of the members

Sources	*No. of members*	*Percentage of total*
Curtailing the expenditure	32	24.62
Saving from the income	98	75.38
Total	130	100.00

Source: Field Survey.

Most of the members save small amount from their income (75.38%). But, it is not possible always, because income generation influences expenditure pattern also. Therefore, members of groups curtail their expenditure to save fixed amount in terms of thrift.

Occupations

Table 17.8: Primary occupations of the SHG members before SHG

Occupation	*No. of members*	*Percentage*
Spinning	54	41.54
Handloom weaving	2	1.54
Farming	14	10.77
Agricultural labourer	20	15.38
Bidi rolling	4	3.07
Mid-day meal cooking	15	11.54
Maid servant	3	2.30
Only house work	6	4.62
Private Tutors	5	3.85
Small business	5	3.85
Tailoring	2	1.54
Total	130	100.00

Source: Field Survey.

Table 17.9: Primary occupations of the SHG members after SHG

Occupation	*No. of members*	*Percentage*
Spinning	52	40.00
Handloom weaving	7	5.38
Farming	12	9.23
Agricultural labourer	13	10.00
Small business	13	10.00
Bidi rolling	4	3.07
Mid-day meal cooking	15	11.54
Only house work	3	2.31
Private Tutors	5	3.85
Goat Rearing	3	2.31
Tailoring	3	2.31
Total	130	100.00

Source: Field Survey.

If we compare Tables 17.8 and 17.9 we see that there is a significant occupational change due to join the SHG. About 12.30 per cent women start small business. Here small business includes petty business, shop keeper, business of cloths, processing of *chira* and *muri* and concrete pole. Many members have undertaken self-employed remunerative activities which fetch them more income.

Table 17.10: Monthly household income before and after joining SHG

Monthly income in Rs.	*Before joining SHG*		*After joining SHG*	
	No.	*Percentage*	*No.*	*Percentage*
1000-2000	65	50.00	28	21.54
2001-3000	40	30.77	59	45.38
3001-4000	22	16.92	35	26.92
4001-5000	2	1.54	5	3.85
5001 & above	1	0.77	3	2.31
Total	130	100.00	130	100.00

Source: Field Survey.

Table 17.10 shows the various income distributions of the members before and after joining the SHG. The comparison obviously shows that the levels of income have changed during post-SHG situation. The number of members whose monthly income was below Rs. 2000 has been reduced from 50 per cent to 21.54 per cent after joining the SHG. It is very clear that monthly income of the members has been improved after joining the

SHG. Similarly, the other income levels have also been increased during the post-SHG situation. Thus, we can say that microfinance has indeed helped the rural poor households to improve their level of income.

Table 17.11: Monthly Savings of the members before and after joining SHG

Monthly savings in Rs.	*Before joining SHG*		*After joining SHG*	
	No.	*Percentage*	*No.*	*Percentage*
No saving	90	69.23	—	—
Upto 50	23	17.69	75	57.69
51-100	10	7.69	30	23.08
101-200	4	3.08	16	12.31
Above 200	3	2.31	9	6.92
Total	130	100.00	130	100.00

Source: Field Survey.

Table 17.11 gives us the information on monthly savings pattern of the members before and after joining the SHG. From the table we see that whereas 69.23 per cent members had no savings before joining the SHG, the same percentage become nil after forming SHG. Similarly, other savings levels have also been increased after formation of SHG. Thus it can be said that SHG helped the rural poor households particularly the

Table 17.12: Loan Utilisation Pattern of Members

Loan Utilisation	*No. of members*	*Percentage*
Invested in the activity	26	20.00
Household consumption	9	06.92
Spent on education	13	10.00
Spent on healthcare	14	10.77
Spent on purchase of asset (land, gold jewellery etc.)	17	13.08
Agriculture	12	09.23
Others (marriage, festival etc.)	10	7.69
Use for old debt repayment	7	5.38
House alteration and construction	6	4.62
No loan	16	12.31
Total	130	100.00

Source: Field Survey.

rural poor women to save and consequently helped them to build up self-reliance in the family as well as in the society.

Table 17.12 shows the loan utilization pattern of the members. The internal loan amount as well as bank loan credit are used for various purpose by the members. Members usually invest the loan purposefully towards the improvement of quality of their lives. It is seen that greater number of members (20%) used their loan for capital formation in their activities. Members also used their loan for children education, healthcare and purchase of land and gold jewellery, household consumption, old debt repayment, house alteration and construction.

V. Findings and Conclusions

This chapter describes how microfinance through SHGs plays an important role for the livelihood of the rural poor. The rural poor population particularly the rural poor women are able to largely satisfy their credit needs by joining SHG. The major findings that emerge from our study can be outlined as follows.

First, the analysis of annual household income of sample members for both pre-SHG and post-SHG situation showed that there was substantial increase in the annual income of the households in post-SHG stage. Further, when sources of income of SHGs are analyzed, we find substantial increase in household income from self-employment in non-farm activities such as livestock, handloom weaving, business and so on. In fact, we find there was a shift in the composition of activities due to join the SHG.

Second, we find that a significant number of members started savings only after joining the groups (70%) and the rest have been able to increase their savings in the post-SHG situation. The study found that apart from savings in SHG, the members also started their savings in LIC, post office, and so on.

Third, we find there was a shift in the purpose of loan taken. While previously the loan was taken mainly for consumption purpose and cultivation, the same is taken mainly for business and allied activities in post-SHG situation. It is found that due to increase in income of the members in the post-SHG situation, their need for loan for consumption purpose had substantially reduced.

Forth, it is found that besides economic improvement, the social outlook of rural women has undergone a radical change. The involvement in the group significantly contributed in improving the self-confidence of the members.

Thus, it can be concluded that microfinance is a successful step in providing access to finance to the rural needy people of Nadia district subject to some difficulties faced by the members as highlighted above. The process has enabled a large number of people to exercise various options to challenge poverty. The programme, indeed, helped in improving the household conditions of the beneficiaries. However, the following recommendations may be noted for further betterment of the working of the SHGs.

- One major limitation that is being faced in Nadia district is the problem relating to BPL list which keeps a large number of poor families, who ought to have been supported under the SGSY programme outside its fold. To improve the growth rate of SHGs, Panchayat representatives are yet to be careful, so, that really needy families are not excluded.
- Periodical monitoring of the SHGs can be effectively done by the district, block and Gram panchayat level.
- To improve better co-ordination between bankers SHGs members, frequent SGSY meeting at different level should be conducted.
- To improve and set up proper marketing for various products of SHGs, farm and non-farm linking is essential.
- To organize entrepreneurship development, training programme and infrastructural support of the government in a proper way are needed.
- Access to bank credit should be increased by taking various simple operational decisions.

References

Barr, M. S. (2005). *Microfinance and Financial Development*, p. 278.

CIDA and Microfinance (2002). *A Poverty Reduction Approach*, Policy Branch.

Hossain, F. and Z. Rahman, (2001). *Microfinance and Poverty: Contemporary Perspective:* University of Tampere: University of Administrative Science, Finland. Co-published by: Helsinki: Service Centre for Development Co-operation. pp. 163. http://www.uta.fi/~kumoho/pub.html

Kabeer, N. (2001). "Resources, Agency, Achievements: Reflections on the Measurement of Women's Empowerment", in *Discussing Women's Empowerment—Theory and Practice*, SIDA Studies No. 3.

Kar, S.C. (2009). "Poverty and Social Exclusion: A case study of an Area Economy of North Bengal", presented at the *National Seminar of Centre for the Study of Social Exclusion and Inclusive Policy*, University of Calcutta.

Khandker, S.R. (1998). *Fighting Poverty with Microcredit: Experience in Bangladesh*. New York: Oxford University Press.

Khandelwal, A.K. (2007), "Microfinance Development Strategy for India", *Economic and Political Weekly*, Vol. 42, No. 13, pp. 1127-1135.

Kirkpatrick *et al.* (2002). *Handbook on Development Policy and Management*, p. 173.

Mayoux, L., (1999). *For Access to Empowerment: Gender, Issues in Microfinance*, CDS, Virtual Conference.

Murdoch, J. (2000). "The microfinance schism", *World Development*, Vol.28, No. 4, pp. 617-629.

Murray, U. and Boros, R. (2002). "A Guide to Gender Sensitive Microfinance", *The Socio-Economic and Gender Analysis (SEAGA) Programme*, FAO, pp. 10-11.

Moll, H., (2005). "Microfinance and Rural Development: A long term perspective", *Journal of Microfinance,* Vol. 7(2), pp. 13-23.

NABARD (2002). *SHG-Bank Linkage: NABARD and Micro Finance*, 2001-2002.

Rao, V. M. (2002). "Women Self-help Group: Profile from Andhra Pradesh and Karnataka", *Kurukshetra*, p. 16.

Robinson, M.S. (2001). *The Microfinance Revolution. Sustainable Finance for the Poor*. The World Bank, Washington DC.

Swain, B, B. and Nayak, G. (2008). "Micro Credit through Self-Help Groups" in Das, S.K., Nanda, B., P. and Rath, J. (Eds.) *Microfinance and Rural Development in India*, New Century Publications, New Delhi.

Yunus, M., (2003). *Banker to the Poor*. New York: Public Affairs.

Yunus, M. (2004). "Grameen Bank, Microcredit and Millennium Development Goals". *Economic and Political Weekly*. 39 (36): 4077-4085.

UNIFEM (2009). *Reducing Women's Poverty and Exclusion.*
http://www.unifem.org/gender_issues/women_poverty_economics/at_a_glance.php

18

Handloom-Oriented Livelihood of the Weavers of Nadia

A Case Study of Santipur

Mahasweta Bhattacharya and *Ananta Kumar Bhukta*

I. Introduction

It is a well-known fact that we are crossing the present era of Liberalization, Privatization and Globalization (LPG) world. This economic scenario comprises of deregulated trade, investment and finance across the globe with the two very common objectives of reducing abject poverty and high degree of inequality in the distribution of income and wealth persisting perpetually among the people. Surprisingly enough, we are observing ever increasing inequality in the distribution of per capita real income and wealth (the traditional barometer representing development) among the people of the low and middle income countries than that in the high income-earning, industrially advanced countries of the universe. But we could not yet practically materialize these two very objectives for almost all the countries of reducing for whom LPG was primarily taken into consideration. In the Arjun Sengupta's report which Government of India had to accept finally after a long debate that during 2001 and 2005, 77 per cent of the Indian population could not spend even Rs. 20 per day when the GDP growth rate was 8 per cent to 9 per cent resulting in economic inequality, illiteracy, child labour, crime, violence on women, malnutrition among children. The GDP growth rate is subsequently found decreasing from 6.2 per cent (in 2010-11) to 5 per cent (in 2011-12). This made the scenario much more grave. The consequence is that the gap in the level of average well-being among the people of different regions of our country is getting wider and wider. We thus opine that the LPG policy taken originally for reducing income inequality and poverty alleviation across the country has not become effective at least to our desired level. Rather it leads to an exclusive, rootless and jobless growth for us. The situation thus reminds us the necessity for composing effective economic plans for the specific regions to provide at least a moderate push to arrest such deceleration. Through such decentralized grass-root area based regional planning in the underdeveloped regions of a country, using their own potentials, in the desired directions we can achieve a harmonious balanced growth all-over the country and reap all those benefits mutually. Through such area-wise need-based regional planning, we can substantially enhance "ability and entitlement" of the downtrodden people inhabiting there and bring them back into the mainstream as suggested by Prof. A.K. Sen and simulate own growth process in a sustainable manner.

As I am professionally placed in the district of Nadia, West Bengal and according to the prescribed area of discussion we are interested to concentrate our thinking on rural development of the district here. This district as we know is a place of historical and religious importance to the people of all categories and as such it is termed as secular place. The places of this district are primarily depended on agricultural activities although the district is not agriculturally such developed mainly because of less productivity of soil and absence of variety of product, lack of irrigation facilities, improved seeds and fertilizer etc. A number of attempts have already been made in different directions in setting up agro-based industries so as to stimulate agro-based industrial venture of the district. Next to agriculture we find wide importance of the textile sector here, the two decentralized sectors under this industry are the handloom and powerloom potential to grow steadily. We think it necessary to take all possible steps for continuous improvement of these two sectors in this district and along with the people associated in these two sectors in the name of "Handloom weavers" and "Power loom workers".

II. Objective of the Study

Historically, it is a fact that this art of weaving actually originated in a few villages, now located in Bangladesh (e.g., Tangail etc.) and the partition of Bengal afterwards shifted them in the adjacent areas of India—

at Santipur, Nabadwip, Ranaghat, Chakdah etc. wherefrom the handloom and powerloom sectors started as initial spurt. These people with their high quality technical knowhow easily earned their name and fame, both regionally, nationally and even internationally within a short period of time. But with the passage of time we also find here a number of decelerating factors surrounding this art, mainly of capital scarcity, degrading raw materials and finally inadequate market avenues.

The objective of our study is to analyze the socio-economic status of the people associated with weaving in Nadia, to study the exact nature and degree of income inequality persisting among these artisans, to offer possible measures that be taken towards reduction of such high degree of income inequality and to suggest necessary measures to make this decentralized sector cost-effective and at the same time competitive enough compared to powerloom mill sectors for its own survival.

III. Methodology

Through complete and comprehensive questionnaire data are collected from 30 per cent-40 per cent of the handloom weavers from five selected centres (namely Rahaghat, Santipur, Chakdah, Haringhata and Hanskhali) having concentration of handloom weavers in the district. Observations are taken at random following the prescribed Random Number Table from the available list of handloom from each block.

IV. Geographical Location of Nadia

The geographical boundary of Nadia district comprises Bangladesh in the east, Bardhaman and Hoogli district on the west, Murshidabad district on the North and North-West and North 24 Parganas towards south and south-east. Situated on the main rail route connecting Howrah/Kolkata and New Jalpaiguri (NJP) including parts of North-Eastern states, the Nadia district can easily be accessed by rail. The major railway stations are Nabadwip Dham, Ranaghat and others with regular trains to Kolkata/ Howrah/NJP/Guwahati. The International Rail Link connecting India and Bangladesh will pass through Nadia District with Gende as the last railway station at Indian Border. Bifurcated by National Highway-34 on the North and East, the district can also be accessed by road from other parts of the country (Fig. 18.1).

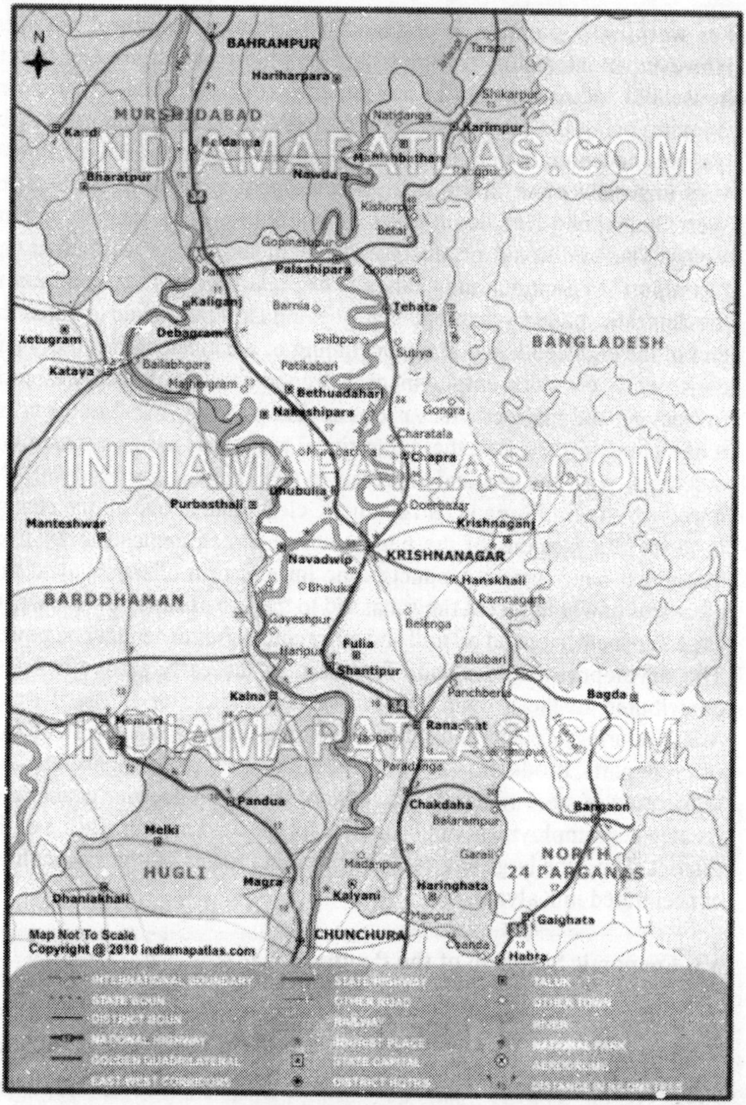

Fig. 18.1

V. A Brief Introduction of the Industry in Nadia

The district of Nadia is essentially an agricultural district and the bulk of her working population is engaged in various agricultural pursuits. However, an interesting feature is that here more people are engaged in household industries than in any other part of the State. Handloom-weaving being the main household industry, a considerable number of weavers concentrate in this particular district. Nadia district occupies a very important place in the field of Handloom industry in the State of West Bengal and Handloom plays a pivotal role in its socio-economic status. The traditional production on "Jamdani Saree" of Nabadwip, "Santipuri" of Santipur and "Tangail" of Fulia zone has been popular in the domestic market years together. This industry flourished towards the end of the eighteenth and at the beginning of the nineteenth century and consistently provided employment to a good number of people directly in weaving and indirectly its various ancillary activities and in the sense it has a long history. But, these traditional household industries received a setback with the gradual increase in the cost of raw material, the introduction of mill-made and synthetic cloths and above all the change in tastes and fashions of the people which turned demand away from traditional hand-woven products. The introduction of mechanical and electrical power in recent times has led to the rise of such new industries as power-loom, rice and oil mill and other enterprises depending on power. The development of Kalyani Township in the early sixties has also contributed to the growth of various new industries in the district. Manufacturing of plants and machinery for tea industry and manufacturing of cycle parts, production of yarn, rolling of steel rods, angles, etc. and fabrication of steel materials are some of the new industries which have created new employment opportunities for the working population of the district. Thus, the large and medium sized industries of this district have concentrated in Kalyani.

VI. Economic Scenario of the People of Nadia

As per 2011 census, 72.19 per cent population of Nadia district lives in rural areas of villages. The total Nadia district population living in rural areas is 37,30,897 of which males and females are 19,22,578 and 18,08,319 respectively. In rural areas of Nadia district, sex ratio is 941 females per 1000 males. If child sex ratio data of Nadia district is considered, figure is 958 girls per 1000 boys. Child population in the age 0-6 is 3,92,543 in rural areas of which males were 2,00,525 and females were 1,92,018. The child population comprises 10.43 per cent of total rural population of Nadia district. Literacy rate in rural areas of Nadia district is 71.50 per cent as per census data 2011. Gender-wise, male and female literacy stood at 75.65 and 67.08 per cent respectively. In total, 23,86,942 people were literate of which males and females were 13,02,721 and 10,84,221 respectively. According to the population census, 2001 in Nadia, every fifteenth male worker is employed in the household industries (like hand weaving) whereas this proportion is barely thirty per thousand in the entire State.

Table 18.1: Distribution of population according to categories of workers by sex, 1991 and 2001 in Nadia District

Industrial Categories	*Year*	*Population Number*			*% of Total Population*
		Male	*Female*	*Total*	
A. Total Main Workers	1991	1029267	80564	1109831	28.81
	2001	1306217	311064	1617281	33.60
1. Cultivator	1991	322477	3131	325608	8.45
	2001	291921	25964	317885	6.60
2. Agricultural Labourers	1991	287744	17225	304969	7.92
	2001	342511	32922	375433	7.80
3. Household Industries	1991	154584	35812	190396	4.94
(mainly handloom)	2001	87319	97597	184916	3.84
4. Other workers	1991	264462	24396	288858	7.50
	2001	584466	154581	739047	15.36
B. Marginal Workers	1991	5435	14931	20366	0.53
	2001	85571	123637	209208	4.35
C. Non-workers	1991	955139	1766761	2721900	70.66
	2001	1058837	1927638	2986475	62.05
Total Population	1991	1989841	1862256	3852097	100.00
(A+B+C)	2001	2450625	2362339	4812964	100.00

Source: Census of India, 1991, 2001.

Table 18.1 shows that about 30 per cent of the total population residing in this district is engaged in various industrial and agriculture pursuits and are termed as main workers here. Among the main workers, almost five per cent of the district populations are performing household industrial activities, mainly hand-weaving, clay models and sweet making etc. The percentage of marginal workers is negligible here. But surprisingly enough, a large proportion of the population (70%) were found to be non-workers in this district in the Census Report, 1991. They mainly comprise of children, women, old and invalid people. As the census data for 2011 is not available the recent scenario could not be depicted.

As per the data collected from the Directorate of Textile, Government of West Bengal following are the scenario of the handloom industry of West Bengal for the time period from 2000-01 to 2010-11 (Table 18.2).

Table 18.2: Progress of Handloom Industry in West Bengal

Particulars	*Unit*	*2000-01*	*2001-02*	*2007-08*	*2008-09*	*2009-10*	*2010-11*
Production of Handloom Societies	Million metres	679.00	650.00	921.20	902.78	893.76	862.08
Handloom Co-operative Societies	Number	2203	2203	2199	2213	2214	2214
Sales turnover – (a) West Bengal State Handloom Weavers Co-operative Society Ltd.	Rs. Crore	50.65	48.89	31.00	40.00	49.00	53.30
(b) West Bengal Handloom and Power-loom Development Corporation Ltd.	-do-	48.35	33.46	—	—	—	—

Notes: As per "Handloom and Powerloom Census" conducted in 1995-96 by Government of India, the total employment in Handloom Sector is 6,66,514.

As per the records collected from Handloom Development Office, Santipur, there are 69,713 weavers in the rural area of Santipur in 2011. Out of these weavers an exclusive survey conducted for over 222 weavers, it was found that about 70 per cent respondents belong to Scheduled Castes and Tribes or Other Backward Castes (Table 18.3).

About 70 per cent of them live in "Kancha" Houses. The usual age of entry of workers here is 15 years and they work up to 70 years. The academic levels attained by the respondents are given in castes (Table 18.3).

Table 18.3: Weavers under the purview of Handloom Development Office, Santipur as per Weaver Census 2012

	Name of Area	*No. of weavers*
Rural Area	Ranaghat I	21,332
	Ranaghat II	3,491
	Santipur Block	69,713
	Chakdah	5,787
	Haringhata	1,846
	Hanskhali	3,725
Urban Area	Santipur Municipality	55,814
	Birnagar Municipality	1,977
	Chakdah Municipality	57
	Coopers Municipality	1,662
	Ranaghat Municipality	41
	Taherpur Municipality	339
	Total	1,65,784

Table 18.4: Academic attainments of the sample respondents

Academic status	*No. of respondents*	*%age*
Illiterate	52	23.43
Read up to class IV	59	26.57
Up to class VII	43	19.36
Above class VIII	68	30.64
Total	222	100.00

Source: Field Survey Conducted during 2010-11 (March-April).

Thus, about 50 per cent of the workers have not got education beyond class four. The more alarming situation is their earning situation. Taking Rs. 2000 per month that can offer at least one full meal in a day as the minimum subsistence level of living for an average representative family consisting of 4-5 members of our sample respondents about 80 per cent of the workers live below the subsistence level.

The "Saris" manufactured in this area are of different qualities and those can be classified into three categories—one is fine quality precious item, in the name of "Jamdani and Tangail" prices of which start from Rs. 400-500 and rise up to Rs. 2000 depending on the count of yarn used and quality of die designing and other necessary implements used. These are produced in Jacquered looms with different attractive designs in the entire body. Weavers can earn Rs. 80 to 100 as profit from each of them meeting all expenses for inputs. Next we have noticed medium quality

"Size-pare" sari prepared in "jacquered looms" with simple designs inside, prices of which range from Rs. 300 to Rs. 500 and meeting all expenses weavers can earn profit of Rs. 50 to 60 from each unit. And the coarse qualities called the "Janata Sari" are woven by the entrepreneurs and big master weavers. These are produced with the yarn of 80 count in the ordinary looms (called Mattha) having no jacquered facility and hence no designing inside. They are sold within Rs. 200 where the wage rate is Rs. 50 to 60 for each unit. During our investigation we have also learnt that the cost for yarn and the wage are the two main components of the total cost of production. The wage rate is found to remain more or less constant. Collective bargaining by the weavers is found to be not effective. But the prices of yarns are ever increasing leading to cost of production and prices for finished items and thus making them less competitive in the open market with the similar items produced in the mills and powerlooms. Therefore, the most important problem is the rising yarn prices and enough attention should be paid to it in order to make their prices stable.

The resultant income distribution is found to be distinctly unequal as given in Table 18.5.

Table 18.5: Inequality Table

Sample Respondents classified into income classes by Rank	*Mid Value*	*%age Share of income*	*Cumulative %age of income-classes*	*Cumulative %age of income*	*Inequality*
1	*2*	*3*	*4*	*5*	*6*
(0-20) Lowest One-fifth	10	5	20	5	15
(20-40) Second One-fifth	30	11	40	16	24
(40-60) Third One-fifth	50	18	60	34	26
(60-80) Fourth one-fifth	70	23	80	57	23
(80-100) Highest One fifth	90	43	100	100	0

The data collected are classified into three categories – (i) weavers producing and selling individually, (ii) weavers producing and selling under Co-operatives, and (iii) weavers producing and selling under Mahajans. The co-efficient of variation of income of weavers are calculated for these three types of marketing outlets. Table 18.6 shows the result of co-efficient of variation.

Here, CV_1 for the first group (i.e., weavers producing and selling individually) is having least variation. So, this group is detected as the most consistent in generating surplus among the three. We suggest most

Table 18.6: Result of Co-efficient of Variation

I.	$C.V_1$ (weavers producing and selling individually)	0.21
II.	$C.V_2$ (weavers producing and selling under Co-operatives)	0.70
III.	$C.V_3$ (weavers producing and selling under Mahajans and others)	0.31

encouragement to this mode of production and selling for accelerating the pace of surplus generation. This is important because one needs equality in income generation along with higher levels of income. Thus, one needs to ensure better income for this group of income for this group of income earners. This will simultaneously generate more and more self-employment in the handloom sector, reduce rural-urban migration and minimize undesirable population pressure on the nearby urban economy and at the same time reduce the extent of disguised unemployment in the agricultural sector. They can, therefore, effectively avert risk and uncertainty of production and maintain a steady surplus with greater marginal productivities. So, the individual modes of production and selling in these two sectors must be given more support for accelerating the pace of surplus-generation and less income inequality.

From this statistical analysis we can also draw the Lorenz Curve:

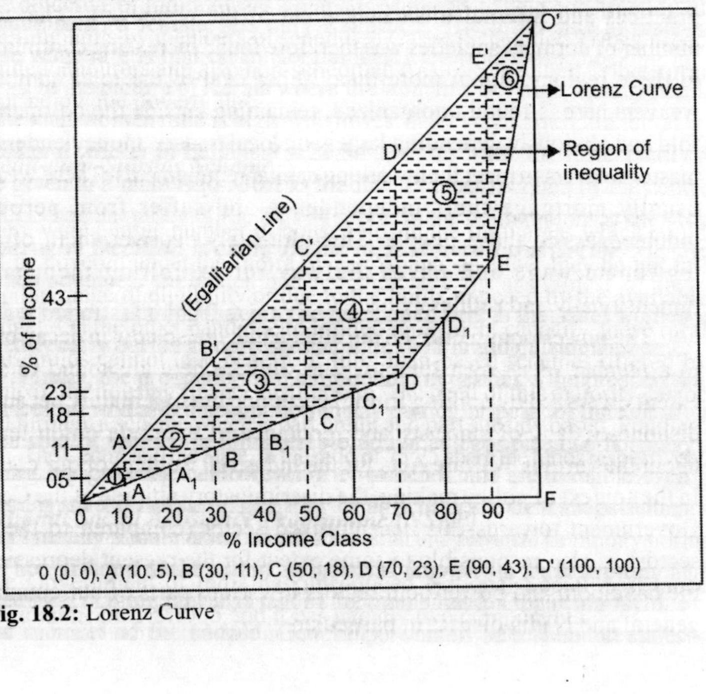

Fig. 18.2: Lorenz Curve

$$\text{Here value of Gini Coefficient} = \frac{\text{Area of OABCDO}'}{\text{Area of OFO}'}$$

$$= \frac{2975 \text{ sq. unit}}{5000 \text{ sq. unit}}$$

$$= 0.595 = 0.60$$

Here, value of G is 0.60, which denotes that there is inequality among the earnings of the weavers of Nadia District of West Bengal.

VII. Conclusion

The scarcity of working capital, lack of adequate marketing facility and insufficient supply of hank-yarn are the three main hurdles responsible for the gradual deterioration of the traditional cotton textile industry in the district. With a view to solve these problems as far as possible, along with a number of important other measures, a good number of handloom cooperatives were set-up here by the government. But, in the course of our investigation in five selected handloom weaving centres in this district, many of these societies became non-viable mainly because of corrupt practices and internal mismanagement of the organizers. The actual number of dormant societies was therefore found increasing continuously in these regions. Again more than 70 per cent of the total number of weavers here is found unorganized, remaining outside the co-operative fold and obviously depending largely on local traders, moneylenders and master weavers to meet their working capital requirements. These weavers usually mortgage their independence and suffer from perpetual indebtedness to these people. This ultimately deprives them of their legitimate wage and paves the way for exploiting them multi-dimensionally and ruthlessly.

The powerloom sector, on the other hand, is also now in decay owing to a number of its own reasons. The workers here are found to some extent organized by nothing fruitful is coming out of it mainly because of dishonesty, lack of sincerity and ignorance of the trade union leaders about the various Welfare Acts for the industrial workers of our country. In the context of policy making, the discriminatory attitude of the Central Government towards this decentralized sector (compared to the mill sector), is also responsible to some extent for the present depression in the handloom and powerloom sectors in various parts of our country in general and Nadia district in particular.

With the constant efforts of both the Central and State Government in the form of financial and technical assistance, a significant amount of progress have been achieved in the field of product diversification and the skilled weavers of this district are now engaged in production of value added fabrics which has penetrated in the global market also. Government of India has introduced export oriented project scheme with the provision of improved training, upgradation of looms, seed capital, Design development and publicity etc. and some Co-operative societies are undergoing commercial production for export. In this modern era, the consumers taste and preferences are changing day by day and to meet the need, modern technology is being introduced in conformity with diversity and versatility of products.

References

Bouchand, J. and Mezard, M (2000): "Wealth condensation in a simple model of economy", *Physica A*, p. 282.

Census of India 1991, 2001 and 2011.

Government of India (1996): *Handloom and Powerloom Census*.

Government of West Bengal (2011): *District Human Development Report-Nadia*, pp. 88-90.

Government of West Bengal (2011): *Salient Statistical Information of Handloom Industries as on 31.3.12*, Handloom Development Office, Santipur, Nadia.

Government of West Bengal (2012): *Block-Wise Weavers Identity Cards Distribution Report*, Handloom Development Office, Santipur, Nadia.

19

Forest Dependence of Households

A Study on Joint Forest Management in the Districts of Bankura and Paschim Medinipur in West Bengal

Sebak K. Jana, Bipul De and *Mamataj Uddin Ahmed*

I. Introduction

Non-Timber Forest Products (NTFPs) are an important source of livelihoods for the rural population all-over the world. Rural communities depend on forest to meet subsistence needs like food, fodder, litter, and fuel wood. Different studies reveal that a significant proportion of the world rural population is highly dependent upon forest resources (Piya *et al.*, 2011). Joint Forest Management (JFM) as the term indicates is the management of forest by more than one party. In India the two parties are—the Government represented by the forest department and the people living in villages in the fringe areas of forest. Under this system forests are being protected by the Forest Protection Committees (FPCs). The primary purpose of JFM is to give users a stake in forest benefits and a role in planning for the improvement of forest conditions and productivity. West Bengal is the pioneer state in India in initiating Joint Forest Management. As on March 2012, there are 4,281 FPCs in the State comprising of total number of 4,98,808 members protecting the total forest areas over 5,67,599 ha. (Government of West Bengal, 2012). The development of Forest is indispensable for the improvement of living standards because of less availability of agricultural land and unavailability of alternative occupations in rural areas. FPC members collect different types of non-timber forest products (NTFPs) from the forest which is used for different purposes in addition to food, fodder and fuel.

The importance of JFM is well documented in the literature. Shankar (1998) discusses the probable consequences of fuelwood extraction on biodiversity and explores management options to meet energy requirement and to conserve biodiversity. According to Dutta *et al.* (2004) NTFP extraction becomes an important incentive for forest preservation—perhaps the only incentive, given that the quarter share of felling returns or the awareness regarding environmental benefits are both very small—and the first is also uncertain. If this is recognised, enhancing the returns from NTFP should become a major objective of the state. This would involve discussing the mix of species in plantations with the villagers, so that useful varieties are grown more. They point out that fuelwood or fodder production should not be the only objectives—all useful or commercially viable varieties should be grown in accordance with demand. They suggest that the forest department and other state organizations can think of developing processing units in the villages and can be involved in the marketing of the processed goods. According to Singh *et al.* (2005) in case of NTFPs, there is market failure as well as institutional failure and there are possibilities for private-public-partnership (PPP) in cultivation, processing, value addition and marketing of timber as well as non-timber forest products. According to Das and Sarkar (2008) forest income plays the dominant role in reducing measured income inequality for poor households who are relatively asset poor and also live below poverty line. According to Sunderlin *et al.* (2006) populations living in or near forests have a high poverty rate and they are often among the poorest of the poor and they tend to be disproportionately dependent on forest resources. The paper of Rao (1998) delineates the impacts of JFM activities on the vegetation and development of Eastern Ghats region of Andhra Pradesh and presents the case of four villages representing four forest divisions. He argues that NTFP productivity is to be maximised as the present level of production is very low because of their low abundance and poor genetic vigour. According to Mishra *et al.* (2004) greater attention should be paid to the processing and marketing of NTFPs as they can provide increased income only through value addition and development of appropriate marketing channels. Various dimensions of dependence of households on forests have been addressed by various authors like Jodha (1990), Government of West Bengal (2012), Shankar (1998), Dutta *et al.* (2004), Singh *et al.* (2005), Das and Sarkar (2008), Sunderlin *et al.* (2006), Mishra *et al.* (2004) and Jana *et al.* (2012).

The main objective of the study is to assess the dependence of households on forest by estimating the value of Non-Timber Forest Products (NTFP) collection by households in the FPC areas and to find the determining factors of NTFP collection.

II. Data Collection and Study Area

The data collected for this study is mainly primary in nature. The primary data has been collected from the selected FPCs of the districts of Paschim Medinipur and Bankura. We have selected 17 FPCs belonging to three forest ranges namely Patrasayer, Barjora and Sonamukhi in the district of Bankura. The name of the FPCs are Padmapukur, Gabera, Bangladanga Palasbani, Balsi, Chandni, Banagram, Dhanipara, Madhabpur, Kayma, Palsona, Brindabanpur, Tiura, Pathormora, Kalyanpur, Jasra, Kusumkana. From these 17 FPCs in Bankura, we have selected 150 households for our survey. We have selected six FPCs namely Dhanyardihi, Rampur, Chhargora, Dhaboni, Jemuasole and Pathrisole in Amlagora forest Range in the Rupnarayan forest division in the district of Paschim Medinipur, West Bengal. Our sample consists of 220 households from four ranges, chosen by the method of stratified random sampling. It is to be pointed out that we are only taking about the local population who has a direct connection with the forests.

III. Household Characteristics and Responses

Let's take a quick look on the household characteristics of the surveyed respondents on the basis of some different parameters like family size, caste compositions, average livestock holdings, asset holding status, socio-economic characteristics, savings and lending per household, problem areas, benefits enjoyed by different activities etc.

IIIA. Family Size

We have selected 220 households from 23 FPC areas. The district-wise number of households is as follows: Patrasayer-50, Barjora-50, Sonamukhi-50, Amlagora-70. The average family size in the whole sample is calculated as 5.8, the average number of adult members is 3.82 and the average number of kids is 1.85. District-wise family size for the surveyed household is presented in Table 19.1.

Table 19.1: Average Family Size of the Households

Items	*Bankura*	*Paschim Medinipur*	*Total*
HH size	5.67	6.10	5.81
No. of kids	1.67	2.26	1.85
Dependent Adult	3.81	3.84	3.82

Source: Primary Survey.

IIIB. Caste Composition

The caste composition of the sample households in the FPCs has been presented in Table 19.2. Our sample comprises of SC-34.6 per cent, ST-50.9 per cent, OBC-5 per cent, General-9.5 per cent. The table shows the existence of SC and ST communities in the surveyed areas in a greater extent than OBC, or even General communities in total population. It also indicates the greater dependence of the socially and economically backward communities on forest related products and the joint forest management as well.

Table 19.2: Percentage Composition of Castes of the Selected Households

Category	*Bankura*	*Paschim Medinipur*	*Total*
SC	43.33	15.71	34.55
ST	38.67	77.15	50.90
OBC	7.33	0.00	5.00
General	10.67	7.14	9.55
Total	100	100	100

Source: Primary Survey.

IIIC. Average Livestock Holding

Average livestock holding per family is reported in Table 19.3. The average animal holding per family is as follows: cow-2.19, goat-0.56, Buffalo-0.08 and Pig-0.09. The table also shows that in Paschim Medinipur district, the average livestock holding of cow, buffalo and pig is greater than that of Bankura. It indicates that the dependence on forest for the grazing of livestock is less in Bankura than Paschim Medinipur.

IIID. Asset Holding Status

Asset holding status of the households is presented in Table 19.4. Of all

Table 19.3: Average No. of Livestock Holding per Household

Livestock	*Bankura*	*Paschim Medinipur*	*Total*
Cow	1.65	3.36	2.19
Buffalo	0.00	0.26	0.08
Goat	0.82	0.00	0.56
Pig	0.00	0.27	0.09

Source: Primary Survey.

the sample households the percentage of households having different assets are as follows: radio-16.36 per cent, TV-4.0 per cent, cycle-73.18 per cent. Of the 220 households surveyed 98.18 per cent households are card holders of MGNREGA, 66.18 per cent of households are BPL and 100 per cent of the households have Ration Card.

Table 19.4: Asset Position of the Households Selected (% hhs)

Asset	*Bankura*	*Paschim Medinipur*	*Total*
TV	4.00	2.86	3.64
Cycle	64.67	91.43	73.18
Radio	14.67	20.00	16.36
BPL	66.00	72.86	68.18
MGNREGA	99.33	95.71	98.18
Ration Card	100.00	100.00	100.00

Source: Primary Survey.

IIIE. Socio-Economic Characteristics

We have presented some more socio-economic characteristics of the households in Table 19.5. The average education level is measured in terms of highest education i.e. class attained by the head of the households. The average education of the head of the households is 2.54 with 2.49 in Bankura and 2.63 in Paschim Medinipur. The average distance of the forest from the households is calculated as 0.61 kms. The average participation rate in the FPC meeting is calculated as 65 per cent with 68 per cent in Bankura and 60 per cent in Paschim Medinipur and the average agricultural landholding is 0.35 acres. The percentage of BPL families are respectively 66 per cent and 72.8 per cent in Bankura and Paschim Medinipur respectively.

Table 19.5: Socio-Economic Characteristics of the Households

Characteristics	*Bankura*	*Paschim Medinipur*	*Total*
Education	2.49	2.63	2.54
Male (%)	80.67	92.86	84.55
Female (%)	19.33	7.14	15.45
Distance (km)	0.69	0.43	0.61
Participation	68	60	65
Land (Acre)	0.17	0.73	0.35
BPL (%)	66.0	72.8	68.1

Source: Primary Survey.

IIIF. Benefits Accrued from NTFPs by Different Activities

The activities that are important to develop the economic situations of surveyed households are shown in Table 19.6. We have classified different forest activities in six categories like grazing of livestocks, collection of fruits, collection of leaves, collection of fire-wood, collection of medicinal plants etc. The data reveals that the most important activity of the surveyed people across the districts is the 'collection of leaves' followed by 'collection of fire-wood'. The leaves are collected for preparing indigenous plates made by stitching the leaves of the *shal* tree, *kendu* leaves which are used as wrappers in making '*bidis*'. The medicinal plants are not available in the surveyed areas in Bankura.

Table 19.6: Percentage of HHs Benefited from NTFPs by Different Activities

Activities	*Bankura*	*Paschim Medinipur*	*Total*
Grazing of Livestocks	65	93	74
Collection of Fruits	66	69	67
Collection of Leaves	99	100	100
Collection of Fire Wood	95	100	97
Collection of Medicinal Plants	0	66	21

Source: Primary Survey.

IV. Collection of NTFP and the Extent of Dependence

The benefits from NTFPs are in the form of—

- *NTFP used directly by the collector*—The main items are firewood and fodder followed by food such as potatoes, mushrooms and mahua and items of HH use such as reeds or grasses that are converted into mats or brooms or items needed in hut construction. Attempts also have been made to obtain data on the collection of medicinal plants and items used for ritual or ornamental purposes.

- *NTFPs collected for sale after or before processing*—The main items are indigenous plates made by stitching the leaves of the *shal* tree, *kendu* leaves which are used as wrappers in making *bidis*, and shal seeds which can be pressed to produce oil.

Annual Value of NTFP

The people depend very much on Non-Timber Forest Products (NTFPs) for their livelihoods. From our field survey we have noted that households collect different types of non-timber forest products from the forest. We have estimated the value of NTFPs from the forest for each household by imputing the value of non-marketed products also. The value of NTFPs collection per household varies from Rs. 1,55,841 to Rs. 5,841. District-wise estimated values of different NTFPs are presented in Table 19.7.

Table 19.7: Annual Value of NTFP Collection (in Rs.) per Family

Different Items	*Bankura*	*Paschim Medinipur*	*Total*
Fire-wood	7808.47	12729.67	9374.30
Dry leaf	4975.36	0.00	3392.29
Green leaf (plate, wrapper)	5944.11	24737.69	11923.88
Grass	1091.73	8804.03	3545.65
Mushroom	3710.33	424.90	2664.97
Kendu	1631.83	0.00	1112.61
Mahua	2724.27	0.00	1857.45
Fruits	308.00	192.63	271.29
Honey	216.60	0.00	147.68

Source: Primary Survey.

IVB. Average Number of Days Spent to Collect NTFP

Average number of days going to forest for NTFP collection per family is given in Table 19.8. As the table shows FPC members mainly go to the forest for collection of leaves, fire-wood and grass. This reveals that poorer households are more dependent on fuelwood and since they have less land and livestock ownership they could not use the intermediate forest products. The product like 'mushroom' is very much occasional and the availability of such a product actually happened only for two to three weeks in a year. The average number of days spent by the surveyed households to collect '*mahua*' fruit and other fruits is also significant and showing the high dependence on NTFP. Paschim Medinipur shows higher dependence on forest for grazing cows compared to Bankura.

Table 19.8: Average Number of Days per Year Gone to Forest for Different NTFP Collection by a Family

Different Items	*Bankura*	*Paschim Medinipur*	*Total*
Fire-wood	199	66	157
Dry leaf	167	0	114
Green leaf (plate, wrapper)	162	159	161
Grass	105	255	152
Mushroom	8	3	6
Kendu	20	0	14
Mahua	162	0	110
Fruits	112	3	77
Honey	1	0	1

Source: Primary Survey.

IVC. Dependence on NTFP

The villagers are dependent to a significant extent on the forests and NTFPs. The forests provide different resources to the community—fruits, materials to make houses and tools, leaf, firewood etc. The dominant use of the forest is to obtain fuelwoods for domestic energy consumption and for the sale. The forest dependence measured in terms of NTFP income as a percentage of total income is calculated as 42 per cent in Paschim Medinipur and 75 per cent in Bankura. The natural advantage of the forest fringe people is that most of the NTFPs have their harvest seasons during late winter and early summer at which time the agricultural activities are at their low. Some of the products like leaves, fire-wood, grass etc., are harvested throughout the year depending upon their availability.

In order to get to know the exact impact of the influencing variables on the NTFP income, a regression analysis was done using the following multiple linear regression model:

$$\text{NTFP} = b_0 + b_1\,\text{EDU} + b_2\,\text{DIST} + b_3\,\text{PART} + b_4\,\text{LAND} + b_5\,\text{HSIZE} + b_6\,\text{ST} + b_7\,\text{BPL} + u_i$$

Where,

- NTFP = Annual NTFP income of the Household (Rs.)

- **EDU** = Education level of the head of the household (years)
- **DIST** = Distance of the forest
- **PART** = Dummy variable representing the participation in FPC meeting
- **LAND** = Land possessed by the family (in acres)
- **HSIZE** = Household Size
- **ST** = Dummy variable representing whether the household is ST
- **BPL:** Dummy variable representing whether the household is BPL
- u_i = random error term

The regression results are reported in Table 19.9. The estimated regression coefficients have been presented in order of level of significance. The 'Adjusted R^2' value of 0.341 implies that about 35 per cent of variation in the NTFP is explained by the regression model. The significant 'F' value indicates that a significant relationship exists between weighted linear composite of the independent variables as specified by the model and the dependent variable.

Table 19.9: Estimated Regression Results

	Unstandardized Coefficients	*t*	*Sig.*
(Constant)	2656.078	0.561283	0.575197
EDUC	–792.793	–1.86505	0.063556
DIST	–3730.83	–1.13689	0.256869
PART	3936.275	1.6204	0.106633
LAND	6155.906	2.226706	0.027019
HSIZE	4212.171	8.056028	0
ST	5354.574	2.129569	0.03436
BPL	5845.103	2.287014	0.023182

Adjusted R^2 = 0.341; F = 17.2 (Level of significance = .000).
Source: Estimated from Primary Survey Data.

The results show that significant positive factors affecting the NTFP income are HHSIZE, LAND, ST and BPL and the significant negative factor is education level. The results suggest that larger the household size, the family being ST and BPL, higher the participation, larger the NTFP collection. Higher education level discourages going to forest for NTFP collection.

V. Conclusion

Our study clearly reveals that the people, particularly the tribal people, living in forest fringe areas depend very much on forest resources particularly NTFPs for deriving their livelihoods. As there are still fewer avenues for improving the living standard in these regions, the forest based livelihood development strategies should be explored further and a supportive joint forest management policy can play the crucial role to solve the problem of poverty. Hence, forest management policy needs to be directed at utilization and maintenance of forest resources so that sustainable development of poorer community is ensured.

References

Das N. and D. Sarkar (2008): "Distributional Aspect of Forest Income: A Study on JFM and non-JFM Forest Dependent Households", http://mpra.ub.uni-muenchen.de/15330.

Directorate of Forest (1996): *Regional Workshop on Joint Forest Management, West Midnapore Division*, 27-28 February. Jhargram.

Duttta Madhumita *et al.* (2004): "Forest Protection Policies and Local Benefits from NTFP: Lessons from West Bengal", *Economic and Political Weekly*, Vol. 39, No. 6 (Feb. 7-13), pp. 587-591.

Government of West Bengal (2012): *State of Forest Report, 2011-12*.

Jana S., S. Datta Roy and M. Ahmed (2012): "Household Dependence on Forest—A Case Study on Joint Forest Management in Rupnarayan Forest Division, Paschim Medinipur District, West Bengal", in R.K. Sen (Ed.), *Forest Management and Sustainable Development*, Deep and Deep Publications Pvt. Ltd., New Delhi.

Jodha, N.S. (1990): "Rural Common Property Resources: Contributions and Crisis", *Economic and Political Weekly*, 30-06-1990, pp. A65-A78.

Mishra T.K. *et al.* (2004): *An Omnibus of Non Timber Forest Products of India*, Daya Publishing House, New Delhi.

Pasa, S. (1992): "CPRs and Rural Poor: A Micro Level Analysis", *Economic and Political Weekly*, XXVIII (46): 2499-2503.

Piya Luni *et al.* (2011): "Collection and Marketing of Non-Timber Forest Products by the Chepang Community in Chitwan District of Nepal", *MPRA Paper No. 35389*.

Rao, Kameswara (1998): "Vegetation and Non-Timber Forest Products Assessment under JFM in Eastern Ghats of Andhra Pradesh," http://hdl.handle.net/10535/615

Ravindranath N.H. and P. Sudha (Eds.), (2004): *Joint Forest Management in*

India: Spread, Performance and Impact, University Press India Pvt. Limited.

Shylajan, C.S. and G.S. Mythili (2005), "Community Dependence on Non-Timber Forest Products: A Household Analysis and Its Implications for Forest Conservation", *IGIDR*, WP 2007-05.

Singh, K.D. *et al.* (2005), "Exploring Options for Joint Forest Management in India", *Forestry Policy and Institutions Working Paper*, A World Bank/ WWF Alliance Project, FAO.

Sunderlin, W.D. *et al.* (2006), "Forests, Poverty and Poverty Alleviation Policies", *Background Paper for World Bank Policy Research Report*, World Bank.

Uma Shankar, R. Hegde and K.S. Bawa (1998), "Extraction of Non-Timber Forest Products in the Forests of Biligiri Rangan Hills, India. 6. Fuelwood Pressure and Management Options", *Economic Botany* 52: 320-336.

Index